WHAT IF THERE HAD BEEN NO PORT IN THE VALE?

Startling PORT VALE Stories!

JEFF KENT

Best wishes,
Jeff Kent

WITAN BOOKS

Jeff Kent was born in 1951 and educated at Hanley High School in Stoke-on-Trent. He gained a second-class honours degree in International Relations from London University in 1973 and lectured at several colleges in North Staffordshire.

He is a prolific writer on a variety of subjects and has previously published ten books: *The Rise And Fall Of Rock*; *Principles Of Open Learning*; *The Last Poet: The Story Of Eric Burdon*; *Back To Where We Once Belonged!: Port Vale Promotion Chronicle 1988-1989*; *The Valiants' Years: The Story Of Port Vale*; *Port Vale Tales*; *The Port Vale Record 1879-1993*; *Port Vale Personalities: A Biographical Dictionary of Players, Officials and Supporters*; *The Potteries Derbies* and *The Mysterious Double Sunset*.

Jeff was the editor of and the main contributor to *The Mercia Manifesto: A Blueprint For The Future Inspired By The Past*; *A Draft Constitution For Mercia* and *The Constitution Of Mercia*. He also edited Denis Dawson's autobiography, *Port Vale Grass Roots: From Supporter To Groundsman And Back Again* and Cyril Kent's autobiography, *A Potteries Past*. In addition, Jeff was the historical adviser to the Port Vale video histories, *Up The Vale!: The Story of Port Vale FC* and *The Millennium Documentary*.

He was a pioneer of Green music, has performed benefit concerts for several environmental and humanitarian organisations and has released four albums: *Tales from the Land of the Afterglow, Parts 1 & 2*; *Port Vale Forever* and *Only One World*. Consequently, his biography has gained entry into the *International Who's Who In Music Volume Two: Popular Music*. He currently plays percussion in the Glorishears of Brummagem morris dance band.

Jeff was the convener of the Confederation for Regional England from 1999 to 2000 and of the Mercian Constitutional Convention from 2001 to 2003. Also, he has been the co-ordinator of The Mercia Movement since its formation in 1993 and the convener of The Acting Witan of Mercia since its foundation in 2003.

He has supported Port Vale for 55 years, since being taken at the age of four to watch his cousin, Harry Poole (the club's second-longest-serving player), make his first-team debut in 1956. Jeff acted as the chairman of the Port Vale Supporters' Group from 1992 to 1994, was the co-ordinator of the Save The Vale campaign in 2003 and served as the convener of Vale Supporter Links, also in 2003. He is a season ticket holder in the Bycars Stand and, like many others, rarely misses a home match regardless of the club's fortunes.

Witan Creations
2011 Main Catalogue

WTN 001: *Butcher's Tale/Annie, With The Dancing Eyes* – Jeff Kent & The Witan (animal rights protest single), 1981 - £2.50, including p & p.

WTN 027: *The Mercia Manifesto: A Blueprint For The Future Inspired By The Past* – The Mercia Movement (128-page radical political manifesto), 1997 - £8.25, including p & p.

WTN 030: *Only One World* – Jeff Kent (13-track environmental concept CD), 2000 - £11.15, including p & p.

WTN 032: *A Draft Constitution For Mercia* – The Mercia Movement (20-page draft constitution for an independent Midlands), 2001 - £2.20, including p & p.

WTN 033: *The Mysterious Double Sunset* – Jeff Kent (203-page study of the extraordinary phenomenon), 2001 - £14.55, including p & p.

WTN 038: *The Constitution Of Mercia* – The Mercian Constitutional Convention (22-page constitution of independent Mercia), 2003 - £2.20, including p & p.

WTN 059: *A Potteries Past* – Cyril Kent (214-page life and times from 1915 to 1962), 2010 - £16.55, including p & p.

(All other publications and releases by Witan Creations are now out of print or unavailable from the catalogue.)

WHAT IF THERE HAD BEEN NO
PORT IN THE VALE?

First published in November 2011 by Witan Books, Cherry Tree House, 8 Nelson Crescent, Cotes Heath, via Stafford, ST21 6ST, England.
Telephone: (01782) 791673.
E-mail: witan@mail.com
Website: www.witancreations.com

WTN 060

ISBN 9780 9529152 8 7

A Cataloguing in Publication record for this book is available from the British Library.

Design and cover concept: Jeff Kent.
Cover artwork: Gary Devreede.
Editorial advisers: Sue Bell, Gill Evans and Phil Sherwin.
Main research: Jeff Kent, Phil Sherwin and Pete Wyatt.
Printed and bound by: Hanley Print Services, Units 90 & 79, Shelton Enterprise Centre, Bedford Street, Shelton, Stoke-on-Trent, ST1 4PZ. Tel. (01782) 280028; E-mail: gstock1@btinternet.com.

Front cover photo: The penalty that was awarded to West Bromwich Albion against Vale in their F.A. Cup semi-final at Villa Park on 27 March 1954.
Back cover photo: Part of the queue at Vale Park on 20 March 1954 for tickets for their F.A. Cup semi-final against West Bromwich Albion a week later.

Dedicated to those who would Valiants be

ACKNOWLEDGEMENTS

I should like to express my thanks to the following people and organisations for their invaluable assistance, not credited elsewhere, in the production of this book: Colin Askey, Mike Baggaley, Bill Bell, Birmingham Central Library, Blackpool Central Library, Blackpool Football Club, Bill Bratt, Marta Cox, John Cross, Derby Local Studies Library, Brian Herbert, Peter Holme, Gary Kelsall, Cyril Kent, Ray King, Bill Lodey, Simon Lowe, Wade Martin, Ian McPherson, Terry Miles, National Football Museum, Harry Poole, John Poole, Dave Porter, Port Vale Football Club, Lindon Roberts, John Robinson, Del Rudge, John Rudge, *The Sentinel*, Tony Sharkey, Phil Shaw, Allan Staples, Stoke on Trent City Archives, Stoke-on-Trent City Council, Stoke-on-Trent Register Office, Pete Stonier, Robert Thorley and Martin Tideswell.

ILLUSTRATION CREDITS

Illustrations were kindly supplied by the following:
City of Bayeux – 1; Getty Images – 3; Tony Hill – 6; Ray Johnson – front cover, 9; Jeff Kent – 5; *The Sentinel* – back cover, 2, 7, 8, 10, 11, 12, 13, 14; Stoke-on-Trent Register Office – 4.

Contents

Preface

Many people are familiar with the key words of Robert Burns' poem, *To a Mouse*: 'The best-laid schemes of mice and men often go askew.' They nicely encapsulate the simple, but profound, idea that there are myriad, and hardly understood, forces in the universe which are relevant and at times critical in determining the outcomes of situations. Great individuals are able to take many of these factors into account when making decisions, in order to maximise their chances of achieving favourable results. However, frequently, if not always, there are vital elements in play, which are unknown or not properly comprehended, that have a crucial bearing on the consequences of actions undertaken, often leading to unexpected denouements. Indeed, the world that we live in is so complex that it may well be that nothing is a foregone conclusion! What chance of success then do the plans, other than the simplest ones, of ordinary men and women have?

In the twentieth century, science became virtually a sacred cow, which, it was believed, could explain everything rationally, if sufficient data and time were available. However, the passage of time has suggested that science in itself is only a theory and that there is no inevitability in the universe. That might be an uncomfortable conclusion to live with, but one of the greatest modern thinkers, Stephen Hawking, has acknowledged that there exists an 'uncertainty principle', which 'introduces an unavoidable element of unpredictability or randomness in science' at the most fundamental level.

If that is the position in science, then how much certainty can there ever be with regard to the affairs of human beings, who are by nature emotional and volatile? Add in the complexity of human relationships and the result is a cauldron of swirling intangibles. Indeed, the Austrian novelist, Robert Musil, wrote, 'History is like the way of a man sauntering through the streets, diverted here by a shadow, there by a crowd of people, and finally arriving at a place that he had neither known of nor meant to reach.' Thus the idea of chaostory has developed in recent years as an offshoot of chaos theory in science. According to the latter, the laws of nature are so complex that much of what happens appears to be random and, once the highly unpredictable element of mankind is thrown into the mix, the waters become so muddied that it is extremely difficult to perceive any clarity of purpose or direction at all.

Nevertheless, within this twilight world, in which we live, there are pivotal moments in time when significant real choices exist, each of them leading to divergent routes and different futures. Indeed, our path through life appears to be rather like that of an ant climbing a tree. Every so often, the ant comes to a fork in the branch that it is on and the choice of which new one to take will lead to an entirely different destination in each case. Further up the tree, more and yet more choices appear and the nature of the continuing journeys, as well as the outcomes, are dissimilar in every situation.

The history of Port Vale is the same. Obviously, the club is where it is now, but it arrived here along a series of extremely tortuous roads, which in the main, if not always, did not have to be taken. There were innumerable possible other routes which could have been selected or stumbled across and their potential existence was no less real than that of those which were actually travelled upon. Vale have had a specific and mainly identifiable history, but also there were numerous alternative histories of the club that were once possible. Thus there was never any inevitability that the club would be precisely, or even roughly, where it is today. Its history could have been radically different in numerous ways and many moments in Vale's past can be identified as points in time where the way ahead parted from the route anticipated. Therefore, in this book, I have taken on the task of identifying key situations, and many minor ones, in the club's history where its future could have been disparate if only certain events had happened differently, as they so easily could have done.

Consequently, I have attempted to write a counterfactual or virtual history of Port Vale in order to examine what could have occurred, as well as describing and explaining what actually happened. Therefore, I have accepted the grand role that chance has played along the way and tried to make sense of apparent chaos. I have also attempted to take into account the butterfly effect, whereby small and apparently insignificant events can lead to monumental long-term consequences.

There are few, if any, events more likely to lead to dissimilar outcomes than sudden and unexpected deaths, not just for the individuals concerned, but also for those left behind them. Thus, for instance, Vale did not expect their great goalscorer, Frank McGinnes, to die at the age of 22 on the eve of their first season in the Football League and their frequently wretched performances during the 1892-1893 campaign can be attributed, at least in part, to the unanticipated loss they had suffered. However, what would the world have held in store for McGinnes and Vale had he in fact survived, as might have been expected? To try to answer those questions, I have attempted to guesstimate the main alternative outcomes that seem to have been possible at the time.

I have also approached thirteen other major turning points in Vale's history in the same way in this book, explaining how the events arose, how they may well not have done, what the effects of them were and how possible alternative futures may have affected the circumstances and progress of the club.

I hope that the outcome of my labours is that I have provided an entertaining and informative alternative history of Port Vale Football Club for the great pleasure of the readers. That would (almost) certainly be a much more preferable outcome for me than discovering the book is in the event received so badly that I wish I had chosen a different option than writing it in the first place!

Jeff Kent,
Cotes Heath,
November 2011.

1 No Port In The Vale

Most of the long-suffering band of Port Vale fans grudgingly accept that the club they support currently exists in the shadow of their local and big brother rivals, Stoke City. Those who know their history will realise that that is the normal state of affairs and that respites from Vale playing second fiddle in the football world of the Potteries have been few and far between, the golden age of the 1990s now being a distant memory. However, for Vale still to be such a long-standing member of apparently the most famous football league in the world is no mean achievement, especially as Stoke-on-Trent is the smallest city in England to boast two professional clubs. The accomplishment is the greater still if it is considered that the club might well never have existed in the first place because there could quite easily have been no port in the vale. However, as to why that might have been, or not been, requires some painstaking explanation, which will unfold (or might not) below!

The Pennine mountain chain, which the forms the “backbone of England”, stretches from the valley of the River Tyne in the north to that of the Trent in the south. In the north of Staffordshire, a spur juts westwards from the main uplands and falls, quite steeply in places, to the Cheshire Plain. The foothills of this protrusion mark the southernmost point of the Pennines and dominate the urban area known as the Potteries.

Because of its altitude, the poor soils of the uplands and its exposure to westerly frontal rainfall, North Staffordshire has always been relatively unfavourable for even subsistence farming and, as a result, until the Industrial Revolution, its population was low. In 1086, approximately 1.4 million people lived in England, but perhaps only 15,000 of them inhabited the whole of Staffordshire, including the more fertile farming areas in the middle and south of the county. Indeed, Staffordshire seems to have been the least densely populated of all the shires in Anglo-Saxon England.

The source of the third-longest river in England, the Trent, is at Biddulph Moor, just to the north of the Potteries. Although unobtrusive in its early course, the Trent flows 170 miles to the Humber Estuary and dominates the drainage pattern of the Midlands.

One of the first tributaries of the Trent from the west is the even less noticeable Fowlea Brook, which joins the main river in Stoke-upon-Trent. The brook flows south-southeast from its source at Harecastle, near to Kidsgrove, and runs just inside the city boundaries of Stoke-on-Trent for much of its short course.

Between the valleys of the Trent and the Fowlea Brook is a long ridge, on the western slopes of which are located the three most northerly towns of the Potteries: Tunstall, Burslem and Hanley. Burslem was named Barcardeslim in the 1086 Domesday Book and was a very small farming settlement within the Lyme Wood, which stretched from Market Drayton to almost Ashton-under-Lyne. Barcardeslim was inhabited only by a villein and four bordars (both types of peasants, tied to the land) and their dependants. Between them, they had a plough. To illustrate the insignificance of the settlement, Lec (Leek), itself a village of no great importance, was at that time populated by fifteen villeins and thirteen bordars and their dependants and had six ploughs.

Burslem grew slowly around the crossroads of the route from Newcastle-under-Lyme to Leek and that linking Tunstall and Hanley, but, even by about 1680, it still had less than seventy dwellings. Burslem continued to be an isolated settlement in the early part of the following century and most of its inhabitants remained, at least in part, farmers, eking out an existence from the poor land surrounding them.

The few people who had heard of Burslem at that time would most likely have considered it near impossible that the village would soon grow rapidly in size and eventually become the "Mother Town" in a major industrial city with a population of 275,000 by 1951. Indeed, the lack of development of Burslem up to that point must have made it seem obvious to all and sundry that it would remain a backwater in a county that itself was still a sparsely-populated backwater in England.

In 1700, London was the largest city in Europe, with an estimated population of 675,000, but a century earlier it had only had 250,000 inhabitants and was an urban exception, not the rule. It was a world trade centre and the hub of a growing empire. Probably the second-largest city in England at the start of the eighteenth century was Bristol, which very likely had a population of under 30,000. In comparison with even much lesser cities than those, Burslem paled into complete insignificance.

The expansion of Burslem really began in the second half of the eighteenth century and its size almost doubled between 1800 and 1829, with a number of new streets being built and Waterloo Road, running south from the town, being opened in 1817. In the second half of the nineteenth century, the town expanded rapidly westwards, down the hill towards the Fowlea Brook, and to the southeast, in the direction of Cobridge. By 1857, Burslem had two town halls, to celebrate its newly-found status as a bustling industrial town, and a third one was constructed in 1911.

Why was it that Burslem undertook the most unlikely transition from an upland village on the periphery of English affairs to a sprawling industrial town in a city of world renown? Was there anything inevitable about the dramatic change and when it occurred? Or did it happen by chance, through the combination of a series of accidental events? Indeed, could it actually have been otherwise? Also, however did such a place, for so long insignificant, manage to spawn and support a professional club that became one of only twelve founder members of the Second Division of the English Football League in 1892?

It is well known that the rapid growth and alteration in the character of Burslem from a farming village to an industrial town was part of the phenomenon called the Industrial Revolution, which is generally accepted to have begun in Great Britain in the eighteenth century and which did much to create the modern Western world. Prior to the Industrial Revolution, England was primarily an agricultural country, with the majority of people living in the countryside and off the land, but, as a consequence of industrialisation, the population became essentially urban, with a relatively small number of agribusinessmen dominating vast tracts of sparsely-populated rural land.

Attempts to identify answers to questions through the study of history tend to lead to yet more questions and, whilst it is simple to say that Burslem's transformation occurred because of, and as part of, the Industrial Revolution, why did the village industrialise and become a manufacturing town when the vast majority of others did not? Indeed, many of the largest towns in England in 1700, such as York, Norwich and Oxford, grew at a much slower pace than the new industrial urban areas and never really became manufacturing centres in classic Industrial Revolution style.

Furthermore, was the Industrial Revolution itself inevitable? If so, did it have to have first happened in Great Britain? In turn, if that was ineluctable, did it have to have occurred in the places that it did? Finally, did it have to have taken place when it did?

A determinist historian, supporting the linear progress theory of history, might well answer yes to all those questions because its notion supposes that the Agricultural Revolution inevitably superseded gatherer-hunting and that in turn the Industrial Revolution outmoded farming, in technological triumph on the path to earthly paradise. A Marxist determinist historian would no doubt be in agreement as to the inevitability of the events, but for a different reason: feudalism was (largely) replaced by capitalism, which itself would then be succeeded by socialism and finally by communism, through class struggle, although these developments currently seem unlikely to happen. Or, of course, the various economic changes over time could have been part of God's plan, not that mere mortals can understand what that might be or how it might come about. Alternatively, there might have been a master plan by brilliant businessmen or other great individuals in the eighteenth century to create an entirely new kind of world. Or perhaps the dramatic changes were all an accident, a chance consequence of the combination of uncontrollable intangible elements and the individual, and often divergent, wills in action of mainly (but not entirely) powerful human players.

There is never a perfect place in the past to start a story, but the late Anglo-Saxon period provides a vital focal point to consider how events might have unfolded differently to how they actually did. Before the Norman Conquest of 1066, Barcardeslim was a remote settlement in the northwest of Mercia, which was one of the six earldoms of the regional confederation of England. Although its boundaries had fluctuated since it had emerged in the sixth century, Mercia was essentially the central area of England, which is today most commonly known as the Midlands.

The Anglo-Saxon political system was decentralised, so that most decisions on their local areas were taken by the villagers themselves. The majority of English people lived as freemen in stable farming communities, which were bonded by common customs and traditions, kinship and co-operative effort on the land. Because the Anglo-Saxons were primarily subsistence farmers, with a sustainable, organic, open-field system, which had long been perfected, little changed from one generation to the next. It did not need to. Anglo-Saxon communities worked to live, not lived to work, and the frequency and length of their festivals are testament to the amount of leisure time that existed for most people beyond the essential tasks that needed to be completed. Amongst the sports that English people played at the time were a game which evolved into cricket and another which was a type of football.

In 1066, England had been fundamentally at peace for fifty years and tales of the wars against the Danes (which had ended in 1016) must have seemed almost as distant as stories of the Second World War do today. Anglo-Saxon England had a mainly northern outlook and much in common, especially culturally, with its Germanic neighbours, the Danes, Norsemen and Frisians. It must have been unimaginable to almost all of the English people at the beginning of 1066 that the world that they and that their ancestors had known for so long was about to be shattered by a sinister threat emerging on the other side of the Channel in northern France.

The Battle of Hastings, which was fought on 14 October 1066, is, of course, the most famous event in English history and quite rightly so because the Norman Conquest of William the Bastard, which followed, destroyed Anglo-Saxon England and thereby ended its era, which had lasted for six centuries. That would matter not a jot to the readers of this book except that the events of 1066 had a crucial influence on the development of Barcardeslim and whether there would eventually be a port in the vale.

Chance played a crucial role in the outcome of the Norman invasion of England and was vital in securing its unlikely success. The prevailing winds in England are southwesterlies, blowing from the Atlantic Ocean, as is clearly illustrated by the regular rainfall that the country receives. In August 1066, the Norman armada was waiting to cross the channel on a southwesterly or southerly wind and land in the south of England. A large Anglo-Saxon army (the fyrd), under King Harold Godwinesson, was stationed on the south coast, ready to deal with the Normans when they arrived, but the wind persistently blew from the east, and then later from the north, and kept the invasion force in harbour. The following month, the English provisions ran out and Harold was forced to disband the fyrd so that the harvest could be collected, which was vital.

A few days afterwards, the wind finally changed to a favourable direction for the Norman armada and it put to sea for the crossing to England, but was intercepted by the vastly superior Anglo-Saxon fleet. The Normans had a torrid time in the battle that followed, but, before the English sailors could complete their victory and destroy the armada, a storm suddenly arose and they were forced to break off the action. The unexpected intervention of the elements therefore rescued the bulk of the Norman expedition and it was able to gain port in the Somme estuary in northern France.

By then, the northerly winds, which had kept the Normans in harbour, had brought a huge Norse army to Yorkshire to attempt the conquest of England. A dash north by King Harold, with forces that he could muster at short notice, brought him upon the Norsemen at Stamford Bridge, near to York, on 25 September, and there the Norwegians were annihilated in an epic battle, which marked the beginning of the end of the Viking Age. As luck had it for the waiting Normans, the English losses in manpower were irreplaceable.

By chance, two days after the Battle of Stamford Bridge, the wind in northern France changed from north to south and the fortunate Normans were able to cross the Channel and land in Sussex unopposed. They had over two weeks to prepare for the arrival of King Harold and his depleted English army.

Like the Battle of Waterloo, the epoch-changing struggle at Hastings (or, more accurately, Senlac) was 'the nearest run thing you ever saw'. The outcome of the battle could have gone either way and the future of England and therefore the rest of the world could have been very different. It is nearly impossible to pick a precise moment which proved decisive in chaotic events like wars, but the famous story of the arrow in the eye at Hastings is worth mentioning. The struggle between the Englishmen and the Normans had ebbed and flowed all day, but, according to the twelfth century poet, Robert Wace, late in the afternoon, apparently by chance, Harold was struck in his right eye by an upwardly-fired arrow and, not surprisingly, was immobilised. The same event also seems to be depicted in the Bayeux Tapestry. If the story is true, he must, as a result, have lost control over the direction of the English resistance at a crucial time, leaving their forces virtually leaderless, so that the turning point of the battle had been reached. The outcome, of course, was that Harold was killed and the English army annihilated.

William "the lucky Bastard" he may have been, but the Norman duke, who consequently became the new king of England, was not a man to let opportunities slip. He quickly dismantled the ancient, decentralised Anglo-Saxon democracy and concentrated all power in England in his own hands as a hereditary absolute monarch. Not surprisingly, he is now, of course, known as William the Conqueror. England had been well and truly vanquished and became the first colony of the Norman (and later British) Empire, to be plundered at will. The land was no longer treated with care to ensure its sustainability; it became purely a resource to provide profits for the leading members of a foreign power and other freebooters who arrived in England to grab a share of the kill. The people were reduced in status from freemen to 'subjects of the crown', which they remain in law even today. The feudal system was imposed on the people and the land and, as a result, a huge underclass of English serfs became tied to foreign, and mainly French-speaking, lords. The Anglo-Saxons were so thoroughly dispossessed of their lands that by 1086 only one per cent of them retained their original holdings, which were otherwise handed over to their conquerors. The English people at large became overburdened sub-tenants, forced to carry out a series of onerous obligations and make various payments to the lords for the "right" to farm their own land.

Before the cataclysm, Alward, an English freeman, had held the land in Barcardeslim, but by 1086 he had disappeared from the settlement, which had become controlled by Robert de Toeni, a Norman nobleman. Toeni had Stafford Castle constructed to control the local natives, gained the name Robert de Stafford and was listed in Domesday Book as holding the lordships of 150 scattered settlements in England!

Had there been no Norman Conquest, it is inconceivable that England and Barcardeslim would have been the same as they are today, or even very similar. Prior to 1066, England was non-expansionist and seemed to accept the existing boundaries of the land. Had the world of the Anglo-Saxons continued uninterrupted, it is reasonable to project that England today would have been independent of the other countries of the British Isles and similar in most aspects to Denmark and Norway, with which there were very close connections until the Conquest. If England had managed to resist the Norman invasion and the consequences of the Conquest, it is likely that the country would have had a still primarily northern outlook, a much smaller population and considerably less industry, with an industrial revolution (certainly on the scale of that which happened) never having occurred. It is also probable that farming would have been much more significant; that there would have been stronger community bonds and a less individual outlook in society, and that the people would have had a much greater say in the important decisions made about their local areas, if not been fundamentally in control of them.

However, because of the aggressive policies of the Normans and their descendants, England became embroiled in a series of bloody wars in the British Isles and on mainland Europe for several centuries, which were followed by similar struggles across the globe as the exploitative British Empire was established, to the great advantage of the upper and, later, the middle classes. The people at large became impoverished and were for centuries (and arguably still are) forced to work long hours to make ends meet.

The difficulties that the settlers at Barcardeslim must have experienced in farming their relatively infertile land can only have been exacerbated by the Conquest in having additionally to support a lord in luxury and work on his land as well as their own. Life obviously became a struggle and the inhabitants found that a second occupation was very helpful, and perhaps even critical, in them being able to sustain themselves.

As luck would have it, Barcardeslim was located on Coal Measures, which contained clay suitable for making pottery. There was initially plenty of local timber available from the Lyme Wood for the firing of the clay and, when the trees eventually became scarce, the ground of the coalfield itself supplied long-flame coal, which was highly suited to performing the same task. So the inhabitants of Barcardeslim began to manufacture small pots as a sideline, to top up their income. Although North Staffordshire remained relatively sparse in population, the Burslem farmer-potters increasingly found outlets for their wares in nearby market towns, such as Newcastle-under-Lyme and Uttoxeter.

In 1686, Robert Plot's ground-breaking book, *The Natural History Of Staffordshire*, was published and in it the author noted that Burslem was a village 'of scant houses and thatched buildings', but was also where 'the greatest pottery they have in this county is carried on'. At the time, the village had about twenty farm buildings with an adjoining small pottery kiln, so clearly Burslem had found a profitable occupation that supplemented farming or vice versa.

A plan of the settlement in 1750, by Enoch Wood, shows Burslem still to have been a village, surrounded by fields, croft land and meadows, but within it are marked a number of 'potworks', there having been 23 in total around that time. There were also a few shops, but they were mainly of the kind that would be expected to be found in a farming community, for example four smithies, two butchers', a joiner's and a cobbler's.

With the impoverishment of the general population of England after the Norman Conquest, the numbers of people in the country had gradually, but almost relentlessly, risen, from the 1.4 million of 1086 to around six million in 1750. The major cause of this was the removal of peasants from the land by the lords, who initially wanted their holdings for profitable enterprises, such as the creation of hunting forests, sheep farms and vineyards. This dispossession of peasants led to many of them drifting to the towns in search of work, but finding poverty and being forced to increase the numbers of children they had, in the hope that the employment of their offspring would bring more income into the home.

Then, from the 1530s, the lords made a deliberate attempt to transform the farming system of England from peasant agriculture into a capitalist enterprise, so that even larger numbers of people were removed from the land, with the re-employment of some of them as wage-slaves. The consequent enclosures created a huge army of landless and unemployed labourers, living in grinding poverty, and the wholesale depopulation of the countryside at that time was only prevented by a series of riots and rebellions.

The resultant increasing growth of the size of towns meant there were large numbers of people removed from the supply of food and this created a further opportunity for profit-making farming. Therefore, six million acres of land were enclosed in England and Wales by the lords and other large landowners between 1700 and 1850 and converted into private farms. As a result, the ancient, communal, open field system was almost entirely destroyed. Because fewer labourers were needed under the new system, huge numbers of villagers were entirely dispossessed of their land. Some of them found re-employment as poorly-paid agricultural labourers, but many sought work in the towns, commonly the nearest ones to them.

The congregation of large numbers of unemployed people in the towns provided a potential source of cheap labour for existing and aspiring capitalist entrepreneurs and underpinned the remarkable transformation of England by the Industrial Revolution. The grinding poverty of the new urban masses meant that employers needed only to offer the lowest survival wages, longest hours and harshest conditions to attract workers for their enterprises. The effect was an unprecedented boom in industry and an unparalleled surge in the population as the birth rate rocketed because child labour was much in demand. The population of England and Wales soared to 8.9 million in 1801, almost 18 million in 1851 and 32.5 million in 1901.

Burslem was just one of the numerous small-scale industrial centres in England that dispossessed farmers, from land enclosures, moved to in search of work. In addition, the development of the village's pottery industry was assisted not least by the enclosure of its own fields, which made the making and sale of pots a necessity for the bulk of its inhabitants. With the availability of cheap labour, Burslem's pottery industry expanded quickly in the second half of the eighteenth century, motivated by the potential profits available by satisfying the rapidly-increasing demand from the country's burgeoning population. So the village soon became a thriving industrial town, with a population of 16,090 by 1841, 22,971 by 1871 and 42,444 by 1921. Also, following the construction of the Big House Works in 1751, the first pottery to have a tiled roof in Burslem, increasing numbers of "pot banks" were purpose built as factories, independent from the homes of the owners, which was a radical departure from the farmhouse-kiln tradition. Farming then fell by the wayside because making pottery became much more profitable (for the factory owners).

The problem that the Burslem pottery manufacturers faced was in the transportation of their fragile goods to market. Because of the location of the town near to the sources of the River Trent and its upper tributaries, transport by water was impossible. Furthermore, even in the mid-eighteenth century, the "roads" in and around Burslem were effectively little more than tracks, rutted with potholes and sometimes impassable in the winter because of mud and floods. They were therefore most unsuitable for the movement of pottery, the more so because the main form of transportation was by mule trains. Not surprisingly, breakages were frequent and journeys were slow and therefore costly. Consequently, the primitive system of communications acted as a serious restraint on the expansion of Burslem's booming industry.

The position was helped in 1763 when the route from Cheshire to Lichfield was made into a turnpike road, of much better quality, as far south as Burslem. By the same Act of Parliament, a turnpike, named Pack Horse Lane, was also created, which ran westwards from the town to Trubshaw Cross. Particularly once the Trent and Mersey Canal had come to Longport, this latter turnpike road became of considerable importance. The new turnpikes were an improvement on the existing "roads" and allowed the finished pottery to be moved by wagons, as well as mules, but they did not revolutionise the movement of the fragile goods because only relatively small quantities could be carried at a sedate pace, especially to ensure that the amount of breakages was minimised.

Burslem was by then exporting increasing quantities of pottery to Ireland, Continental Europe, North America and even as far afield as Africa and the West Indies. The potential of the trade was enormous for the manufacturers, but it was most laborious for them to get their ware to the main ports of Liverpool, Bristol and Hull for export. The nearest navigable river was the Weaver, from Winsford north, which was twenty miles away.

In 1757, the first modern English canal, the Sankey Brook Navigation, was opened, to transport coal from St. Helens, and other nearby places on the Lancashire Coalfield, to Liverpool. Its success inspired the Duke of Bridgewater, who owned mines at Worsley, in Lancashire, to promote the building of a canal to Manchester, seven miles away. The duke's problem was that the cost of transporting his coal by packhorse to the rapidly-growing cotton market town meant that his selling price was near prohibitive. The Bridgewater Canal opened in 1761 and was a tremendous success because the duke was able to reduce his prices by about half and still make a handsome profit.

These successes proved the catalyst for the construction of the remarkable 93-mile-long Trent and Mersey Canal, which transformed the transportation of pottery from Burslem. The visionary pottery manufacturer, Josiah Wedgwood, fully realised the immense commercial advantages that would result from the building of the canal and was its greatest advocate. The route was surveyed by James Brindley, the engineer of the Bridgewater Canal, and work began on it in 1766. It took eleven years to construct and Brindley had died before it was completed in 1777, but its creation was a major feat of engineering. From its maximum height of 408 feet at Etruria, the canal descended to the River Mersey through 35 locks and to the Trent by 40, but the greatest achievement was the building of the 3,000-yards-long tunnel through Harecastle Hill, northwest of Tunstall, which was called 'the eighth wonder of the world'.

From Harecastle Tunnel, the new canal ran broadly south-southeast down the Fowlea Valley, thus transforming the hitherto insignificant vale into a key highway in the new industrial England. The canal passed approximately three-quarters of a mile to the west of Burslem, down the hill at Longbridge, so named from the 100-feet-long structure carrying the Burslem to Newcastle packhorse road over the Fowlea Brook and the marsh that surrounded it.

The Trent and Mersey Canal gave Burslem waterway access to Liverpool and Hull, and the opening of the Staffordshire and Worcestershire Canal, from Great Haywood to Stourport, in 1772 also linked the town with the River Severn and Bristol. The short distance that the finished pottery goods had to travel to the canal on the relatively sound turnpike road meant that Burslem had become very accessible to numerous inland markets that the new waterway connected, as well as to the major coastal ports. Not surprisingly, a number of wharves soon opened along the canal in the proximity of Burslem, which provided the town with outlet ports.

Although the canals were very slow and primitive in comparison with modern transport systems, they had advantages so decisive compared with the roads of the time that Burslem and the numerous other growing industrial towns were able to expand on an unprecedented scale as the phenomenon of the Industrial Revolution got into full swing. Inland water transport was smooth and therefore ideal for the movement of fragile pottery goods, so there were few breakages, which led to a significant reduction in supply costs. Also, barges enabled the carriage of products in much greater bulk than could be achieved with mules and therefore there was a further saving on transportation costs. Another advantage was that, even allowing for time spent negotiating locks and tunnels, goods could generally be delivered more speedily on the canals than on the roads of the time. All these benefits enabled much larger profits to be made by manufacturers, few more so than those producing fragile items in landlocked upland settlements like Burslem.

The most important of Burslem's canal ports was at Longport, as Longbridge became renamed in 1777. Before the canal had been cut, Longbridge had comprised only a few cottages, but it grew quickly as a port and a manufacturing centre in its own right, with its first factory being built in 1773. Following the success of Longport, Westport developed a short way along the canal to the north and Middleport and Newport not far to the southeast. All these canal ports were in the Fowlea Valley, on the east side of the brook. So, down the hill to the west of Burslem, to deal with the booming trade, there developed a veritable valley of ports – the port vale.

The settlement at Longport grew quickly and sprawled eastwards as Burslem expanded rapidly westwards, so that eventually there became a continuous urban area between the two. Likewise, the building of houses and factories in Middleport and Newport followed the arrival of the canal until the whole area to the east of it became urbanised.

Although the origins of Port Vale Football Club remain disputed, there is general agreement that it was formed in Burslem's docklands in the vicinity of the Trent and Mersey Canal. Indeed, Enoch Hood, the celebrated co-founder of the club was born in 1861 at 48 Navigation Street, Middleport, and several of Vale's other early, and quite possibly founding, players are known to have been living in the valley of ports at the time. Therefore, had there been no port in the vale, there would have no doubt remained little settlement in the Fowlea Valley west of Burslem and so it is hard to believe that there would ever have been a Port Vale Football Club and most certainly one of note. To suggest otherwise would seem to be irrational.

It might be argued that, had Josiah Wedgwood not been born, there would never have been a Trent and Mersey Canal and consequently no port in the vale. Although Wedgwood was the main proponent of the canal, he was not the only individual who could see the potentially immense commercial advantages that a navigable new waterway through the Potteries would offer. Indeed, the Company of Proprietors of the Navigation from the Trent to the Mersey included the Duke of Bridgewater; the MP, Earl Gower, who was also Viscount Trentham; Thomas Anson, the MP for Lichfield; the Birmingham metal manufacturer, Matthew Boulton, and the ironmaster, Samuel Garbett, as well as Wedgwood and many other local manufacturers and landowners. With such an array of powerful, wealthy and pioneering individuals involved, it is unimaginable that none of them would have promoted the idea of a canal if Josiah Wedgwood had not existed. Huge potential profits beckoned the initiative of bold entrepreneurs in an age of opportunity and they were not essentially dependent on the existence of very specific individuals.

Of course, it can also be maintained that the real canal pioneer was the Duke of Bridgewater, who has been called the 'father of British inland navigation' and whose efforts preceded those of Wedgwood. Therefore it can be argued that, once the duke's canal had proved highly successful, the canal age was inevitable, irrespective of the other individuals who would, in the event, become involved in developing it. However, had the duke's engagement to the dowager Duchess of Hamilton not been broken off in 1758, he might well have spent his life in London society or elsewhere and not have devoted himself to his estate at Worsley and the development of canals.

In turn, perhaps the construction of the Trent and Mersey Canal and the development of the ports in the vale can be attributed to James Brindley. Had he not built the Bridgewater Canal for the duke, he may never have surveyed the Trent and Mersey Canal and been the driving force behind its construction. Perhaps Brindley was the real genius of the canals and the duke a lucky entrepreneur who happened upon him. Having said that, the duke clearly recognised the outstanding talents of Brindley, who had been born to humble parents in the Derbyshire hills, was illiterate and rarely resorted to writing or drawing! Also, had the Duke of Bridgewater's love life, his ambitions and his wealth and the circumstances of the age been different, Brindley might have simply have worked his way up from being an apprentice millwright to a qualified millwright and been unknown to history.

Furthermore, the Sankey Brook Navigation preceded Brindley's and the Duke of Bridgewater's involvement in building canals and so they already had an example to work from. In that case, perhaps they were merely carrying on more of the good work that had gone before, produced by the Sankey Brook Navigation Company and their engineer, Henry Berry. Even their ideas were inherited from the ancient Egyptians, Greeks and Romans and not created in isolation from the construction of canals in the Netherlands, most notably in Amsterdam, the previous century.

According to this reasoning, it seems that trends and not individuals were responsible for the creation and development of the Burslem docks, the ports in the vale, and therefore, indirectly, Port Vale Football Club. It may well be that none of the canal pioneers in modern English history was so important as to have been an irreplaceable individual, without whom there would have been no canal age. So it might appear that the foundation of Port Vale Football Club was inevitable.

However, the construction of the canals did not occur in isolation. They were not built for the sake of having splendid waterways. Perhaps the development of the canals was a catalyst for the Industrial Revolution, but the canals, and the railways that followed them, were also key servants of industrial expansion. The age-old conundrum comes to mind: which came first, the chicken or the egg? Industry or transport?

Without a considerable increase in demand from industry for a new, more efficient form of communications to transport raw materials to factories and finished goods to market, it is inconceivable that a national canal network would have been built, let alone within ninety years of its commencement. In turn, there could have been no upsurge in industry without a sufficient demand for its products and an available cheap labour force willing to make them, so that large profits became achievable. The increasing home and world population meant more goods were wanted and needed, especially textiles, which made up sixty per cent of British exports by 1850. A fair proportion of the sales of clothes were to England's urban poor, who had largely made their own garments before they had been removed from the countryside by land enclosures, which in themselves were crucial in providing a desperate mass of townspeople prepared to work at almost any price.

The main reason why the countryside was depopulated was because the lords realised that compact land holdings, without the peasants and their open-field strips, could be farmed extensively, with the maximisation of profits. Capitalist agriculture on an unprecedented scale then became possible. Prior to the Agrarian Revolution of the eighteenth century, there had been limited potential for selling food for profit, except around the large towns, especially London, because most people had worked on the land as subsistence farmers. Having said that, the enclosures of the sixteenth century had sown the seeds of agribusiness by removing sizable numbers of small farmers from the land, many of whom had drifted to the towns and been forced to become purchasers, instead of producers, of food. In the towns, with either low-paid jobs or no jobs, the poverty of most of the dispossessed farmers grew and so did the sizes of their families, as they sought the alleviation of their situations through the potential employment of their children.

Without land enclosures and the resultant drift to the towns, it is highly unlikely that a population explosion would have occurred in England from the eighteenth century onwards, not least because subsistence farmers tend to regulate their own numbers as there is a maximum amount of mouths they can feed. And without the population upsurge, it is extremely doubtful that the Industrial Revolution would have occurred because there would have been insufficient numbers of consumers and producers.

In turn, any successful business venture needs capital to support and promote it, as to which concept most fans of the almost perennially underfunded Port Vale Football Club would surely testify. The increasing acquisition of overseas colonies in the seventeenth and eighteenth centuries provided cheap resources, especially cotton, which formed the bedrock of industrialisation. Huge profits were generated by merchants from the Triangular Slave Trade with West Africa and the

Americas, with the result that much larger amounts of money came into circulation. The accumulation of this greater wealth in turn provided the capital needed for the undertaking of very large-scale projects, like the building of factories, which then employed the desperate masses in the new industrial towns. As British trade expanded and purpose-built industrial workplaces became more common, the philosophy of capitalism became respectable and admired and would-be entrepreneurs were increasingly attracted to its notion of speculating to accumulate. Or it could be that the notion of acquisition itself was the reason for the establishment of the colonies, so that an expansionist ideology amongst people of power and wealth was the catalyst for increasing overseas trade, and the developments that followed, rather than the consequence.

So it could be that the Trent and Mersey Canal, the valley of ports and Port Vale Football Club were created by the eighteenth century transport revolution or the Industrial Revolution or land enclosures or the boom in population or the acquisition of cheap resources or the increase in the amount of money in circulation or the development of a capitalist way of thinking or a combination of any numbers of these factors. Alternatively, perhaps it was only the chance coalescence of these elements, and many more besides, that produced the conditions which eventually led to the development of the vale of ports. As the factors seem interconnected, it could be that, had one or two of them not been in place at the time, the preconditions for dramatic change would not have been present. Therefore, it could well be that the right circumstances for the founding of Port Vale Football Club came about purely by chance and that there was nothing inevitable about it.

However, most interestingly, it can be argued that the origins of the very system in England that underpinned all of the factors leading to the industrial and transport revolutions occurred by the unlikeliest combinations of chance. In attitude, there is little to distinguish the eleventh century Norman Empire, based on England, from the British one which succeeded it. Indeed, it is not possible to differentiate the two because the former gradually developed into the latter. Avarice and individualism were key characteristics of the Normans, which became embedded in the post-1066 ruling class in England and defined their outlook on the world that lasted until colonialism and industrialisation and beyond. There may be centuries beyond the Norman Conquest and the heyday of the Triangular Slave Trade, but the common attitudes of the successful players were all too similar. The connections between the Slave Trade and the building of the ports in the vale were very strong too, even though they may not seem obvious at first sight.

Had the democratic subsistence farming communities of the Anglo-Saxons not been crushed by the Norman Conquest, we would now live in a very different country, most probably with a much smaller population, but with a considerably higher percentage of the people living in the countryside and engaged in agriculture. It is very doubtful that there would have been industrialisation and urbanisation on anywhere near the scale that took place, in which case an inland waterway transport revolution would not have been required. Consequently, Barcardeslim would perhaps have developed gradually only into a large village or a very small town and never become called Burslem. Without the rapid growth of Barcardeslim and the other settlements in the Potteries area, it is highly likely that a canal connecting North Staffordshire to the coast would never have been built. Therefore, the ports in the vale would not have existed and so there could not have been established a Port Vale Football Club in the Fowlea Valley. Despite these projected radically different circumstances, it is possible that football could still have developed into a very popular sport in England and that there could still have been participating teams from North Staffordshire, including one called Barcardeslim or something similar, but the name Port Vale would have been entirely absent from the fixture lists.

It is interesting to speculate on what might have been, but is it really conceivable that life in England could have been so dramatically different today from how it is? Because everything that exists at any time is the product of past events, which seem not to have been predetermined, then the answer is that indeed it could, especially as a result of outcomes that seemed unlikely when they occurred. Moreover, in world history, very few situations have been so radically altered by such an unlikely combination of events as those that took place in and around England in the fateful year of 1066.

Could it really be that the foundation of Port Vale Football Club was a result of King Harold Godwinesson being hit in an eye by an arrow at the Battle of Hastings on 14 October 1066? Probably not, but not because the events were separated by more than eight centuries or that there appears to be no obvious connection between them. The Battle of Hastings was a seminal event in world history and two dramatically different futures, particularly for England and its people, depended on its outcome.

If Robert Wace is to be believed, it was late in the day when great misfortune struck Harold and by then the battle had very probably already been lost by the English. Also, if Harold was struck by an arrow, it did not hit him entirely by chance. It is doubtful that any arrow was specifically aimed at him because William, the Norman duke, had belatedly commanded his archers to fire upwards into the air, over the protective shield wall of the English army. There followed a cloud of arrows descending from the sky on the mass of Englishmen gathered on the ridge at Senlac. Many Anglo-Saxon warriors must have consequently been struck by these missiles, some of them being seriously injured and others killed. So, although it is extremely doubtful that Harold himself was a specific target, the Norman stratagem proved to be highly successful by knocking out the enemy commander. In contemporary parlance, it could be argued that Duke William had cleverly made his own luck.

Even if the story is true, Harold's injury very probably made no difference as to which side won the battle, but it may well have affected the scale and importance of the Norman victory. Had Harold remained fit and well, it is possible that the English army could have fought a retreat to the vast woodlands of Andredsweald, a short distance to the north, and remained a significant future threat to the Norman invaders. However, it is doubtful that a manoeuvre so tricky could have been completed successfully at such a critical time, when the English army was under full assault from the Normans. Also, as Harold had no quality reserves and the Normans received very significant reinforcements shortly after the battle, it seems that the Conquest would have been successful anyhow, although it may have taken longer and been even more bloody. So, even if it is true that Harold had the great misfortune to be struck in an eye by an arrow, it does not appear to have led, albeit indirectly, to the foundation of Port Vale Football Club.

The directions that the winds blew from during the key stages of the 1066 campaign, however, are another matter. It is quite remarkable how consistently the winds favoured the prospects of the Normans, so much so that they were arguably the greatest single factor leading to the Conquest.

Although William's armada was ready to transport his invasion force to England in August 1066, the east and then north winds that blew prevented it from doing so. Little did he realise that the wind was actually blowing to his advantage because Harold had assembled a very large army in the south of England to crush him. Then, when the wind changed direction and enabled the Normans to set sail, the elements intervened again as a storm got up and allowed them to escape in the nick of time from the clutches of the much stronger Anglo-Saxon fleet in the Channel.

Unfortunately for Harold, the north wind, which had prevented the probable annihilation of the Norman army, sped southwards to England a vast Norwegian invasion force. The scale of the loss of Anglo-Saxon military manpower in the destruction of the Viking host then meant that Harold was left to face the Normans with a significantly depleted force, especially in the quality of its soldiers.

Finally, the weather had a great impact on events once more. While the English army was recuperating in York from its titanic struggle against the Norsemen, the wind blew from the south and enabled the Normans to land in England without opposition and gave them ample time to secure their bridgehead before Harold could return to oppose them. Thus, the uncanny intervention of the elements played a decisive role in transforming the Norman invasion of England from a wild adventure into an era-changing conquest.

Had the elements behaved in an altogether more likely and predictable fashion, the odds are that the combined Anglo-Saxon fleet and army, with their full force to bear, would have destroyed the Normans. Having said that, Harold's land forces would very probably have paid a significant price for their success in such a struggle, suffering considerable losses themselves, especially from William's crack troops, the knights. In that case, they would have been less well able to have dealt successfully with the Norse invasion, which would have followed. It may have been that the Norsemen this time would have been the eventual victors and conquered England. However, had that been the outcome, the long-term future of England would almost certainly have been very different than it turned out to be through the Norman Conquest. The Norsemen had a very similar culture and language to the Anglo-Saxons and their previous incursions had ultimately led to them quietly settling down as farmers alongside the English in a society that was little changed by the process. Thus, although Cnut of Denmark had conquered England in 1016, only 26 years later an Anglo-Saxon king (Edward the Confessor) was peacefully elected to the throne and most everything returned to normal.

Therefore, even had the Norsemen been the ultimate victors in the 1066 three-way struggle, the probability is that England would quickly have absorbed them and carried on much as before. However, the Normans were radically different, with a strange language and customs alien to the Anglo-Saxons, and had a propensity to greed, aggression and conquest, which fundamentally changed England and its people forever.

In conclusion, it may be at least an exaggeration to say that a chance arrow, which apparently struck King Harold of England, led, centuries later, to the formation of Port Vale Football Club, but had the winds of 1066 not behaved in such an unpredictable and uncanny manner, it is exceedingly unlikely that there would be such a team in existence today. In that case, the Vale supporters can only speculate as to what they would be doing on their Saturday afternoons instead of following their favourites. Dare it be mentioned that one possibility is that they would be following Stoke City and calling them the pride of Staffordshire! Perhaps, therefore, they have a lot to thank or blame William the Bastard for, even though he did not realise what the outcome of his efforts would be over eight centuries later!

2 The Tall Tale Of 1876!

It is, of course, well known and almost universally believed that Port Vale Football Club was formed in 1879, as an offshoot of the Porthill Victoria team. It would be potentially insulting the knowledge of the readers of this book to repeat once again the details of Vale's long-accepted origins, but, for the purpose of introducing the intriguing story that follows, it is necessary to take that risk.

Although a written record of the formation of Port Vale has never been found, it is known that Enoch Hood was the football team's first captain. In 1926, Hood told *The Staffordshire Sentinel* that Vale had begun their existence as an athletic club formed to play cricket, which was 'mixed with a little football' after the first few months.

The earliest known existing record of the foundation of the club has been traced to *The Football Annual* of 1883, edited by the renowned football pioneer, Charles W. Alcock. The publication was highly respected and, in the absence of stronger evidence, its detailed statistics are generally regarded to be accurate or at least as accurate as are available. In that year, the annual listed Vale's year of formation as 1880 and, because the date is in such close proximity to 1879, it is likely that Alcock was close to the truth. However, it is doubtful whether that year has ever been locally proposed as a serious contender for the year of Vale's foundation and, as a national publication, it is difficult to regard the annual as reliable a source of information of footballing details in North Staffordshire as local sources. For example, the 1883 annual inaccurately listed F. Gater, instead of Samuel Gater, as Vale's secretary.

The best local information on the formation of the club was not surprisingly provided by the *Sentinel*. On 22 September 1900, the newspaper published an article, which described how, in 1879, members of Porthill, 'a most prominent team,' were discontented because it was inconvenient to travel to the field on which they played, which was quite possibly off Pitgreen Lane, in Wolstanton. Therefore, according to the *Sentinel*, they had a meeting one evening in Limekiln Lane [presumably Limekiln Road], Longport, at which 'the members who desired to play nearer home were present and it was then decided to start an entirely new club'. The newspaper stated that a second meeting was held some days later at a hotel in Amen Corner, Longport, when detailed arrangements for the organisation of the new club were agreed upon. Seemingly, it was at this gathering that the name Port Vale was chosen. As Longport was but one of the sites of a series of wharves along the Trent and Mersey Canal for the loading and unloading of barges in the valley of ports, the name Port Vale is an unremarkable and perhaps rather obvious one to have chosen for the new club.

Although it was published 21 years after the event, this matter-of-fact account has a strong ring of authenticity about it and is only one year out of step with Charles Alcock's date of Vale's origin. The story seems to have been accepted by the newspaper's readership (and therefore, presumably, by the club's officials, supporters and founding players) because no following critical letters or amendments to the original article were printed. The published story appears to have been regarded as true because it was repeated at least four times up to 10 March 1928 and the foundation year of 1879 was stated at least eight times until

24 August 1931. Also, of course, it has been accepted as correct by the club and its supporters ever since.

A foundation meeting in a hotel is not only believable, but fairly likely as drinking houses were very much a part of working-class life at the time, even for children. This was substantiated by Paul Molloy in his book, *Recreation In Newcastle-under-Lyme 1837-1900*, in 1982. He said, 'Sporting clubs, particularly in the later decades of the century were based in the pub.'

The likelihood of Vale's formation occurring in 1879 is further affirmed by three other key pieces of evidence:

The first of these is the fact that the club's ninth annual meeting was held on 24 August 1887. Therefore, the first such meeting took place in 1879, assuming that the one which founded the club was regarded as the initial annual meeting.

The second piece of evidence favouring 1879 is an appeal by Vale's chairman, Robert Audley, in a letter which was published in the *Sentinel* on 18 May 1907, asking for businessmen to step forward to help save the club. He said that, 'Unless capital is forthcoming, there must be an end to an organisation of 28 years' standing.' For Audley to have got his arithmetic bang on, it is likely that the year of 1879 was well known at the time to have been the date of Vale's foundation. Although, as the chairman of the club, he should have had a reasonable idea of Vale's origins, especially as they were still well within living memory, the precision of his figure suggests a certainty of knowledge.

The third vital piece of evidence indicates that Vale were formed in 1879 as an offshoot of the Porthill side and therefore substantiates the 22 September 1900 *Sentinel* article. The *Sentinel* reported three matches played by team called Porthill Victoria in the 1878-1879 season. They beat Middleport True Blues 3-1 at home on 23 November 1878 and won 1-0 at Mow Cop Rovers 2nd the following Saturday before losing 2-1 at home to Brownhills Pottery 2nd on 4 January 1879. In the second of these games, John Hood scored the winner, whilst the consolation goal in the last of the matches was bagged by E. Hood. It is highly likely that this John Hood was Enoch's elder brother, who was usually known as Jack and who almost certainly soon became a founder of Port Vale, whilst there is every probability that E. Hood was none other than Enoch Hood himself. Because Enoch was a forward and Jack made history by scoring Vale's first ever goal, their sharpshooting for Porthill Victoria adds to the evidence connecting the two clubs.

The dates of the Porthill Victoria games fit nicely into the *Sentinel's* account of Vale's origins and help to indicate the following likely sequence of events: Porthill Victoria were competing in organised football matches against other teams in the 1878-1879 season; various members of the side (including Enoch and Jack Hood) were dissatisfied with playing their home games in Wolstanton and they therefore formed Port Vale, very probably for the next campaign, which started in the autumn of 1879. In addition, after the 1878-1879 season, nothing further was recorded about Porthill Victoria until 29 March 1884, by when Vale had become a team of some note. It is unknown whether Porthill Victoria folded following the defection of a number of their players to Vale and later re-formed or were established as a new club. However, any way round it makes no difference to the origins of Port Vale.

Enoch Hood was born on 10 January 1861 at 48 Navigation Street,

Middleport, close to the Trent and Mersey Canal in the vale of ports. The family were still in the area in 1871, in Ford Street (which is now Eyre Street), but by 1881 they had moved to Porthill. By then, Enoch was living in Watlands View and Jack in Queen Street and therefore they were very close to Porthill Victoria's playing field. However, the football matches took place on Saturday afternoons after the players had finished work for the day, which could be quite late. By that hour in the winter, there was little time left to fit in a game before it went dark. Enoch and Jack Hood were employed as potters, as was Billy Poulson, a probable founding member of Port Vale, who lived at 31 Stubbs Street, Longport. Their most likely workplaces were therefore factories down in the port vale and, after several hours' hard work, they must have undertaken an unwelcome slog up the hill to Wolstanton, in a race against the increasing twilight in midwinter, to fit in a game of football. Therefore, a team playing in a field close to the factories in the valley of ports would have been a much more attractive option to them and the founder members of the new club who lived in the vale would have no longer had to travel so far to get home after each match.

The choice of the name Port Vale for the new team follows neatly from the above explanation of events. The majority of football clubs were (and still are) named after the place in which they were formed, as were Porthill Victoria themselves. Along the banks of the Trent and Mersey Canal west of Burslem at that time were Westport, Longport, Middleport and Newport, containing the main docks of the area, and Port Vale Wharf, Port Vale Street, Port Vale Corn Mills and Port Vale House were all in the vicinity. There were numerous football teams in and around Burslem in 1879, but the name Port Vale was not used by any of them, so it was vacant and therefore ready to be adopted, especially by players who already had an affinity with the area. Also, the breakaway footballers had played for Porthill Victoria on the hill above the Fowlea Brook and the new club was based in the valley below, so Port Vale was a natural, and perhaps the most obvious, choice of name to have selected. Finally, the veracity of the team being called after the Port Vale place name is supported by a near contemporaneous article in the *Sentinel* on 1 February 1887.

So it was that Port Vale began their long history in 1879, playing in the meadows in the Fowlea Valley, mainly against other local teams. Although no written documents pertaining to the club's origins have ever been discovered, and almost certainly never will be, the accepted story above of Vale's formation is greatly supported by the available evidence, is known to have been believed for well over a century and seems eminently sensible and logical. Indeed, at this late stage, unless some incontrovertible evidence near miraculously appears to challenge the long-agreed foundation story, it must be accepted as the factual account of what actually happened.

Having said that, wild revisionist ideas on a whole range of established facts abound in the modern world. One of the great masters of writing fantastic fiction as "fact" was the twelfth century cleric, Geoffrey of Monmouth, the author of the *Historia Regum Britanniae*. His "history" book claimed that the British Isles had once been inhabited by a race of giants, traced the ancestry of the English monarchs to the Trojans, denied that the Romans had ever conquered Britain, stated that an army of Africans had helped the Anglo-Saxons to establish England and did much to create King Arthur. More remarkable still is the fact that

Geoffrey's fantastic work was widely celebrated, even though it was utterly worthless as a piece of history.

A second example of making myths to try to fix facts occurred in the latter half of the twentieth century when it became popular amongst the new far right to deny that the genocide by Nazi Germany of around six million Jews in the Second World War ever took place, despite overwhelming evidence to the contrary. The mainstream history books have not changed their stance on the subject as a result, but there remain considerable numbers of people in complete denial of the existence of the Holocaust.

Even more far-fetched is the incredible claim by the writer and ex-broadcaster, David Icke, that accepted history is almost entirely wrong because the world is in "fact" ruled by a secret group of reptilian humanoids called the Babylonian Brotherhood, who include in their ranks none other than the current monarch of the United Kingdom, Queen Elizabeth II, and the American musician, Kris Kristofferson! According to Icke, human beings were created in a breeding programme by the Anunnaki, a race of reptilian creatures from the Draco constellation! Although many people are easy prey to crazy counter-establishment ideas, Icke's claims have so far gained him relatively few followers, but much ridicule.

Nevertheless, it is fair to say that even the longest-standing and most accepted of wisdoms are only as strong as their ability to beat off the challenges to them that may arise. It may well be that nothing is set in tablets of stone and that all beliefs are purely statements of the times in which they exist, however certain they may seem to be. Thus the Biblical version of creation, which appears to have been almost entirely accepted in the Western world not much more than a century ago, has now been largely swept aside by scientific explanations of the origin of the universe, such as the Big Bang concept. However, it could be that science itself is just another theory.

So, in the light of the challenging world in which we live today, just how secure is the 1879 Porthill Victoria offshoot explanation of the origins of Port Vale Football Club? Pretty safe, it would seem, as it has so long stood the test of time. However, nothing is certain and it is always feasible that its doom could be just around the corner. However, what could the nature of any revisionist claim possibly be?

Suppose, for the sake of argument, that a counter-version of Vale's date of origin suddenly appeared approaching fifty years after the club's foundation, say in 1926. How might this have come about and what could have been the reactions of the club's founders, officials and supporters to it? To investigate these questions, actuality needs to be suspended in favour of the, hopefully, imaginative story which follows.

Let's assume that in fiction world, on 16 January 1926, the *Sentinel*, the long-standing proponent of the established view of the club's formation, suddenly, and without any explanation, quoted January 1876 as the date of the great event. Although such a possibility is scarcely believable, if it had occurred, it would surely have shocked the newspaper's readership, the club's founders and the then current officials so much that there would have been considerable correspondence on the subject. However, suppose that there was none and then, only eleven days after the newspaper article, matter of fact, Vale held their jubilee celebration in the Queen's Hall, Burslem, which was attended by 2,000 people. One can only speculate as to what would have attracted them all to commemorate unquestioningly, at such a high-profile event, a date which had never previously been suggested as marking the origin of the club. Such an occurrence seems inconceivable, but, of course, fiction is stranger than fact.

The readers of this book will appreciate that poetic licence can enable the fantasy world Enoch Hood to give the only apparent explanation of the occurrence of the mystery jubilee to the *Sentinel*, to be dutifully reported in its pages the following day. It is, of course, to be expected that Hood's account of the events would have solved the strange puzzle, but what if he had made no reference whatsoever to the traditional foundation story and date? Also, what if he had simply recalled, seemingly out of the blue, that Vale had started playing cricket in April 1875 and included football from 1876? Clearly, the fiction world story would deepen because it would then need to be asked as to why his account had never come to light before and how he knew the exact month when Vale came into existence and began playing cricket 51 years previously if there was no founding document. The obvious solution would be that Hood had kept a diary, but had, all the time since then, kept his knowledge to himself, as had all of Vale's other founder members. However, suppose he had never written a diary. How then could he possibly have had such precise facts at his disposal after approximately fifty years? Perhaps that could be explained by saying that teenagers are renowned for their rapid recall of the specific dates when they first started playing a particular game with their friends and that the memories of old men remain so perfect that exact details of past times can be conjured up with ease. Alas, neither is true because people's accurate recall of precise dates, even in their own lives, is unusual and so the presentation of such arguments would be akin to taking a lamb to await slaughter.

A plausible explanation of this fiction world conundrum is that, as Vale's jubilee of 1929 was approaching, a journalist from the *Sentinel* took it upon himself to seek out Enoch Hood and ask him questions about the foundation of the club, without expecting his answers to deviate from the established facts. It could be that the correspondent was very surprised by Hood's answers, but dutifully repeated them, whilst making no attempt at investigative journalism to try to square the circle. In that case, the opportunity for an extremely interesting debate on the intriguing different options, which surely would have created the greatest interest, was entirely missed.

Alternatively, Hood might have made vague remarks about when the monumental formation event occurred, something like: 'Oh, I suppose it must be coming up to fifty years by now. It seems a very long time ago. We started off playing cricket and then a bit later we began to have a go at football because there was nothing to do in the winter otherwise.'

In this case, his interviewer could have interpreted Hood's mention of fifty years as being a literal figure and regarded him as meaning Vale's foundation had occurred half a century before at that precise, or near-precise, moment, instead of being a rough estimate of time past. Also, Hood's apparent specific mention of April as being the start of Vale's cricketing activities could fairly easily be explained by the journalist having made the neat statement from more vague comments because the cricket season then began in that month, just as it does now. Another possible interpretation of Hood's revelation is that he could have been describing the start of his own involvement with organised sport, which preceded Port Vale. Alternatively, it might have been that the *Sentinel* journalist did not realise that that Hood was essentially referring to his own beginnings and not those of the club in the valley of ports. Even in the fiction world, it therefore could be that the Enoch Hood story did not contradict the long-accepted date of 1879 of Vale's origins.

However, suppose at the hypothetical jubilee celebration, Vale's chairman, Sampson Walker, himself had referred to 1876 as being the club's formation date. He would have been corroborating Enoch Hood's story and vice versa, which would have added to the credibility of both their versions of history. Having said that, it is inconceivable that either Vale's chairman or their co-founder would have stood up at their jubilee celebrations and said: 'Well, of course, this isn't fifty years after the real date the club started. It's actually in three years' time. So I've no idea why we're here tonight, but I suppose we may as well carry on enjoying the event anyway.' They would have been pilloried! In any case, it is doubtful if Walker would have really known anything about Vale's foundation, except by hearsay, because it had occurred a very long time before and it is highly unlikely that he had been present at the time.

One's imagination could be stretched further by saying that the fiction world *Sentinel* reverted to quoting 1879 as Vale's foundation date only just over two years after the celebrated 1926 jubilee, say on 10 March 1928, and again, for argument's sake, on 24 August 1931. If that had really happened, whatever would the by then bemused supporters have thought about it all. The much-used modern phrase, 'You don't know what you're doing,' springs to mind, but then again what is being projected here is only fiction and its plausibility needs to be suspended. It is, after all, not necessary in the world of fantasy to let the facts get in the way of a good yarn.

To add an amazing new twist to the tall tale, suppose the opinions on the origins of Port Vale of a William Powner, who had no proven connection to the club, had been published even later in the *Sentinel*, say on 1 August 1935. In the world of fiction, Powner might have said: 'Fifty-eight years ago ten or a dozen young men met in Lime Kiln Lane [sic], Longport, and decided to form a football club. All details were settled, with one exception – the club's name. Then one of the company, looking up at the wall, espied the words "Port Vale House" – and that was how Port Vale Football Club came to be founded and how it got its name.'

The fantasy William Powner would, of course, have claimed to have been present at this monumental event, which romantically and neatly marked the very moment of Vale's birth in a sudden, recordable blinding flash of inspiration. Perhaps the readers of this book will regard it as far-fetched, even in a piece of fantasy, for a foundation messiah finally to have appeared well over half a century after the origin of the club, expounding belated words of wisdom. Of course, it needs to be remembered that this terrific tale is only a piece of fiction, even though a fabulous fable it may be!

In any case, the first flaw in this story is that even a mythical William Powner should have known that the name of the street they were in was Limekiln *Road* and not *Lane*. Even more obviously, the gathered company in Limekiln Road would have realised exactly whereabouts they were because at least some, and likely all, of them lived or worked in the vale of ports and so they would not have needed to look up to find a sign containing the words 'Port Vale' for inspiration. Alternatively, it is just possible that the ten or a dozen would-be footballers had no connection with the port vale and had wandered there by accident from somewhere else and then, purely by chance, discovered the very name they wanted on a house. In this case, they would obviously have been vastly less spatially aware than the founders of Stoke, Liverpool, Newcastle United and numerous other place-name clubs. Having said that, a novel full of such near impossibilities would hardly be likely to be in the running for the Booker Prize!

The story's chances would not, of course, be helped if it was shown that there was absolutely no record of William Powner having played for Vale or served them in any official capacity. Also, suppose that the *Sentinel* had nevertheless in 1926 listed him with forty years' connection to the club. That would have left him at least seven years adrift of Vale's foundation and suggested that his fantastic tale had been concocted or, at best, was second hand. However, it could have been that the newspaper had made a mistake with its figures and that Powner therefore had been unjustly represented.

However, just imagine if it so happened that the fictitious William Powner had a poor memory and was all at sea with facts. For example, as previously mentioned, in 1935 he had said that Vale had been founded 58 years earlier, that is in 1877, which made him the only known person, fictitious or real, ever to suggest that the birth of the club was in that particular year. Also, he might have said that Vale had played their first really important game against Preston North End around 1879, whereas even in fiction world the team were only competing against local clubs until 1883. Moreover, suppose Powner was not a modest man and described himself as 'an important member' of the Vale side in their early days, but was actually so vital to their play that he 'soon retired from active playing' to become the club's treasurer, even though his name is absent from Vale's real historical records in both capacities. Perhaps, therefore, the strange claims of William Powner could only ever have made him a character in a world of fiction unless, of course, fact is more peculiar still!

Let's finish our brief visit to fantasy world with a final supposition, one so fantastic that it will surely make the readers of this book laugh about its implausibility, if not drive them to ridicule the whole point of the author having mentioned it. Suppose that, in the real world, the accepted year of Vale's foundation (1879) and the place-name explanation of the club becoming called Port Vale (from the valley of ports) had actually been challenged by the hitherto fictitious cases just mentioned. That is, suppose that the club had really held its jubilee out of the blue, and without explanation, at the Queen's Hall, Burslem, on 27 January 1926 after at least 26 years of apparently accepting 1879 as Vale's date of origin. Also, suppose that there really had been a William Powner, who, on 1 August 1935, had claimed in the *Sentinel* that the club had become called Port Vale purely by chance, after the name of a house that the founder members happened to be standing next to. In addition, suppose that the new explanations had replaced the long-standing accounts of Vale's origins and become the accepted wisdom over time despite their implausibility and a lack of hard evidence to support them. Furthermore, suppose that they had still been in the ascendant today, with the club officials, the supporters and the general public, almost to a man and woman, regarding them as straightforward facts set in tablets of stone. Finally, what if all these suppositions in themselves were actually real and today it *was* generally believed that Port Vale had been founded in 1876 and named after a house? Would that then be fact or fantasy? Would the tall tale of 1876 be the truth or a really ripping yarn?

There is something further to consider in this world of what might or might not have been. That is, if the fiction world turned out to be the real world, what difference would it have made, if any, to the history of Port Vale Football Club?

An important question to ask is how things might have been different if Vale had actually been founded in 1876 instead of 1879. Slight variations in events can lead to monumental changes in outcomes, not least in the long term, as the consequences of the various wind directions around England in August and September 1066 testify. Of course, no-one will ever really be able to predict the possible fine details of alternative scenarios with any degree of accuracy, but some reasonable guesstimates can be made that are considerably more likely than speculative stabs in the dark.

The one certain thing is that if the club's date of origin had been different, the club's history would have differed too. In 1879, Enoch Hood, a known founding member of Port Vale and the club's first captain, became eighteen, whereas he was only fifteen in 1876. Although children matured more quickly into adults in the hard world of Victorian England than they do now, it is difficult to accept that Hood could have been so instrumentally important to Vale in their formative years if he had still been a juvenile at the time. It is common knowledge that young men of eighteen are almost invariably vastly more mature than adolescents of fifteen. Therefore, it is inconceivable that Hood co-founded and captained a football team of players several years older than himself. For him to have taken such a key role, it is likely that most of the other players involved were no older than he was and they, or at least some of them, could easily have been younger. Football really was a man's game at that time, based more on brute force than finesse, and, had Hood's adolescent upstarts tackled teams of full-grown men, it is doubtful that they would have persisted in playing for long.

Although Enoch's brother, Jack, was older than him, having been born in 1857, other early Vale players and possible founder members were not. Joe Baskerville, the team's first recorded goalkeeper, had probably been born in 1861, as had Charlie Simpson, the right-half in the first reported Vale line-up. Half-back Harry Hodgkinson, one of the club's original players, was born in 1862, as were Vale's first known right-back, Ralph Dain, and half-back Billy Poulson, who was a probable co-founder of the club. The first reported centre-forward, Billy Reynolds, was probably born in 1864. Then there was the defender, George Bateman, a close friend of Enoch Hood, who was born in 1865 and was a pioneer of the club or at least a very early player for it. It seems just about possible for Bateman to have been involved in the formation of the first Vale team at the age of fourteen in 1879, but it really stretches the imagination to believe he can have had such a role when he was eleven in 1876.

Therefore, in the very unlikely event that Vale had been founded in 1876, their adolescent players and consequently the club would most probably have been quickly kicked into touch. Football teams were born and died with great rapidity in those days and few lasted for many years. A side of more mature players in 1879 would have stood a much greater chance of surviving the rigours of such a rough competitive sport than would a bunch of juveniles in 1876. So the date of the formation of the club was very probably crucial in determining its longevity. Being founded by Enoch Hood and co. in 1879, Vale had a chance of competing on reasonably even terms with other local football clubs. Had they been formed in 1876, it is doubtful if they would have survived for more than a year or two at most and they may well never have appeared in recorded history.

Had that been the case, in 1892, the by then named Burslem Port Vale would not have been elected to the Second Division of the Football League. That would have left it a club short and given the opportunity for another team to have joined the select few. But which club would that have been? Fifteen had applied in good time for membership of the division, but three of them were rejected: Birmingham St. George's, Long Eaton Rangers and Sunderland Albion.

The first mentioned side were the only members of the Football Alliance (the Football League's main rivals) not to be admitted into the Second Division and therefore they might have been in pole position to have gained entry in Vale's stead. However, they had finished bottom of the table at the end of the 1891-1892 season and had been hammered 4-0 by Sunderland Albion in the first round of the F.A. Cup. Consequently, their credentials were not very impressive and they disbanded that same year because of financial difficulties.

In 1892, Long Eaton Rangers had ended up ninth out of eleven teams in the Midland League, which was considered inferior to the Alliance, and therefore their application was not very impressive either.

That left Sunderland Albion, but they had only managed to finish sixth out of nine sides in the Northern League, the standard of which was regarded as being well below the Football League.

So, had Vale not been in the frame for election to the Second Division, the Football League would have been in a quandary and may have had to have considered further options. There were plenty of other teams around of some importance and the league might well have cast its eyes over them. A speculative guess of which could have seemed the most attractive can perhaps be best made by examining the five new clubs which were admitted to the division the following season and expanded its members from twelve to fifteen (sic).

The most famous today of the five were Liverpool, but they were involved in a wrangle with Everton until June 1892 over which of them was actually the latter, a member club of the First Division. By the time the issue had been resolved by the Football Association, who refused to recognise Liverpool as Everton, preferring instead to endorse Everton as being Everton, it was rather late in the day for Liverpool to be admitted to the Second Division, so their application was rejected and they joined the Lancashire League instead. It is therefore doubtful that Liverpool would have taken Vale's place.

Another of today's famous clubs also joined the Second Division in 1893, Arsenal, who were then known as Woolwich Arsenal. They had become professional, which was very unusual at that time in the mainly amateur south of England, and were involved in an unsuccessful attempt to get a southern equivalent of the Football League up and running. Therefore, 1892 was really a season too early for them to have replaced Vale in England's premier league competition.

Also in contention might well have been Newcastle United, who were still named Newcastle East End until December 1892. They had been invited by the Football League to join the Second Division, but had refused because they thought it would be more profitable to carry on competing in the Northern League. Therefore, had Burslem Port Vale not been in existence, it is inconceivable that it would have made any difference to Newcastle's decision.

The remaining two clubs, Rotherham Town and Middlesbrough Ironopolis, had both won championships in the 1891-1892 season, the former of the Midland League and the latter of the Northern League. As Vale were elected to the Second Division in preference to Rotherham, despite having finished two places below them in the league, it would seem a reasonable bet that the latter's northeastern rivals would have been asked to join the Football League in 1892 if the aforementioned four failed applicants had continued to be rejected. However, of course, we will never know if that would have happened because Vale did indeed become founder members of the Second Division in 1892.

Vale found it to be a struggle in the Second Division and spent only four years there, twice finishing in penultimate position and third from the bottom in the 1895-1896 campaign, as a result of which they were not re-elected. Had there been no Burslem Port Vale in the league that season, then it may well have been that Lincoln City, who had done the double over the Potteries side, would have finished third (and not fourth) from the bottom and therefore been demoted. However, that would have been dependent on their results, and those of the three teams above them, that season against whichever side had replaced Vale in the league in 1892.

Two years later, Vale were back in the fold, not least because of their magnificent 2-1 F.A. Cup win over Sheffield United, the eventual champions of the Football League. Had Vale not been in existence, then it is likely that Nelson, who had polled the highest number of votes of the unsuccessful applicants, would have taken their place in the Second Division.

This time, Vale lasted for nine seasons in the Football League and fared fairly reasonably in the second tier until June 1907 when financial problems forced the club to resign from the league and drove them out of existence. Vale's misfortune proved to be a piece of good luck for Oldham Athletic, who were elected to take their place. However, had Vale not been in existence to go out of existence, Oldham most likely would not have been promoted from the Second Division in 1910 and not finished as the First Division runners-up in 1915.

A mere twelve years after the demise of the old Burslem Port Vale club, an entirely new team, just called Port Vale, put the "Mother Town" back on the map by gaining entry to the Football League and, of course, they have been members ever since. Vale's return to the fold had a very large element of luck attached to it. On 13 October 1919, Leeds City were expelled from the Football League because of financial irregularities and Vale were fortunately elected to take their place in the Second Division, most likely because they had failed by only two votes to gain admittance to the league for the start of the season. Had there been no Port Vale, it is probable that Tranmere Rovers, who had also applied to take the place of Leeds City, would have been elected and joined the league two years before they actually did and a division higher.

In 1929, Vale finished in penultimate position in the Second Division and were relegated. If the "Valiants" (as Vale had by then become nicknamed) had not been in existence, it is very difficult to speculate on which team would have been demoted in their stead. At the end of the season, Bristol City had ended up third from the bottom of the table, but had gained two points from their matches with Vale. However, Swansea Town, who had finished one place higher, had taken three points from Vale and therefore would have dropped below the "Robins" if the Valiants' record had been taken away. However, had there been no Port Vale, presumably another club would have featured in the Second Division in their place and, of course, it is impossible to say how they would have fared against both Bristol and Swansea and whether they would have been so weak that they would have been the ones relegated instead. Having said that, in all the examples that follow, it is assumed that all the relevant teams would have performed equally well or badly that season against whichever club had replaced Vale in the league.

The following season, Vale won the Third Division (North) championship with a then record 67 points. They lost only five games all season, two of which were against the runners-up, Stockport County, who finished thirteen points clear of the third-placed team, Darlington. Therefore, had Vale not been extant, it appears almost inevitable that the "Hatters" would have been the champions instead. The only thing that seemingly could have prevented such a success would have been if the team replacing the Valiants in the division had been even more proficient than Stockport and that is highly unlikely for an otherwise non-league club.

Six years later, Vale finished in penultimate place in the Second Division and were relegated again. Without them, Barnsley, who ended up third from the bottom, could only have been saved from the drop if the team replacing the Valiants had been inept. The "Tykes" did the double over Vale and would have managed only 29 points had those two victories been expunged from the records.

Vale did little further of note in the league until their record-breaking 1953-1954 campaign when they won the Third Division (North) championship by eleven points after suffering just three defeats all season. Had the Valiants not been present, unless their (otherwise non-league) replacements had been a particularly strong side, Barnsley, the runners-up would have finished top of the table and not been the champions the following year.

Only three years after their fabulous success, Vale finished bottom of the Second Division, eight points and goal average adrift of safety. As third from the last Notts County did the double over the Valiants, they would have been deducted four points and ended up in penultimate position if Vale's results had not existed. Therefore, only a very poor replacement club for the Valiants could have prevented the "Magpies" from being relegated.

The following season, Vale were relegated again, despite finishing fifteenth in Division 3 (South), because the bottom half of the two regional Third Divisions were demoted into the new Fourth Division. Without the Valiants and their league record, the hitherto twelfth-placed Colchester United would have been relegated unless the replacement club for Vale had finished in the lower half of the table.

Vale changed grades for the third year running after becoming the inaugural Fourth Division champions in 1959, four points clear of the runners-up, Coventry City. In the absence of Vale's results, the "Sky Blues" would have topped the table on goal average unless the replacement club for the Valiants had been particularly powerful. In the same circumstances, York City and Shrewsbury Town would still have been promoted and hitherto fifth-placed Exeter City would have joined them.

The Valiants remained in the Third Division until 1965 when they finished third from the bottom and were relegated. Had there been no Port Vale in the league and their record been deleted, Walsall, hitherto two places clear of the drop, would have lost their place, unless, as always, the club that had replaced the Valiants had fared worse than the "Saddlers".

Five years later, Vale were promoted from the Fourth Division in third place. Without them and their results, the hitherto fifth-placed Brentford would have been promoted unless the team having replaced the Valiants had overtaken the "Bees".

Vale remained in the Third Division until 1978 when they finished fourth from the bottom and were relegated. Had they not been present and their record been deleted, Plymouth Argyle, formerly two places above them, would have been demoted unless the Valiants' replacements had performed even worse than the "Pilgrims".

In 1983, Vale regained their status by ending up third in the Fourth Division, but the eradication of their playing record would have had a significant impact on the promotion situation. Scunthorpe United, who had finished the season in fourth place and were promoted, had done the double over the Valiants and the deduction of their six points (there by then being three points for a win) would have seen them drop three positions. Unless a strong replacement side for Vale had made the top four, hitherto fifth-placed Bury and sixth-placed Colchester United, who had fared less well against the Valiants, would both have been promoted.

To many people's surprise, Vale finished the following campaign in penultimate position and were relegated. With the erasion of their results, Plymouth Argyle, who were otherwise five points clear of danger in nineteenth place and had done the double over the Valiants, would have been relegated unless the club that replaced Vale had performed more badly than the Pilgrims.

In 1986, the Valiants finished fourth in Division 4 and were consequently promoted. Without their record that season, Orient, who had ended up fifth, would have risen a place and been promoted except if whoever had taken the Valiants' place had done better than the "O's".

Three years later, Vale secured third spot in Division 3 and then entered the four-team play-offs, which they won to return to the Second Division after 32 years. The elimination of their results would have seen ninth-placed Notts County, who had lost both their matches against Vale, move up three positions and into the play-offs, unless, of course, the team replacing the Valiants had proved superior to the Magpies. Bristol Rovers would still have made the play-off final, but whether this time they would have been victorious and therefore promoted in Vale's stead is impossible to call.

In 1992, the Valiants finished bottom of the Second Division and were relegated. With the deletion of their record, Newcastle United would have dropped from twentieth to third from the last and been demoted to the third tier of the Football League for the only time in their history unless the replacement side for Vale had performed worse than the "Toon".

The Valiants regained their status only two years later when they were the runners-up in the Second Division (as the Third Division had by then been renamed). Without Vale's results, Plymouth Argyle would have moved up from third to second and been promoted and hitherto ninth-placed Hull City would have risen to sixth position and qualified for the play-offs, both, of course, if the team replacing the Valiants had not bettered them. Whether, in the changed circumstances, Burnley would have triumphed in the play-offs and been promoted can only be the subject of conjecture.

In 2000, Vale ended their stay in the First Division by finishing in penultimate place, thirteen points and goal difference adrift of safety. The deletion of their playing record would have meant fourth from the bottom West Bromwich Albion would have dropped one position and been demoted if the side occupying the Valiants' place in the league had not fared worse than the "Baggies".

Finally, in 2008, Vale finished second from the bottom in League One (as the Second and old Third Division had been rebranded by then) and were only saved from propping up the table by Luton Town having had ten points deducted for going into administration. With the elimination of the Valiants' results, Crewe Alexandra would have slipped a place to 21st and been relegated to League Two except in the event that the team replacing Vale in the division had performed more poorly than the "Railwaymen".

The removal of Vale's results from their entire Football League career would, obviously, also have affected many more promotion and relegation issues, in a much larger number of seasons, than those mentioned except in the almost impossible event that whichever teams had replaced the Valiants in the league had achieved an identical playing record to them. Therefore, the impact of Vale never having played in the Football League would have been quite considerable and not least to the Newcastle United fans, who, presumably, would have told their manager and chairman a few home truths had they been relegated to the third tier of English football in 1992!

There would have been other significant consequences, in addition to those affecting the Football League, of the Port Vale team of 1876 having not entered recorded history, for example in cup competitions. The Valiants have never won a major trophy and hardly look likely to in the near future, but they did secure the Autoglass Trophy on 22 May 1993 at the old Wembley Stadium. The competition was contested by the clubs in the Second and Third Divisions of the time, being really the Third and Fourth Divisions, of course. Vale beat Stockport County 2-1 in the final, but, had the Valiants not existed, it can only be speculated as to which other side would have had the opportunity to have denied the Hatters the trophy. En route to the final, Vale had beaten Fulham, Northampton Town, Stoke City and Exeter City, so they would all have become contenders, along with whichever team had replaced the Valiants in the Football League.

On 22 April 2001, Vale repeated the feat, albeit that the cup had by then become renamed the LDV Vans Trophy. They beat Brentford 2-1 in the final, but, had the Valiants not have been in existence to enter the competition, the Bees would have had a golden opportunity to have added the trophy to their limited silverware. On the way to the final, Vale had seen off Notts County, Chester City, Darlington, Stoke City and Lincoln City, so those sides would also have been in contention to lift the cup, as well as whichever club was filling the Valiants' place in the league.

In their history, the Vale first team have also won the Birmingham Senior Cup, the Staffordshire Senior Cup three times, the Staffordshire Junior Cup, the Staffordshire Senior Charity Cup twice, the North Staffordshire Charity Challenge Cup three times (jointly on two of the occasions), the North Staffordshire Infirmary Cup three times (twice jointly), the Burslem Challenge Cup, the Supporters' Clubs' Trophy and the TNT Tournament. Obviously, had the Valiants not been in existence in those times, most of the various cups would have been won by other teams instead, but the permutations are too numerous to list. However, on the two occasions that Vale shared the North Staffordshire Infirmary Cup, the trophy appears to have been contested only with Stoke. As the match was a charity occasion, it seems reasonable to assume that, in the event of the Valiants' absence, another side would have been found to play the Potters each year and, clearly, the lucky team or teams would have had the opportunity to have won the cup. However, the Supporters' Clubs' Trophy was competed for, in two consecutive seasons (1959-1960 and 1960-1961), specifically between Vale and Stoke City. Had the Valiants not existed, it is impossible to imagine that Stoke would have gone to the trouble to have played themselves for a cup that only they could win and therefore it is safe to assume that the trophy would never have been invented.

The highly unlikely premature foundation of Vale in 1876, and their consequent almost certain disappearance into the mists of time, would without question have affected the lives of tens of thousands of people, if not more, especially the supporters of the club down the ages, although none of them except the members of the short-lived team and a small circle around them would ever have known it. Nevertheless, it would be interesting to speculate on some of the more important individuals whose lives would have been radically different if the Valiants had not become a professional Football League club.

The legendary Roy Sproson, easily the club's longest-serving player, made all his professional appearances with Vale and therefore, had the Valiants not existed, it is likely that he would not have featured in the Football League at all, especially as Stoke City had already released him as an amateur. Without Vale, the league would also probably not have been graced by many other local stalwarts, such as Harry Poole, Phil Sproson, Andy Porter, Terry Miles, Russell Bromage, Basil Hayward, Stan Steele, Tom Cheadle and Roger Jones and Robbie Earle.

In addition, without the Valiants to launch their Football League careers, it may well be that the following players would never have become internationals: Billy Beats (England), Tom Baddeley (England), Tom Cooper (England), Phil Griffiths (Wales), Ronnie Allen (England), Bill McGarry (England), Sammy Morgan (Northern Ireland), Mark Chamberlain (England), Andy Jones (Wales), Robbie Earle (Jamaica), Anthony Gardner (England), Chris Birchall (Trinidad and Tobago) and James Lawrie (Northern Ireland).

Also, over the years, Vale have had a number of very fine managers, but, without the club to cut their teeth on, two of them may never have exhibited their skills in the world of professional football, namely Gordon Lee and John Rudge. On the other hand, the reputations of Stan Matthews and Dennis Butler would have been considerably better had there never been a Port Vale for them to fail with in their debut attempts at football club management.

Gordon Lee had had a mediocre professional career as a full-back with Aston Villa and Shrewsbury Town, making just 120 Football League appearances. He then became Town's trainer-coach before the Valiants took a chance on him by appointing him as their manager in May 1968. Lee excelled in building a Vale side, primarily based on fitness and teamwork, which was promoted from the Fourth Division in only his second season in charge. He succeeded in maintaining the Valiants' status in the Third Division despite being starved of funds, owing to poor attendances, and thereby attracted an offer from Blackburn Rovers, whom he left to manage in January 1974. He later became the manager of Newcastle United, Everton, Preston North End, KR (of Iceland) and Leicester City, but had it not been for Port Vale, he may well never have had the opportunities which followed.

John Rudge was arguably Vale's finest ever manager, steering the club to three promotions (from the Fourth Division in 1986, the Third Division in 1989 and the Second Division [as Division 3 had by then been rebranded] in 1994, as well masterminding the Autoglass Trophy success in 1993. He had been a journeyman striker for Huddersfield Town, Carlisle United, Torquay United, Bristol Rovers and Bournemouth, scoring 79 goals in 230 appearances, and then became the first-team coach at Torquay. Had Vale's manager, John McGrath, not appointed him as the coach in January 1980, it may well be that Rudge would not have become a highly successful Football League manager. Almost certainly, he would never have been offered the lucrative position of the director of football at Stoke City or have lived in a mini-mansion in Trentham.

The internationally-renowned Stan Matthews, the "Wizard of the Dribble", made the mistake of putting his near-flawless reputation on the line when he became Vale's general manager in July 1965. He had 54 England caps and had been knighted, but was at the helm when the Valiants were expelled from the Football League in May 1968 and was £7,000 out of pocket when he left the club. However, such was the power of his name for him to be fêted that he did not need to rue the existence of Port Vale.

Dennis Butler could be forgiven for not feeling the same. Butler took his one and only job as a Football League manager with Vale in May 1978, but criticism instead of success came his way and his response was to call the supporters 'a bunch of yobbos'. The joy of Port Vale's existence was not uppermost on his mind when he left 'by mutual consent' in August 1979!

Had the Valiants been founded in 1876 and disappeared soon afterwards, there would no doubt have been only one professional football club in Stoke-on-Trent today, Stoke City. Although that would now be catastrophic to the Vale supporters, no other club in or near to the Potteries has ever come close to emulating the success of the big two. The city is the smallest in England to boast two Football League clubs and that is arguably a major disadvantage. However, as Stoke have almost invariably had considerably better support, it is doubtful whether the addition of more possible fans from the north of the Potteries would have made a vital difference to Stoke throughout most of their history. Another 5,000 City supporters would be of no avail to the club today because they would not be able to get into the Britannia Stadium and, even if they could, the Potters would need a lot more than that to help bring in the extra revenue to compete with the big Premier League clubs.

The only real occasion when City missed a major honour by a whisker was in 1947 when they would have been the First Division champions had they won their final game of the season. It could be argued that some more revenue from supporters in the north of Stoke-on-Trent might have made the difference in adding a vital player or two of extra quality. Having said that, the maximum wage made it hard to attract outside footballers to a city with its "Smoke-on-Stench" reputation and the star man, Stan Matthews, to many the key link, was transferred to Blackpool five weeks before the end of the campaign. Therefore, it is difficult to believe that the addition of possibly up to several thousand extra fans would have had more impact than the loss of the maestro at such a vital stage.

An altogether more certain consequence of the imaginative story of Vale having been formed in 1876 is that the organisers of the fictitious 1926 jubilee event would have been a whole lot happier about the foundation year than if it had later been pointed out to them that they had got the date wrong! They definitely would have been left with egg on their faces, having trumpeted the jubilee to the media and got 2,000 people to celebrate it at the Queen's Hall. Had the news about their error filtered through before 1929, they would have had the chance to have had a second go at getting it right, but had they discovered the awful truth after the end of that year, their mistake would have been irredeemable. Also, had the fantasy world misconception not been discovered, the error might well have been compounded by the holding of the club's centenary in 1976!

Finally, the question needs to be asked as to what the consequences would have been had the fictitious Port Vale House story of the club's name origin been believed in preference to the simple port in the vale place-name one. For the obvious to have been missed would almost certainly have been academic to virtually everybody except perhaps for one or two disgruntled Vale historians. However, the club's origins would obviously have seemed altogether more romantic and stranger than they do with the accepted mundane place-name explanation. In addition, the more knowledgeable fans would have been able to have gloated to opposing supporters that Vale were a rare club indeed in not being named after a district, town or city. Also, perhaps today the valiant supporters would have had a stronger affinity to Burslem (within the town boundaries of which lay Port Vale House) than to their real home in the vale of ports. However, any way round, opposition fans would no doubt have continued to ask: 'Where is Port Vale? Is it on the coast, in South Wales somewhere?' Furthermore, irrespective of the nature of Vale's origins, the magic of their name would most certainly still have rung out across the land.

So ends the fantastic story of 1876, happily ever after or otherwise.

Oh, by the way, have you heard the tall tale of how Vale started off as a brickworks team?

3 The Fine Art Of Passing

There were numerous teams in the Burslem area in 1879, which had sprung up as the new craze of football had spread rapidly in North Staffordshire. The *Sentinel* coverage of the sport was still erratic at that time, so there were probably many more sides in existence in the area than those who were important or lucky enough to have had their matches reported. The teams from the Burslem district whose results appeared in the newspaper at least once in 1879 were Burslem, Burslem Hill Top Wanderers, Burslem Rangers, Burslem Royal Albert, Burslem St. John's, Burslem St. Paul's, Burslem True Blues, Burslem Victoria, Burslem Wanderers, Brownhills, Brownhills Pottery, Cobridge Collegiate, Cobridge Rangers, Dalehall Trueblues, Hot Lane, Middleport Wesleyans, Porthill Juniors, Porthill Victoria, Smallthorne Juveniles, Wolstanton and Wolstanton United. Most of these sides, if not all of them, had greater experience than Port Vale, who had very probably only been formed that year.

Wolstanton were first mentioned by the *Sentinel* on 13 January 1877 when they hammered Cocknage 4-0, but may well have been playing before then. They appear to have been quite a good team and were strong enough to beat Leek 3-0 on 26 January 1878. However, on 27 September 1879, they were beaten by three goals (and one disputed) to nil by Burslem Rangers, who lost only two of their seven other reported games that year. Rangers' defeats were both against Middleport Wesleyans, who beat them 2-0 and 1-0 within three weeks in the autumn of 1879. However, in turn, Wesleyans were eclipsed by Oulton (Stone), who were victorious by 1-0 in their match on 13 December 1879. So there were plenty of useful teams around at that time, not least in the Burslem district.

The top club in the area in 1879, though, were Cobridge, who had joined the Staffordshire Football Association as far back as 1872 and changed their name to Burslem for the 1879-1880 season. They rarely lost against local opposition and were a powerful enough outfit to take on sides from outside North Staffordshire. On 12 January 1878, they won 1-0 at Wolstanton despite having to play under the home side's rules, with which Cobridge were unfamiliar, and, four weeks later, they trounced Leek 2nd XI 10-0. In 1879, they reached the final of the Staffordshire Challenge Cup before going down 2-1 to the mighty Stoke, North Staffordshire's most senior and easily their best team. The following season, as Burslem, they also competed in the prestigious Birmingham Challenge Cup and reached the third round, but then scratched from the competition instead of playing their tie at Derby. During that same campaign, on 15 November 1879, they won 2-1 away in a friendly match at Wednesbury Old Athletic, the holders of the Birmingham Challenge Cup, in front of several thousand spectators. However, to give an indication of how inferior even Burslem were to Stoke, they were annihilated 10-0 by them in the first round of the Staffordshire Challenge Cup in the 1880-1881 season!

Therefore, when Port Vale came into existence, most likely in 1879, they faced a great deal of competition from numerous other clubs in the Burslem area, some of which already had very strong teams. The very best of them played powerful sides from outside North Staffordshire and competed in important cup tournaments, but none of them were remotely a match for the local football giants, Stoke. However, the newly-founded Port Vale were complete also-rans, even in the Burslem district, and yet in less than four years they had totally eclipsed all the other teams of North Staffordshire except Stoke. It is difficult to accept that such a meteoric rise in such a short time, by a club founded so belatedly, actually occurred and it really does take some explaining. It is the stuff of which legends are made and yet today it seems that Vale's relatively high status is regarded as a simple matter of fact, if not an inevitable development, no doubt because the Valiants have been a respectable Football League club for so long. However, it is extremely doubtful whether any betting men in 1879 would have been willing to put any money on Vale's imminent remarkable ascent to success.

Clearly, on the surface, Vale were far from well placed upon their foundation to go from strength to strength so rapidly. Indeed, the odds at the time would undoubtedly have been short on them not lasting for more than a year or two, like many other transitory football clubs throughout the length and breadth of England in this age of boom and bust. Obviously, there were factors in play at the time that quickly turned Vale from nonentities into celebrities, even if the impact, or indeed existence, of the elements were not then apparent or predictable.

The very first time Vale entered recorded history was in remarkable fashion on 16 October 1880 when their second team were noted by the *Sentinel* as having beaten Hot Lane 1-0 at home! The same day, Burslem Rangers were reported as having won 1-0 against Norton in front of 'a large number of spectators'. The following Saturday, Vale's reserves (though once more not their first team) again found themselves in print after winning 2-1 at home to Longport Hall, another side of minnows. Their score was alongside those of Burslem Rangers, who this time were defeated 1-0 at Shelton; Middleport Wesleyans, who won 2-0 at Smallthorne Salem, and Wesleyans 2nd XI, who beat Cobridge Rangers 3-0. It was in such illustrious company that Vale adorned the pages of the local rag.

Unfortunately, during the period when Vale's amazing transformation into a club worthy of national respect was taking place, the pages of the *Sentinel* and other publications are entirely devoid of their progress. The first team can be finally said to have appeared in the historical records on 6 September 1882 when the club joined the Staffordshire Football Association. By then, they were well on their way upwards to fame and fortune. The curtain had been lifted rather belatedly, but then a sensation occurred – after a walkover against Cliff Vale in the first round of the Staffordshire Challenge Cup, Vale had the temerity to take on the mighty Stoke at the next stage of the competition on 2 December 1882.

Traditionally, it was believed that Stoke had been founded in 1863, but in 1988 Wade Martin put forward impressive evidence in his book, *A Potter's Tale*, that their formation had occurred in 1868 as Stoke Ramblers. Either way round, they had at least an eight-year, and possibly a sixteen-year, head start over Vale that obviously resulted in their superior experience and support, which has never really been matched by the Valiants. In contrast to Vale's rather vague establishment by young working-class men in the valley of ports, Stoke were able to claim that they had been founded by pioneering ex-public schoolboys and their early players were mainly the sons of gentlemen. By 1882, Stoke were one of the main football clubs in the whole of the Midlands and in a league of their own in North Staffordshire.

Such was the size of the task facing Vale in the Staffordshire Cup in 1882 and they must have been very keen to avoid the kind of drubbing that their opponents had handed out to Mow Cop in the first round of the competition in annihilating them 24-0! However, remarkably, the upstarts achieved a 1-1 draw with their illustrious rivals at home in 'a spirited game'. Vale's heroic efforts must have created a local shock wave almost equivalent to those which reverberated when England lost 1-0 to the USA in the World Cup in 1950 and surrendered their unbeaten home record (to teams outside the British Isles) to Hungary by 6-3 in 1953.

The Staffordshire Cup replay was on the following Saturday, in front of 'a large number of spectators' and both sides were listed in the *Sentinel* as having one back, three half-backs and six forwards. Normality was resumed when Stoke ran out 5-1 victors, but Vale had at last come to the attention of the wider public and they did not look back. The degree of their progress at that stage can be well illustrated by comparing the activities of some of Vale's Burslem area rivals that same day. Whereas Vale had tackled one of the Midlands' oldest and most dynamic clubs in a relatively prestigious tournament, Burslem St. Paul's had beaten East Vale 2-0 at home, Wolstanton United had lost 2-0 at Basford Excelsior, Longport Star had been defeated 2-1 at Cobridge Catholic Boys and Dalehall had gone down 3-1 at home to Alsager Albion, all in mere friendly games.

Having been in the limelight, Vale's matches began to be mentioned in the *Sentinel* on occasions and then more regularly, which was a distinct advantage in putting them on the football map, at first locally and then beyond. That same season, they reached the final of the North Staffordshire Charity Challenge Cup, in which they faced Leek, another club of considerably longer pedigree and higher standing than themselves, on 31 March 1883. Again Vale defied the odds and secured a 1-1 draw, but this time triumphed 4-2 in the replay on 28 April at Stoke's Victoria Ground, where there was 'a good assemblage of spectators', according to the *Sentinel*. So, within four years of their probable foundation, Vale had won a cup of respectable stature.

The next season, their fortunes really took off. They reached the semi-finals of the Staffordshire Cup, winning three matches on the way by a total score of 17-0, and entered the big time by playing a whole series of friendly games against impressive opponents from out of the area, more than holding their own against them overall. On 3 November 1883, they beat Aston Unity 3-1 at home, which led the *Sentinel* to say that they were 'now surely in the first rank of Midlands clubs'. A fortnight later, Vale achieved a splendid 1-0 win at Everton in front of 'a considerable number of spectators'. On 22 December, another away victory followed, this time by 5-3, at Chirk, 'the famous Welsh club'. Then Vale's ability to put lesser sides to the sword was amply illustrated on 2 February 1884 when they annihilated Middlewich 16-0 at home, but the *Sentinel* reprimanded them for playing such inferior opponents. Finally, for the first time, they had two of their players, Billy Poulson and the versatile Charlie Simpson, selected to play for Staffordshire, which they did on 16 February 1884. As a result, the *Sentinel* wrote in praise of 'our two local champions – Stoke and Port Vale' and commented on the latter's 'wonderful success this year'. Vale had truly arrived. They had become the undisputed kings of football in the north of the Potteries and were by then the only rivals to Stoke's supremacy in North Staffordshire.

But how had Vale's rags to riches success come about, especially in so short a time, and how was it that they had managed to surge ahead of clubs who were well in advance of them less than five years earlier? The task of answering the questions posed is infuriatingly difficult because of the lack of source material, so there has to be a fair amount of guesswork involved. Having said that, there exists sufficient evidence for a number of very plausible reasons to be explored to explain Vale's remarkable achievements.

Today, football managers pit their wits against one another, choosing from an almost bewildering array of team formations and tactics to try to achieve victory. Changes to how the game was played generally took place more slowly in the nineteenth century than they do now. Football originally developed from the almost completely unregulated roughhouse street games, of which the amazing Ashbourne Royal Shrovetide match is a notable survivor, but the modern game was born in the public schools, which were mainly located in the south of England. However, it was little less brutal and physical than its forerunner and the main tactic was for the 'flying man' to run as fast as possible, kicking or dribbling the ball towards the opposing goal in the hope of eventually scoring. To maximise his chances of breaking through the opposition defences, he would be supported by his own 'behinds' in a massed pack, who would charge with him straight at the goal. The main aim, therefore, was to use sheer speed, or, much more commonly, brute force to put the ball between the posts. That was the state of the game when Stoke were formed in the 1860s and their Old Carthusian (ex-Charterhouse School) founders would have been well familiar with the tried and tested methods of play.

Even the first F.A. Cup final in 1872, between Wanderers and Royal Engineers, was contested in much the same way, with charging and 'rushes' towards the opponents' goal dominating the match. Deliberate passing of the ball was rarely resorted to and the two sides arranged most of their players in a pack, to chase the ball, as per the convention of the time, with Wanderers (who won 1-0) fielding the traditional formation of one full-back, one half-back and eight forwards, whilst the Engineers deployed a more defensive 2-1-7 system! The same two clubs contested the 1878 final, but they had both become a little less attack minded by then and employed a 2-2-6 formation. Although Wanderers were again victorious, by 3-1, their finesse was still at a premium and two of the goals (one by each side) were scored following a 'scrimmage'.

These top teams obviously had a great influence on the way the game was played and new sides that sprung up tended to copy their approach, although there were considerable variations in different parts of the country, especially those where there was some kind of history of football. Naturally, the older-established clubs tended to follow their own traditions and were reluctant to change, even when superior ideas were developed. Although it is very difficult from early match reports to ascertain the formations that were employed by local teams in and around the Potteries at the time, none of them have become renowned for their revolutionary methods of play and it is therefore reasonable to assume that they were mainly inclined to go along with what was imported from elsewhere. Also, because the first known football club in the area, Stoke, were founded by ex-public schoolboys, then their understanding of the game was very influential on the other local sides that were formed after them. Thus, in the early days, Stoke played a modified form of rugby and brute force, dribbling, rushes and scrimmages became familiar facets of the matches contested in North Staffordshire, although handling the ball gradually went out of fashion.

It can be seen from children's football even today that, without coaching and outside interference, there is a tendency for individuals to run with the ball and dribble and not consider passing unless there is no other option. It seems almost natural, as though the ball is an extension of the self, the centre of the universe. To have the ball is to be important and to lose it, or even pass it to a member of the same team, is to be no-one in the tyranny of the present. Of course, even now not all footballers grow out of this egocentric view. However, by the 1870s, a more effective and efficient form of play gradually started to evolve, based on the new development of passing the ball to other members of the same team.

It is not really possible to say when passing first began or who invented it, not least because there was obviously no description for it before it commenced. Therefore, it may have been occurring for some time before it was specifically referred to. Also, the ball must occasionally have been passed by accident by players to other members of the same side from almost the very beginning of the game, but who is to say whether any specific pass is intended or not? In addition, a fluke pass which led to the scoring of a goal would presumably not be vehemently denied by the lucky footballer. Furthermore, 'combination' became an early word used to describe passing, as well as referring to other forms of co-operative effort by members of a team. So it is not straightforward to know in the early days when a pass had been made or even if it seemed to have been intended.

Nevertheless, it gradually became apparent that accurate passing made the ball do the work and quickly tired out opposing forwards who played in a pack, chasing the leather wherever it went. However, different clubs learned the advantages of passing at different times and, while one or two teams pioneered the new idea, others (especially the public school-influenced sides of the South) actively resisted it, as though it was an evil that would ruin their game. The most lauded practitioners of combination play, especially of short passing, were Queen's Park, of Glasgow, who today remain the only amateur team in the Scottish League. They drew 0-0 with Wanderers in London in a semi-final of the F.A. Cup in its inaugural season (1871-1872) before scratching from the competition. However, their performance proved a shock to the old order as they 'combined with a judicious plan of passing on', according to *The Field* magazine, which left their opponents bewildered. The same year, Queen's Park, who were representing Scotland, again achieved a goalless draw, but this time against the might of England in the first ever international match and, according to *The Graphic* newspaper, 'seemed to be adepts in passing the ball'. Indeed, Queen's Park's revolutionary style of play was so successful that it was eight years after their formation before they conceded a goal and nine years before they lost their first game! Also, packed with players from Queen's Park, the Scotland international side beat England nine times and drew with them on three occasions, in twelve meetings between 1874 and 1886.

In England, Sheffield F.C. (who today play in the Northern Premier League) were, according to Charles W. Alcock, early exponents of 'a certain kind of passing', but more of the long ball type than Queen's Park. As Sheffield were a successful club, their style of play, of course, influenced their opponents, many of whom copied their tactics. Then, in 1873, the Royal Engineers adapted their play to the new combination style, although their conversion had little impact on their rivals in the South.

Even by 1879, the progress of passing throughout the English football world was very patchy and dribbling and running with speed at goal have never been entirely superseded, whilst physique remains very important in the British game, in particular. A study of the *Sentinel* football reports of 1879 shows little evidence of passing being utilised in the local games, although running, kicking, dribbling, shooting and 'individual play' were commonplace, whilst rushing and scrimmages were regular occurrences. The general impression given is of hurried activity rather than scientific methods of moving the ball about. There are occasional references to passing, players combining with one another and 'unanimity', especially in the cases of certain clubs, which suggests that these ideas were pretty novel and that they were being taken up unevenly.

Stoke do not seem to have been one of the pioneers of the new methods, which were most sparsely mentioned in their play in 1879 by the newspaper, although Boothen All Saints and the Birmingham Challenge Cup holders, Wednesbury Old Athletic, were well on the case by then. The former won by one goal (and one disputed) to nil at Macclesfield on 13 December and the performance of their forwards 'was very sharp, with good passing being shown at different points of the game'. The same day, Wednesbury won 5-0 at Leek and the *Sentinel* reported that, 'The visitors played well together and their passing was generally done with extraordinary precision.' However the newspaper said that, 'The passing exhibited by Leek seemed to be devoid of judgement altogether. The dribbling of the Leek men as a rule is far superior to their passing game.' The last comment indicates that at least some sides who introduced passing into their play were not very good at it, at least at first, which was to be expected. Presumably, some of them would have persisted with it and got better, whilst others would have reverted to their tried and tested methods and perhaps remained dinosaurs in a changing world.

Although it would be a sweeping generalisation to say that the long-established clubs resisted passing, whilst new ones were more willing to take it up, there is truth in the statement. Port Vale were a new team in 1879, comprised, as far as can be ascertained, mainly of teenagers with limited experience of playing organised football. As might be expected, they seem to have been considerably more open to new ideas than were the battle-hardened veterans of the older clubs, with their long-established ways of going about things. The adage, 'You can't teach an old footballer new tricks,' aptly springs to mind.

There is written evidence that Vale quickly employed passing as a major part of the way they played the game and it may be that they used combination tactics from their very foundation. Either way, they rapidly embraced the idea of passing the ball, more than likely mainly because it was proving to be a highly successful method of play. Footballers like to win matches, often even by foul means if necessary, with there being no finer example than Diego Maradona's great delight in scoring for Argentina against England with his 'Hand of God' in their World Cup quarter-final on 22 June 1986. By passing the ball, Vale were playing well within the laws of the game, but they were nevertheless playing to win.

The *Sentinel* noted that, in one of their first recorded matches, the 1883 North Staffordshire Charity Challenge Cup replay against Leek, Vale 'played with superior passing that surprised everyone'. The fact that their players achieved 'superior passing' indicates that they had not started using combination play overnight or even recently to the cup game. As is well known, only as a result of dedicated players endlessly practising their skills and understanding together can even a team of full-time professionals hope to exhibit first-class passing in a highly competitive match against determined opponents. Accurate passing is not an easy skill to master and its perfection takes years of application to achieve.

As the known and conjectured founding Vale players worked long hours in factories and suchlike places, they must have had very limited time when they could all get together to hone their artistry, not least in the winter months, when competitive football was arranged, with the early hours of darkness. Although professionalism was not legalised until 1885, it is quite possible that the successful Vale players received financial incentives from a very early stage, but none of them could have been full time in 1883, so payments would not have prevented their lack of time to practise.

Also, although the basic concept of combination play became increasingly known, it is extremely doubtful whether there were any coaches to teach its finer points to the Vale footballers and, of course, there were no televisions on which they could have watched masters of the craft perform, in the hope of copying their approach and techniques. Therefore, it would have taken the early Vale players considerably longer than modern professionals to have achieved such proficiency. The consequence is that their team must have been passing the ball by design, and not chance, for some considerable time and maybe from the club's foundation. In turn, by perfecting the superior combination style of play, Vale must have quickly become successful, which is instrumental in helping to explain their meteoric rise to fame, not least because many, and perhaps most, of their longer-standing opponents would still have been persisting with the dinosaur methods of the public schools.

The crucial importance of passing at the time was illustrated in the 1883 F.A. Cup final, just four weeks before Vale's match with Leek. For the first time, the trophy was won by a working-class, non-southern team, not dominated by public school attitudes and tactics, Blackburn Olympic, who defeated Old Etonians 2-1. The victory marked the watershed between the domination of the old order and the triumph of the new working-class sides, based on their combination play, which proved decisive in this final and thereafter. The journalist William Pickford described how Olympic employed 'short passing' tactics, as well as 'long passing from wing to wing', which forced the Etonians to spend much of their time futilely chasing the ball. In sharp contrast, Arthur Dunn, the inside-left of the latter, persisted in running straight into the Olympic defence and, according to the *Blackburn Standard* newspaper, 'would not pass the ball no matter how many of his opponents he had to face'.

On 17 November 1883, a few months after their superlative display against Leek, Vale secured their previously-mentioned 1-0 victory at Everton. The *Sentinel* report on the match said, 'It soon became evident that the Staffordshire players were the better exponents of the passing game.' Although the Liverpool side were nowhere near the force they were later to become, it is enthralling to realise that, only four years after their probable foundation, Vale could outpass a team destined for the big time.

Also, the *Sentinel* report of Vale's 5-0 defeat at West Bromwich Albion on 16 January 1886 contained an intriguing comment: 'There was an entire absence of those passing tactics which have made Vale so famous.' Albeit that the remark occurred a few years after the rise to prominence of the team, it suggests that Vale had previously become such past masters of combination play that they were renowned for it.

So Vale were fortunately founded during the struggle between the old and new orders of football. It was a time of opportunity for those teams who dared embrace the revolution and, by adopting the passing style of play and working very hard to perfect it, Vale ensured that they were very strongly on the winning side, whilst, other, initially more significant, local sides fell by the wayside, victims of change.

There seems to be a second major reason why Vale prospered when so many of their local rivals failed and that is that they quickly attracted many of the better footballers of the Burslem district into their ranks. Of the eleven players in Vale's first recorded line-up, at least three of them are thought to have joined from other local clubs: Enoch Hood, the outside-right, from Porthill Victoria; Ralph Dain, the right-back, who had probably played for Smallthorne, and the splendid inside-left, Billy Reynolds, who had also probably appeared with the latter team. In addition, there was Harry Hood, the outside-left, who was probably Enoch's younger brother. The following season, Vale were joined by Tommy Clare, a formidable defender, who had played for Talke Rangers and Goldenhill Wanderers. He later moved on to Stoke and gained four England international caps. Billy Rowley, a fine goalkeeper, who had been between the posts with Hanley Orion and Stoke, also joined Vale's ranks that campaign and likewise later became an England international, making two appearances. Many others then followed their example.

At first glance, Vale's ability to boost their ranks with good players from other clubs appears to be a mystery because they were relative latecomers into the game, no more than juvenile Johnny-come-latelies. There is no conclusive explanation of what they had that proved so attractive, but a combination of evidence and conjecture can provide apparent answers to the conundrum.

Firstly, the strongest version of Vale's formation is that they were an offshoot of Porthill Victoria in 1879. The available evidence indicates that Enoch and Jack Hood were amongst the Porthill players who left to form the new club in the valley below and there may have been several others as well. Victoria appear to have been no slouches at the game because they won two of their three recorded matches in the 1878-1879 season, albeit against relatively minor opposition, shortly before the apparent departure of the Hoods and probably others. So the defecting players must have been at least of reasonable ability and some experience, which gave the new Port Vale club a fighting chance at its outset.

Secondly, Jack Hood may well have additionally played for other nearby teams during the seasons he was with Porthill Victoria and Port Vale. The *Sentinel* recorded a J. Hood in the Burslem St. Paul's team on 4 October 1879 and one of their goals, in a 2-0 win at Stone, being scored by Reynolds, who may, of course, have been Billy Reynolds. Just eight weeks later, the newspaper noted that J. Hood had put in a good performance for Wolstanton in their 1-0 victory at Boothen. There is no proof that J. Hood was actually Jack because his surname was, and still is, relatively common in the area and Jack and John were very popular first names. Having said that, there is obviously a strong possibility that one or both of the aforementioned players were Jack Hood. Of course, if he was playing for several sides during the same period of time, it might well have been that other Port Vale founding footballers were doing just the same. Indeed, they may have been involved in such a common culture because arranging matches each weekend, against different opponents, would have been easier said than done during this embryonic and largely anarchic period. The outcome of the practice would have been that the peripatetic players would have got to know a fair number of footballers, especially around their own area. In that case, the Vale founders must have had quite a selection of footballing contacts, including particularly skilful players, whom they could possibly have persuaded to join the new club they had formed.

However, because the Vale founders seem to have had contacts in the football world does not mean that they could get them to join their latest venture. Presumably, there must have been some incentive for the contacts to have become involved. No doubt friendships and friendly relations were a factor, but the opportunity to play for a winning side would have been a considerable attraction. No-one knows how Vale's first games fared, but, because of the team's rapid surge from nowhere to becoming the second-best side in the whole of the Potteries, it is highly likely that they did at least relatively well from the outset, probably at least in part from their adoption of the passing game. As is well known, success breeds success and, if Vale were frequently victorious, outside players would have become keen to have joined the bandwagon. The acquisition of better players would obviously have been a recipe for greater success, in which case the club would have been more attractive still to fine new blood and an upward spiral could have been, and perhaps was, set in motion, with the result that Vale became a real footballing force.

The *Sentinel's* 22 September 1900 article stated that Vale had first begun playing at The Meadows in Longport, suggesting that there was an actual football ground there. That is very unlikely as pitches were rare in the late 1870s, because the game was relatively new, and Vale had only recently been formed. The 1879 25-inch Ordnance Survey map of the Port Vale area contains no evidence of a ground, but it does show an expanse of open fields, particularly southwest of Limekiln Road (which was later renamed Scott Lidgett Road), that stretched to the Fowlea Brook and beyond. Although the fields are not named, it is reasonable to assume that they were the Port Vale Meadows, not least because they were conveniently located within the area for the founders of the club to play their football in.

As Vale became increasingly successful, very probably at least partly through their ability to pass the ball and with the addition of more skilful players, local interest in the team grew and no doubt increasing numbers of spectators gathered to watch them play. An article in the *Sentinel* on 1 February 1887 stated that they had aroused sufficient attention, in a couple of years, 'to induce a number of publicans to make a ground for them out of some pit refuse'. This appears to have been Vale's second pitch, at Westport Meadows, in the proximity of the current lake, and it has been commonly asserted that it was used by the club from

1881.

The decision of these businessmen to go to the trouble to create a pitch may well, of course, not have been entirely altruistic and the *Sentinel* reported on 28 March 1931 that the club had to pay a pound per match to play on the pitch. It is unknown whether the team charged spectators to watch them play in their field in Port Vale Meadows, or perhaps had a collection, but they certainly did at Westport, not least so that they could pay their dues. Having said that, their increasing support brought in more money than was required to be paid out and so the club effectively became a business, probably no more than two years after it had been founded!

Although it cannot be proven, it is highly likely that at least some of the profit from playing found its way into the pockets of the players, which would certainly have helped to alleviate their poverty, if only by a little, resulting from their low working wages. Thus the prospect of making some money cannot have hindered Vale's ability to attract skilful players. The fact that the club had their own pitch, if not a proper ground, must have increased Vale's appeal to local footballers because most teams still did not have such a luxury. There was also the lure of the buzz of playing in front of increasingly large crowds and the prospect of local fame for would-be Vale recruits to consider.

According to the *Sentinel*, 'the real awakening of football enthusiasm' for Vale occurred on 27 October 1883 when the team took on the prestigious Preston North End, who had lost only three of their 35 games the previous season and scored 211 goals! The match was staged at Westport in front of a very impressive crowd of 1,500, who apparently paid a penny a time, or two if they felt more generous, to see the home side put up 'a great fight' before they went down 4-1.

So, in approximately four years, Vale had risen from obscurity to become a major entertainment attraction in the Potteries and, from there, they never looked back. A number of factors seem to explain the club's wonderful success in such a short period of time, but it may well be that their players' willingness to embrace the art of passing had proved decisive.

It can be argued that the remarkable and most unexpected rise of Port Vale occurred because, by chance, they were formed just at the right time, but then took full advantage of the marvellous opportunities that were open to them to break the mould. It cannot be proven that the catalyst of the club's success was their players wholeheartedly becoming local champions of the revolutionary combination game and thereby stealing a march on the majority of their rivals, but that appears to be the best explanation of the astounding achievement of a team which looked to be destined to be also-rans at best and, more likely, to fade rapidly into oblivion. Passing was a vastly better method of play than dribbling and infinitely superior to pack rushing and sheer brute force. As Vale seem to have been pioneers of the new style in the Burslem area, they quickly became victorious and thereby attracted skilful players to play for them and increasingly large crowds to watch them. In turn, businessmen saw their potential and provided them with a pitch, instead of a field, to play on, which further increased the local interest in them and enabled the marvellous Preston North End fixture to be arranged, from which there was no looking back.

However, what would have happened if passing had never been invented or if Vale's players had preferred the old kick and rush methods that so many established sides, especially in the South, clung on to? Would they have begun their transient history in obscurity and ended it in obscurity shortly afterwards? As far as they would have ever been remembered at all, would they have been regarded as dinosaurs, who had proved unable to adapt to superior new ideas? Would they have been just brief bit-part players in a football world when the public school-influenced teams still held sway and dominated the F.A. Cup, but whose death knell was at hand? After all, where now in the scheme of things are even the five-time cup winners, Wanderers, or Old Etonians, who won the trophy twice and were the runners-up three times?

Perhaps quite a number of Vale's players would have gone on to join other local clubs and one or two would have appeared for better sides, but for them to have had any lasting success with the latter, they almost certainly would have needed to have familiarised themselves with passing, which was steadily gaining ground as a style of play and came to be the dominant method of moving the ball around. Maybe they would even have dreamed of playing for Stoke, who would have remained the unchallenged football giants of North Staffordshire.

Presumably, the Port Vale publicans would easily have found something better to have done with their time than to have created a pitch for a bunch of youngsters with no aptitude for a sporting craze going nowhere in the Burslem district. Also, no doubt the crowds of people who increasingly followed Vale would have found another short-lived side to support or, more likely, have spent their limited leisure time much more profitably. Some might have got on a train at Longport Station and travelled down the line to Stoke, to watch the impressive side from a rival Potteries town, but that would have involved going to a different part of the world. Of course, that is not something that everybody from Burslem would have wished to do, even without any football rivalry, the Potteries having been still more parochial then than it is now.

Today, passing is taken as the norm in football. Imagine the furore from the supporters of a team if their players never passed the ball to each other for the whole of a single game. No doubt there would be an outcry, if not a riot, even from the fans of the relatively few long-ball specialists. Passing is now ingrained in the consciousness of all football supporters and it is difficult to imagine a time before combination play had been invented. However, had it not been for the art of passing and the willingness of their players to embrace it, Port Vale Football Club would very probably have ceased to exist well over a century ago.

4 Frank McGinnes Lives!

After their 16-0 annihilation of Middlewich in February 1884, Vale continued to make progress and beat Northwich Victoria 4-3 away and Wednesbury Town 6-1 at home before the season was out. Also, on 22 March, they ran Stoke close, losing 5-3 at home in front of a crowd of 2-3,000, the largest ever known gate at their Westport Meadows ground.

Business was booming and it seemed that still more people could be attracted to watch the team, but, for whatever reason, the committee running the club decided that Vale could not prosper further at Westport or that they could thrive better elsewhere. Perhaps the pitch was too open to prevent a fair number of spectators attending for free, maybe it was considered that Westport was too far from the centre of Burslem to reap full advantage of the larger potential available support there or possibly the club had an irresistible offer from businessmen in the town. Any way round, a waste site off Moorland Road, handily placed right next to Burslem Station, was obtained for a new ground on a lease. The club's funds and financial assistance from leading residents in the town enabled the Burslem Football and Athletic Grounds to be constructed from scratch and opened in time for the start of the 1884-1885 season. The stadium included a grandstand, to hold 1,600 spectators, and a quarter of a mile cinder track.

The club then felt sufficiently bold to add "Burslem" as a prefix to their name or possibly the title was a condition of the town's input into the new ground. Either way, it was by then clear that Vale were the key football representatives of the "Mother Town". Only five years after their probable foundation, Port Vale had become a major enterprise in Burslem and clearly intended to stay that way. The team then put the icing on the cake in the opening match on 13 September when they put Everton to the sword, beating them by the remarkable score of 7-0 in front of a crowd of 2,500!

The rest of the season that followed was a resounding success. On 18 October, 3,000 spectators saw Vale beat the mighty Aston Villa's reserve side 2-0 at home and then approaching 4,000 watched them repeat the score against Birmingham St. George's on 24 November, also in Burslem. The crowd rose to nearly 5,000 for the visit of West Bromwich Albion on 7 February 1885, although the match had to be abandoned, with Vale losing 3-2, when the ball burst! To indicate the excellence of the gate, on the same day, only 3,000 turned up for Aston Villa's visit to Stoke. The Valeites (as they had by then been nicknamed) more than made up for the disappointing West Brom affair by annihilating Burton Wanderers 12-1 a week later and then thrashing Stafford Rangers 5-0 in a semi-final of the Burslem Challenge Cup a fortnight after that. On 16 March, Leek were despatched by 5-0 in front of a crowd of 6,000 at Burslem and, five days later, Vale recorded the eighth of nine successive home victories by trouncing Ironbridge 12-0 in the final of the Burslem Challenge Cup! The campaign also ended on a high as the team got to share the North Staffordshire Charity Challenge Cup after drawing 1-1 with Leek in the final in 'a brilliant match' at Stoke's Victoria Ground on 9 May.

The team's marvellous success encouraged the club to form the Port Vale Football and Athletic Company Limited, with nominal capital of £2,000 in shares, and elect a provisional board of directors. The outcome was that Vale became professional and began to pay their top players 2s. 6d. a week. Although the development was a clear triumph for the so-recently obscure Port Vale, ironically it marked the start of endless financial problems for the club as they competed in the big time with teams with much greater support.

The team were also highly successful in the 1885-1886 season and the home attendances held up, although there were no advances on the ground record. The main highlights, not surprisingly, took place in Burslem and included a 9-1 annihilation of Burton Strollers in the second round of the Staffordshire Cup, a 6-0 trouncing of the same team in the first round of the Birmingham Cup, a 7-1 walloping of Davenham in a friendly match and a 6-0 thumping of Crewe Alexandra, also in a non-competitive game. St. George's (Salop) were despatched by 6-1 in the second round of the Birmingham Cup, four 5-0 victories were recorded, Burnley were beaten 5-2 and two 1-1 draws were achieved with the F.A. Cup holders, Blackburn Rovers.

In addition, Vale reached the final of the North Staffordshire Charity Challenge Cup and the semi-finals of the Birmingham Cup, but perhaps their most exciting endeavours were in the F.A. Cup, in their debut season in the competition. They beat Chirk and Welsh Druids before Leek scratched, to leave the Valeites in the fourth round. There they received a bye into the next round, where they beat Brentwood 2-1 at home in front of a crowd of 6,000 on 30 January 1886. Unfortunately, their vanquished opponents protested about the state of the Burslem pitch and a replay at Derby was ordered. That was drawn 3-3 two weeks later, but Vale then withdrew from the competition when they realised they would get no receipts from the second replay at Brentwood's unenclosed ground. Had the original result been upheld or the Valeites have travelled to Brentwood and won, they would have played at Blackburn Rovers in the quarter-finals. As Vale had already drawn twice that season with Rovers (albeit at home both times), it was by no means impossible that they would have beaten them and progressed still further. Blackburn duly won the cup again that year and so what might have been for Vale, had not the Brentwood tie been such a strange affair, is open to speculation.

That summer, the Valeites were on the move again, to a new ground off Waterloo Road, in Cobridge. The Moorland Road pitch had proved a problem and the ground could only be leased for a further six years, so the club cut their losses with it. The new Athletic Ground cost £1,500 to build, much of the money going on a brick grandstand for 1,000 spectators, three shower baths for the players and a gymnasium. The club's funds were further depleted by the engagement of the first (five) players from out of the area.

Although the opening game of the 1886-1887 season was a disaster, being lost 7-0 at home to Preston North End, Vale generally held their own through the campaign. They recorded 6-0 home victories in friendly games against Crewe Alexandra and Padiham, but their greatest success came in the Birmingham Cup, in which they trounced Market Drayton 7-0, Southfield 6-1 and Birmingham Excelsior 7-1 to reach the semi-finals of the competition. Also, the club's record gate was smashed when approaching 8,000 people turned up to watch the Valeites beat Accrington 3-2 in a friendly on 15 November.

The team's performances tailed off somewhat in the 1887-1888 campaign and the size of the crowds attending their home matches remained more or less static, perhaps at least in part because football and friendly matches were no longer a novelty. Nevertheless, the Valeites achieved several very convincing victories, most especially in their home games against Walsall Town (by 6-0), Nottingham Forest (7-2) and F.A. Cup semi-finalists, Derby Junction (10-0), in friendlies, and Tunstall (7-0), in the Staffordshire Cup. However, an 8-1 mauling at Mitchell's St. George's was a humiliation and Vale finished 37th in the national averages tables, which was not remotely good enough to get them inclusion in the newly-formed Football League. However, they did gain admission to the Football Combination, which consisted of twenty clubs that had missed out on the big prize.

For the first time, in the 1888-1889 season, the Valeites found playing to be a struggle. They gained only 18 points from their 26 matches in the Combination, which, perhaps fortunately for them, collapsed before its fixtures had been completed. Also, Vale made barely any headway in any of the cup competitions and were trounced 8-1 by Blackburn Rovers at home and by 7-1 at Bootle. For the following campaign, the Combination was replaced by two new leagues, the more important of which was the Football Alliance, a second division all but in name. The Valeites' performances had been so poor that they gained inclusion in neither and were forced to return to organising friendly games. The club seemed to have hit a brick wall.

As it turned out, new hope had already arrived – in the form of Francis (Frank) McGinnes, 'the best centre-forward that ever left Scotland'. McGinnes had been born at 14 Strand Street, in Kilmarnock, Ayrshire, on 14 May 1870 and was a prolific goalscorer, who had played for Halliwell before joining Vale in April 1889. He was one of the "Scottish Professors", who emigrated to England to play professionally at a time when football north of the border was officially strictly amateur. Many of the Professors first joined clubs in Lancashire because of the county's proximity to Scotland, as did McGinnes, with his Bolton-based team. It was while he was with Halliwell that he came to Vale's attention with a bang by scoring all their five goals in their 5-1 trouncing of the Burslem side in a Football Combination game on 15 December 1888. By then, he had gained a redoubtable reputation as a marksman, so the Valeites, who had become desperate for success to return, snapped him up and took on his no doubt relatively hefty pay packet.

Although great things must have been expected of McGinnes, his debut for Vale, at centre-forward, ironically against his old club, Halliwell, in a friendly match at Cobridge on 15 April 1889, passed without him being involved in any sensational play or scoring any goals, although the *Sentinel* said that he 'shaped very well'. McGinnes also played in three of the team's final four games of the season, but his quiet start with his new club continued because he did not score in any of those either.

He finally got on target with the only goal of an exhibition match on 24 August, in which the first team took on the reserves before the start of the new season proper. He followed that up by scoring in the next game, a 1-1 draw at Cobridge against his old club, Halliwell, on 2 September, but was described by the *Sentinel* as being 'much too selfish' and persistently shooting from twenty to thirty yards out. Five days later, Vale annihilated Chirk 9-0, but McGinnes struck only once. Then, on 9 September, the Valeites lost 3-0 at home to Blackburn Rovers, with the *Sentinel* noting that McGinnes would shoot from anywhere. Worse than that, when Vale's inside-right, Bob McSkimming, was about to score, McGinnes 'foolishly' tackled him and then shot over the bar. It was therefore becoming clear that he would not necessarily get goals, but that he was so desperate to do so he did not seem to think of doing anything else.

McGinnes (or McGinnis, as the *Sentinel* almost invariably spelled his name) only scored once in the following six matches, but he struck four times in a 6-1 thumping of Burton Wanderers on 5 October. It had taken him a while really to make his mark, but he could no longer be ignored as a goalscorer by the Vale supporters.

He notched a hat trick in a 9-0 trouncing of Rotherham Town on 9 November and scored another three goals a fortnight later in a 5-2 win against Northwich Victoria. McGinnes continued to hit the target from time to time until he bagged a further hat trick in a 7-1 thumping of Derby St. Luke's on 1 February 1890. He then scored in most of the remaining games to the end of the season and played in the first Vale side ever to beat Stoke, on 29 March, after sixteen previous attempts! He had the honour of scoring the winning goal, assisted by the Valeites' inside-left, Jimmy Ditchfield, as the ball was rushed over the Stoke goal line in front of over 7,000 spectators. Not surprisingly, the *Sentinel* said that the Vale team were 'the best eleven' that 'they'd ever been able to put into the field'. However, McGinnes was not finished there because he claimed his fourth hat trick of the campaign in a 5-1 thrashing of Walsall Town Swifts on 3 May and, a week later, scored with a twenty-yard 'daisycutter' in a second home victory by the Valeites over Stoke, this time by 3-1.

After a quiet start at the club, McGinnes had proved to be a resounding success in his first full campaign, despite his tendency to selfish play and a policy of shoot on sight. He had notched a then Vale record 33 known goals in a season and probably many more because another 23 scorers for the team throughout the campaign were not given. As he had made only 43 known appearances, his goals ratio was obviously extremely impressive.

In its 30 August preview of the 1890-1891 season, the *Sentinel* sang the praises of McGinnes and said he 'has few equals'. Vale had become founder members of the twelve-club Midland League and were optimistic about their prospects of doing well in it, not least because of the shooting prowess of their star centre-forward. So as not to disappoint, he made a sensational start, banging in sixteen known goals in his first 13 appearances, which included two hat tricks – in a 4-4 draw with Newton Heath (who later became Manchester United) in a friendly on 8 September and in a 7-2 thrashing of Long Eaton Rangers in the league five days later, both at home. A week after that, the Valeites gained another league point by drawing 2-2 with Kidderminster despite McGinnes persisting in shooting as soon as he got in the opponents' half! After three matches, Vale were top of the table and everything augured well, but all had been played at home and two defeats, both away, followed, McGinnes notwithstanding.

On 18 October, the Valeites hammered Derby Midland 4-0 in the league, with McGinnes notching one of the goals, but the *Sentinel* complained that he wanted the ball on his toe and wouldn't run for it! The marksman was then missing for two matches at the beginning of November because of 'a bad knee' and completely lost form on his return, scoring only once in ten appearances! Indeed, following a 5-0 hammering at Lincoln City in the league on Christmas Day,

McGinnes was moved to the left wing for Vale's visit to Gainsborough Trinity on Boxing Day. The outcome was that the visitors were annihilated 11-0 and McGinnes resumed as the centre-forward in the next game!

In January 1891, McGinnes rediscovered his form and hit eight known goals in five matches, including a hat trick in a 7-0 mauling of Leek in a friendly at Cobridge on the 3rd. However, he came in for some very rough treatment at Derby Junction, two weeks later, when his legs 'bled freely' by half-time and, nine days afterwards, he was unable to do anything to prevent the Valeites being trounced 12-0 at Aston Villa (who were third from the bottom of the Football League) in the second round of the Staffordshire Cup!

On 14 March, McGinnes bagged his fourth hat trick of the campaign in an 8-0 thrashing of Warwick County at home in the league and, on Easter Monday, scored with a tremendous shot to earn Vale a 1-1 draw in a friendly at Stoke, the leaders and eventual champions of the Football Alliance. The *Sentinel* described him as being the 'finest man on the pitch' in this match and 'clever and [for a change] unselfish'. Five days later, McGinnes followed up by claiming four goals in Vale's 5-0 drubbing of Northwich Victoria, again in a friendly match.

However, amidst frustrations in a Derby at Stoke on 27 April, McGinnes had a furious row with Vale's right-half, Billy Elson, about the ineptitude of the latter's passing. According to the *Sentinel*, Elson's reply 'ought to have caused his marching orders at once'! Having managed completely to distract one of his own players from the task in hand in this game, McGinnes then proved his real worth to the team by scoring his fifth and last hat trick of the season in a 7-0 trouncing of Burton Wanderers on their own ground in a semi-final of the North Staffordshire Charity Challenge Cup on 2 May. He then finished the campaign successfully as a member of the side which drew 1-1 at Stoke a week later in the final of the competition and shared the trophy.

Outside his barren spell in November and December, McGinnes had proved to be an absolute revelation in front of goal and had improved his scoring from his impressive total the previous season. The team had performed poorly in finishing third from the bottom of the Midland League and being knocked out of the F.A. Cup in the second qualifying round, but McGinnes had scored a new club record 41 known goals (with twelve Vale goals unaccounted for during the campaign) in just 47 known appearances. Considering the standard of the side he was playing in, the scale of his success clearly made him a giant amongst minnows.

McGinnes was made the team captain for the 1891-1892 season and got right into his stride straight away, bagging thirteen goals in his first eight games! During his purple patch, he scored seven times in two home matches within three days, claiming a hat trick in a 7-1 trouncing of Loughborough Town in the Midland League on 19 September and then banging in all four of Vale's goals in a 4-3 win against Sheffield Wednesday in a friendly two days afterwards. The same month, two separate incidents occurred, which well illustrated different sides of his mercurial temperament. Firstly, he scored with a sublime 'swift back shot' during a 3-2 home defeat by Burton Wanderers in the opening league match on the 5th, but, when Vale entertained Derby County in a friendly nine days later, he failed to hit the target in a 3-3 draw against ten men and 'spent the match grumbling'! Also, on 26 September, although McGinnes scored in a 4-0 home beating of Doncaster Rovers in the league, he missed the first penalty ever seen on Vale's ground, by shooting straight at the opposing goalkeeper. In addition, the *Sentinel* was very critical of him in the same game, complaining that he 'won't run more than six yards for the ball'.

Despite his fine September marksmanship, McGinnes was something of a law unto himself and was suspended by the club for 'refusing to follow the committee's orders' during the 4-2 home defeat by Burton Wanderers in the first qualifying round of the F.A. Cup on 3 October. Without him, Vale lost their next match 4-1 away, ironically to the same opponents, in the league. Not surprisingly, he was then reinstated, but his form went off the boil, perhaps because he became unsettled through his suspension. Consequently, he scored only four known goals in his next eleven known appearances, which was a poor haul by his standards.

Irrespective, McGinnes was the jewel in the Valeites' crown and Stoke took the opportunity to try to prise him from their grasp. He was offered fifty pounds and a guinea a week to play for them and Stoke suggested to Vale that they should accept thirty pounds in compensation for losing his services. Fortunately for the Valeites, they were unwilling to release their main marksman and so McGinnes lost his chance to grace the Football League.

Nevertheless, the prized centre-forward found his shooting boots again and notched six known goals in the same number of matches from 19 December to the end of January 1892. One of his successes was a terrific shot at Stoke, in a 2-2 draw in a friendly on Boxing Day, which 'was loudly applauded'. However, the *Sentinel* described him as being 'idle' in a 5-2 defeat at Walsall Town Swifts in a friendly on 23 January, even though he registered one of Vale's goals. Two days later, McGinnes was having such a stinker in the Valeites' 4-0 beating of Burton Wanderers at home, in the fourth round of the Staffordshire Cup, that there were shouts from the crowd of, 'Fetch him off!' He promptly improved and it was noted that he performed well five days later in his next game, a 6-3 home league victory over Rotherham Town, in which he scored.

In February, McGinnes' marksmanship went off the boil again and he notched only two known goals in five appearances that month. The club then planned to rest him, but he played in Vale's next match because of a shortage of numbers. However, on 19 March, he got back into his stride by scoring his second hat trick of the season, in a 5-1 hammering of Derby Junction in a league home game. Then, in April, he bagged four goals in as many league matches, to help Vale win all of them and finish the season third in the league. In addition, he produced a splendid piece of play in a home friendly against Stoke on 18 April when he set up the winning goal. He tricked the opposing defenders by arguing about the distance they were standing from a free kick and then quickly touched the ball to Vale's inside-right, Meshach Dean, who fired home, as Stoke's goalkeeper, Billy Rowley, watched in amazement!

McGinnes scored his last ever goal as a consolation in the Valeites' 6-1 thrashing at Northwich Victoria in a friendly on 30 April and his swan song as a centre-forward took place in sensational style in the final of the Staffordshire Charity Cup at Stoke on 7 May, but in front of only about 1,000 spectators. Vale beat their old Potteries rivals in their own back yard for the first time ever, by 2-0, but not before McGinnes had been 'warned for his foul charging' and then sent off for attempting to trip the home side's right-half, Davy Christie. McGinnes refused to leave the pitch and it was two minutes before he could be persuaded to go, to the accompaniment of 'loud groans'. Sadly, McGinnes never set foot on a football pitch again.

After his very impressive start, the 1891-1892 season had perhaps proved a little disappointing for Vale's ace marksman, but he had still banged in 35 known goals in 46 known appearances, with the scorers of at least 22 of the team's goals throughout the campaign unaccounted for. Of course, with such a large number of the goalscorers unknown, it is highly likely that McGinnes' tally was in reality considerably greater than has been recorded and he had finished streets ahead of the team's next top scorer. Also, his ratio in the league of goals scored to appearances was particularly impressive because he had hit the target 18 known times in just 20 games played, with nine Vale scorers unrecorded. It is therefore probable that he actually scored more goals in the league than he made appearances.

In May, Vale found themselves rewarded for their relatively successful Midland League campaign by gaining admission into the Second Division, which was being established by the Football League for the forthcoming 1892-1893 season. As eleven of the fourteen new teams that were accepted came from the Football Alliance, it was quite an achievement for the Valeites to be one of the other three lesser clubs who were included in the expanded premier league. Obviously, there was much joy amongst the Vale players, officials and supporters at the step up into the big time and there was some confidence that they would do well, not least because they had a goalscorer par excellence.

However, the irreplaceable Frank McGinnes became ill during the close season and unfortunately died, at the age of 22, on 25 June at 74 Pitt Street, in Burslem, from a combination of nephritis, vomiting and exhaustion, just ten weeks before Vale's first ever Football League match. In announcing the sad news, the *Sentinel* said that, 'McGinnes was considered to be one of the finest centre-forwards in the country.' Then, on 3 September, the day of Vale's Football League debut, the newspaper reported that: 'There is an unusual quietness at the start of Port Vale's season. The death of Frank McGinnes has cast gloom, but one man doesn't make a team.' It was a fine tribute indeed to the great marksman that the anticipation of one of the most important moments in the Valeites' history was so much overshadowed by his loss.

Vale's initial Second Division match was at Small Heath (who later became Birmingham City) and Billy Beats was selected to replace McGinnes as the team's centre-forward. Beats had been born in Wolstanton on 13 November 1871 and had played for Porthill Victoria before joining the Valeites, probably in the autumn of 1891. He had made his debut at centre-forward in the 4-1 defeat at Burton Wanderers on 10 October 1891 when McGinnes had been suspended by the club. Beats cannot have impressed greatly because he was not picked again until 12 March 1892, but he played regularly thereafter. By the end of the campaign, he had made eleven appearances, right across the forward line, but only once at centre-forward, when McGinnes had been injured. However, Beats had scored just once and therefore wasn't remotely ready to stand in the boots of the great marksman.

Despite his selection, Beats was not destined to feature in Vale's first ever Football League match because he contrived to miss the train to Birmingham and his ten team mates were hammered 5-1 by Small Heath! For the next league game nine days later at Ardwick (who later became Manchester City), Wallace Bliss, a summer signing with 'a dead shot', was selected as the centre-forward, but he made little impact in a 2-0 defeat. He made eight more appearances in the same position, but scored only twice and lost his place in the side in December. He was released at the end of the season. Beats and half-back Fred Farrington were given a game each in the problem position without scoring, but, on 3 December, the former was tried again and kept the position until the end of the campaign and beyond. He played there in eleven league games and one Birmingham Cup match, but hit only four goals, a fraction of the number that McGinnes would have been expected to have attained. Beats was also Vale's centre-forward in their all-time record Football League home defeat on 10 December when they were annihilated 10-0 by Sheffield United! At the end of the season, the Valeites finished in penultimate position and had to suffer the humiliation of having to apply for re-election.

Although they fielded nearly the same side at the start of the 1893-1894 campaign, Vale were remarkably fast out of their blocks and won all their opening seven league games, scoring thirty goals and conceding only seven in the process. Beats banged in nine of the goals and the Valeites sat proudly at the top of the table, well on course to feature in the end of season test matches for promotion to the First Division, in only their second year in the league. However, on 7 October, Vale were annihilated 8-1 at third from the bottom Ardwick and a spectacular collapse followed, in which they won just six of their remaining twenty games, to finish seventh out of fifteen teams! Nevertheless, Beats was ever present at centre-forward throughout the season, with 32 appearances in total to his name, and he finished as the leading scorer, with sixteen league goals, as well as four in cup competitions. Despite the Valeites' spectacular collapse, Beats' marksmanship had come on leaps and bounds.

Vale opened the 1894-1895 campaign dramatically differently than the previous one, recording just two victories and four draws in their first 23 league games. Although a late revival ensured that they finished ahead of the bottom side, Crewe Alexandra, the Valeites were obliged to seek re-election for the second time in three years. Beats appeared in all except two of the thirty league matches, in most of which he again played at centre-forward, but he only scored six times. He also played in three known cup games, bagging just one recorded goal.

By then, the club's financial position had become so precarious that meetings were held to decide whether to continue or not. However, the immediate problem was resolved in June 1895 through the sale of Beats to First Division Wolverhampton Wanderers for eighty pounds and a benefit match guaranteed to raise fifty pounds. In total, he had scored 32 known goals for Vale in 97 known appearances. So McGinnes' replacement went on to play in the top flight of the Football League and he later became an England international, gaining two caps.

In summary, Vale made rapid progress between 1884 and 1887, but their fortunes then declined until 1889 when they managed to procure the services of the fabulous centre-forward, Frank McGinnes. Over the next three seasons, his amazing marksmanship did much to revitalise the team and get them elected into the Football League. Unfortunately, his premature death had a disastrous effect on the side's performances in their debut 1892-1893 Second Division campaign and his long-term replacement, Billy Beats, was nowhere near able to match McGinnes' goalscoring record, even though he became an England international!

As McGinnes died at such a young age, very probably not having reached the peak of his career, the question is: what might have happened had he lived?

At the end of their initial season in the Second Division, Vale finished in penultimate place, just two points behind fourth from the bottom Lincoln City. However, because of a vastly inferior goal average, they were actually three points adrift of safety from having to apply for re-election to the league. As the Valeites *were*, in the event, re-elected, it can only be an academic exercise to ask whether the extra goals that McGinnes would probably have scored would have secured the three points necessary to have prevented their humiliation of having to do so.

Vale's centre-forwards that league campaign (Beats, Bliss and Farrington) bagged only six goals out of the team's total of thirty in 22 matches, a very poor haul by any standards. During his time with the Valeites, McGinnes' known goals accounted for exactly a third of the team's total in the matches he played. Also, his ratio of goals scored per games played while he was with Vale was 0.778, which made him well over twice as prolific as Beats as a marksman. In addition, McGinnes' ratio would almost certainly have been significantly higher had the 56 unknown goalscorers, in the matches in which he appeared, been recorded. Even allowing for the fact that the standard of the Second Division was appreciably higher than that of the Midland League, it is difficult to imagine that a fit McGinnes would not have scored enough extra goals for Vale during the whole of the season to have secured more than two further points.

The Valeites drew three league matches and lost three by the odd goal during the 1892-1893 campaign, but in only one of those six games did a Vale centre-forward bag a goal. Also, one of the odd-goal defeats was suffered, by 2-1, at Lincoln City, who finished in the last safe place, fourth from the bottom. Had the Valeites scored just once more in that match, they would have ended the season on level points with their opponents. Because of their inferior goal average, Vale would therefore have required just one additional successful strike in any of their five other key games to have avoided having to apply for re-election. Surely it would not have been beyond the ability of an ace marksman like McGinnes to have put a single effort over the line with so many matches at his disposal.

The Valeites finished the 1893-1894 campaign nine points adrift of third-placed Notts County, who then lost their test match play-off 4-0 against the First Division's third from the bottom side, Preston North End, and thereby failed to get promoted. Vale have never competed in the top flight of English football in the whole of their history, but would it have been possible with McGinnes in full flow for them to have gone up there that season? It is asking an awful lot for a change of centre-forward to have been able to have made a difference of ten points (because of an inferior goal average) over just 28 games, with the old formula of two points for a win, but could it have been done?

The best prospect the Valeites would have had to reduce the deficit would have been if the scoring of an extra goal in both matches against County would have gained them two more points and thereby decreased their rival's total by the same number. That would have put County on 37 points and Vale on 32.

Unfortunately, in the real world, Vale lost their initial encounter 6-1 and it seems that it would have been beyond the power of even McGinnes to have salvaged anything on that occasion, especially as he had never scored five known goals in a match for the Valeites. The return fixture at Cobridge was won 1-0 and so it is impossible that any further points could have been gained from that game. Therefore, Vale would have had to have found ten more points from their other matches.

The Valeites lost four of their league games by the odd goal and drew four more. Had McGinnes been in fine form in all those matches and notched an extra goal in each, eight more points would have been gained. However, Beats scored in 2-1 defeats both at Newcastle United and at home to Walsall Town Swifts, so, if McGinnes had replaced him as the centre-forward, he would have had to have hit the target twice on each occasion. Also, Beats put the ball away twice in Vale's 2-2 draw at Lincoln City, so, according to the same logic, McGinnes would have needed to have bagged a hat trick in that game to have gained an extra point for his team. However, had McGinnes and Beats successfully played alongside one another and notched their conjectured and real goals, and had the actual scorers in the key matches also stood, then the additional eight points would have been gained.

Even then, two more points would have been needed for Vale to have played in the end of season test matches and had a chance of being promoted to the First Division. They lost two league games by two goals and two additional successful strikes in both by the prolific McGinnes would have turned them into draws and achieved the extra ten-point target by a whisker. However, the marvellous marksman would have had to have been in the most fantastic form of his great career to have produced all those goals as required whilst playing at a standard sometimes higher than he was used to.

It is clearly very doubtful whether the great goalscorer could have been so consistently successful at just the right moments, but suppose he had. Could Vale have beaten Preston where Notts County failed? North End had easily the best overall record of all the Football League clubs and had become known as the 'Invincibles'. They had been the champions in the first two seasons and the runners-up the following three years, so it was a shock that they had finished in such a lowly position at the end of their sixth campaign. It appears to have been a blip because they climbed up to fourth the next season. They had finished the 1893-1894 campaign just one point from safety and had no trouble hammering Notts County 4-0 in their test match. As County had conceded only 31 goals in the league, compared to Vale's 64, it is difficult to imagine what the Valeites could have done to have kept Preston's score down. They would certainly have needed McGinnes if they had met the 'Invincibles', but they would have required a steel curtain as well! Therefore, the odds of Vale making the First Division had McGinnes lived are slight, but it is not impossible that they could have done so.

There is a greater likelihood that McGinnes would have made a fundamental difference to the key outcome of The Valeites' 1894-1895 league season. It was one of struggle and they finished in penultimate position, six points behind fifth from the bottom Rotherham Town and safety from a re-election plea. Beats was the centre-forward in 23 of Vale's 30 league games, Billy Eardley appeared there four times and Alf Wood, Jim Mason and Charlie Mason did so once each. Beats was the only one of them to score in the position and he managed just six successful strikes. There was clearly room for McGinnes to have made a significant impact.

The Valeites drew 1-1 at home with Rotherham that season and lost the return 2-1. Beats was the centre-forward on both occasions and did not score. Had McGinnes been in his place and bagged a goal on each occasion, Vale would have gained two more points and Rotherham had two fewer. That would have reduced the gap between the two sides to just two points, but the Valeites would almost certainly have had an inferior goal average. Therefore, three extra points would have been needed to have avoided a plea for re-election. Throughout the season, Vale drew four league games and lost five times against other teams by one goal. It clearly would have been well within the capabilities of a fully fit McGinnes to have hit the target on three of those nine occasions and so it is feasible that the Valeites, in such circumstances, could have avoided finishing in the re-election zone. However, it would have been immaterial for the future because they were re-elected anyway.

It would by then very likely have occurred to almost permanently cash-strapped Vale that their ace marksman, despite his prowess, had not proved crucial in determining their survival in the Second Division and that even he was unable to help them mount a real challenge for promotion to the top flight, without the team being strengthened. Also, McGinnes may well have realised that First Division football and even greater honours would very probably not come his way with Vale. Therefore, by the summer of 1895, if not earlier, it may well have been that both the club and the player would have become ripe for McGinnes' transfer to a bigger operation.

As Wolves at that time were looking to pay a fee for an impressive centre-forward, it could well have been that they would have approached Vale about the services of McGinnes. Based on the relative proportions of his vastly superior known scoring record to that of Beats, the Valeites might have quoted Wanderers a transfer fee of around £180 and a guaranteed £110 or so from a benefit match. However, that would have constituted an immense payment for the time, so Vale would have been exceedingly lucky if Wolverhampton had been able to find such a huge sum of money and been willing to part with it, even for such a magnificent marksman as McGinnes. As the Valeites were struggling financially, though, no doubt they would have been forced to accept a considerably lower fee for their talisman and McGinnes would have been on his way.

It is interesting to speculate upon how many goals McGinnes would have scored for Vale by then, if he had still been alive and playing for the club. His known total of successful strikes in just over three seasons at the club was 109. However, as his known goals scored represent precisely a third of the team's total in the games in which he played, applying that average to the strikes unaccounted for would add a further 19 to his tally.

In addition, McGinnes appeared 140 known times for the Valeites out of 158 matches they played in total during the time he was with them. If the same proportion of presence is applied to Vale's league and cup games in the three seasons from 1892 to 1895, then he would have made a total of 249 appearances for the club. Had he continued to score at his known rate of 0.778 of a goal per match, his extra 91 appearances would have brought him 71 successful strikes and made his grand total of goals scored for Vale an all-time club record 199. Although his scoring rate may well not have been as high in the stronger Second Division as it had been in the Midland League, it is likely that a consequent reduction in his number of successful strikes would have been more than offset by the extra goals he would almost certainly have scored in the many friendly games which were still played at that time. In that case, it is highly probable that McGinnes would have topped 200 goals during his time at Vale.

When Beats signed for Wolves, his new wages were the princely sum of four pounds a week during the winter and three pounds a week in the summer. As McGinnes had easily outscored Beats at Vale, he might well have hoped for even more, but there is no guarantee that Wanderers would have been willing, or able, to meet his expectations. In Beats' first campaign at Wolverhampton, 1895-1896, his team finished third from the bottom of the First Division and avoided the end of season test matches only by a single point. However, they reached the final of the F.A. Cup, where they were defeated 2-1 by Sheffield Wednesday and, although Beats played at centre-forward, he did not score. The obvious question that follows is, if Wanderers had signed the altogether more prolific McGinnes, instead of Beats, would the magnificent marksman have struck a time or two on the big occasion to have helped to bring the cup back to Wolverhampton?

Two seasons later, Wolves ended up third in the First Division, seven points adrift of the champions, Sheffield United. As they scored one goal more than United, but conceded ten more, it seems that greater defensive strength, rather than attacking power, would have given them their best chance of lifting the title. No doubt McGinnes would have had something to say about the championship race, had he still been playing for Wanderers, but whether his marksmanship could have achieved enough to have made up for their defensive weaknesses can only be an open question.

The season after Beats had left Vale proved to be yet another one of struggle for the Valeites and once more they had to apply for re-election, having finished third from the bottom. This time, though, they were voted out of the league, not surprisingly considering their performances in their four Second Division campaigns. Had the Valeites received a bigger fee from Wolves for McGinnes than they did for Beats, it is very doubtful whether they could have afforded to have assembled a stronger squad that would have enabled them to finish in the safety zone because their finances were in a perilous state. Therefore, the departure of McGinnes for a large fee at that stage probably would not have made a fundamental difference to Vale's future.

However, had McGinnes lived and continued to excel as a goalscorer with the Valeites, the impact on the football career of Beats would most probably have been very significant indeed. While the former was at large, Beats had difficulty even getting into the Vale side, let alone beginning to challenge the main marksman for his position. Upon McGinnes' death, Beats replaced him as the team's centre-forward and, despite the latter's mediocre goalscoring ability, his career then never looked back. Had his rival not died, it may well have been that Beats would have made a handful of further appearances in the Vale team over the next season or two and then disappeared into complete obscurity.

And what might have happened to the fabulous Frank McGinnes himself had fate not dealt him such an awful blow? As has been suggested, he might well have bagged over 200 goals for the Valeites, become a force in the First Division and gained an F.A. Cup winner's medal. As Billy Beats became an England international centre-forward, it is not inconceivable that McGinnes could have become a goalscorer, possibly of great renown, for Scotland. As he was only 22 when he died, it is well possible that he could have continued to be a feared centre-forward for at least ten more years and perhaps scored over 500 goals in his footballing career. However, because he was fundamentally a selfish centre-forward, like many of the great goalscorers, it may well have been that the players around him would have found the ball and therefore the target less frequently!

In 1892, the world was full of possibilities for Frank McGinnes, just as it was for the "Busby Babes" in 1958, but, like happened to many of them, his life was cut off while he was still in his prime. What McGinnes might have achieved had he lived can only be speculated upon, but perhaps thanks should be given for the brief, but exceptionally successful, spell that he was able to enjoy with the Valeites. Maybe the writing of this story will help its readers to preserve the memory of the exploits of arguably Vale's finest ever centre-forward, even though he never scored a single Football League goal for the club. And if indeed the readers are so inspired, then Frank McGinnes still lives!

5 Thank God For Cobridge Church!

After their failure to be re-elected to the Second Division in 1896, Vale rejoined the Midland League, but they did not set the world alight in their first season at the lower level, finishing only seventh out of fifteen teams. With the lack of success, their home crowds dwindled, so that gates of 2,000 became rare and, by November 1896, the club was close to collapse. The following match, at Heanor Town on 5 December, only took place because the home side lent the Valeites the money to get there, though whether it was worthwhile them travelling is arguable because they were trounced 7-1! In the event, the club was saved by the formation of a limited liability company, but the team's main achievement that campaign was winning the Staffordshire Senior Charity Cup, with a 3-0 victory over Dresden United in the final!

The team started the 1897-1898 season even more poorly than they had done the previous year and picked up only three points from their first eight league games. A remarkable turnaround then saw Vale gain twenty points from their following twelve matches and make it through three qualifying rounds of the F.A. Cup before drawing 1-1 against all the odds at Sheffield United, the First Division leaders and eventual champions, in the first round proper on 29 January 1898. Four days later, the Valeites completed the job in the replay at Cobridge by despatching their mighty opponents from the competition, by 2-1, in front of an all-time ground record crowd of 15,000. Although they were knocked out of the cup in the next round, Vale won the Staffordshire Cup for the first time, beating West Bromwich Albion 1-0 in the final at Stoke's Victoria Ground on 5 March. They finished fifth in the Midland League and then received the second-highest number of votes at the Football League's annual meeting, to regain their place in the Second Division. Unfortunately, the club lost £106 17s. 1d. over the season, with the gate receipts of their whole Midland League programme being lower than those from their sensational cup match against Sheffield United alone! Unhappily, their financial failure proved to be a taste of things to come.

For the first few weeks of the 1898-1899 campaign, it seemed that the Valeites were going to surpass their marvellous achievements of the previous campaign because they won their opening six league games, to go four points clear at the top of the table. However, the team then went off the boil and finished ninth out of eighteen sides, with an even worse financial loss than the previous year being registered over the season, this time of £300.

Worse was still to come because the average home crowd in the 1899-1900 campaign dropped by over sixty per cent from that in the preceding season and consequently three of the best players were sold to keep the club afloat. The chairman, Robert Audley, then issued the warning, 'Unless something is done, Port Vale will fall down very much quicker than it got up.' Fortunately, his words were heeded and a supporters' meeting on 7 December 1899 led to the creation of a Shilling Fund, although by the end of the campaign it had raised only £39. On 27 March 1900, Audley announced that the debt had risen to £940 and that £500 was needed for the club to continue. At the end of the season, in which the team had finished a creditable eleventh, it was decided to scrap the payment of summer wages, transfer the most expensive players, cut the pay of those who remained and rely on local, and preferably young, footballers from then on, in an attempt to stop the rot.

The new policy proved relatively successful because £763 10s. 6d. was saved on the players' wages the following campaign, but the total match receipts fell by £235 1s. 5d. and yet another loss was reported, this time of £73 16s. 6d., which increased the total debt to £1,007 12s. 1d. As it turned out, the team finished two places higher than in the previous season, which obviously led to the cheap and local policy being continued!

The team dropped four positions in the league in the 1901-1902 campaign and avoided finishing in the re-election zone only by winning the final game. Nevertheless, a profit of £368 was made, assisted by receipts from eleven cup matches, although the financial success was mostly owing to an Easter bazaar, which raised over £300!

The unexpected turnaround helped persuade the club to scrap the local footballers' policy for the next season, but the gate income dropped by £200 and the club relied on the sale of players to balance the books. In the event, a profit of £112 12s. 2d. was made and the team finished a highly satisfactory ninth in the league.

Vale finished the 1903-1904 season in thirteenth place, just two points clear of the re-election zone, although they won through three rounds of the F.A. Cup, which brought in vital income. Nevertheless, expenditure had risen and league gate receipts dropped, so that a £39 18s. loss resulted despite transfer proceeds.

The following campaign, the team finished third from the bottom of the league and had to apply for re-election. The club's humiliation was not helped by an 8-1 annihilation at Liverpool, the leaders and eventual champions, on 8 April 1905! The gate receipts fell by £152 12s. 1d. and brought in only sixty per cent of the amount needed to meet the club's expenses. Fortunately, Vale were saved once again by the receipt of fees from player transfers, which amounted to £900 and enabled a £140 14s. 8d. profit to be made.

The directors decided to resume the payment of summer wages, to try to attract better quality players, but the team made only the most marginal improvement in the 1905-1906 season by ending up fourth from the bottom. Indeed, a second successive re-election plea was only avoided on goal average and as a result of a consolation goal scored by centre-half Joseph Holyhead near the end of the final match, a 4-1 defeat at West Bromwich Albion on 28 April 1906. The team's failings were further illustrated by 7-0 trouncings they received at Chelsea and in a semi-final of the Birmingham Cup at Birmingham.

The position was exacerbated by an alarming £451 16s. 9d. loss, which was made on the campaign despite stringent economies and the receipt of yet more transfer income from the sales of the best players. The match receipts had fallen by a staggering £280 19s. 4d., which Robert Audley described as 'deplorable'. At £982, they were nowhere near the amount required to balance the club's expenditure of forty pounds or more per week. The secretary, Sam Gleaves, said that Wrexham, who played in the same league as Vale's reserves, took nearly as much gate money and pointed out that if the support didn't improve, 'This club must inevitably cease to exist.'

The outcome was that Vale went for broke for the 1906-1907 season, re-signing centre-forward Billy Beats and engaging several other players from outside the area in the hope that they would prove attractions that would boost the gates. The team made a small improvement in finishing fifth from the bottom of the league, although they only achieved safety from the re-election zone by beating Blackpool 3-0 at home in their final match on 27 April 1907. Perhaps partly helped by the new faces on view, there was a significant increase in the size of the home crowds and Burslem Port Vale recorded their highest ever overall average that season. However, it was not enough to save the club from extinction.

On 18 May, an ominous letter from Robert Audley and Sam Gleaves appeared in the *Sentinel*, appealing for new directors to put money into the club and for more support from the public. It said, 'Unless capital is forthcoming there must be an end to an organisation of 28 years' standing.' Unfortunately, only one supporter answered the cry for help and, on 14 June, the Valeites withdrew from the Football League. The players were increasingly transferred to other clubs as Audley decided that Vale were no longer viable and needed to be wound up.

A further letter, from Audley, was published by the *Sentinel* on 29 June, explaining the reasons why the club had had to fold. There had been an increase in the gate receipts, but Vale had still made a £200 loss on the season. Audley also said that the average takings of the seven previous campaigns had been only £1,500 and they had been supplemented by average transfer takings of £400 a year, a total which 'could not be expected to pay the expenses of a league club'. The bank had refused to loan any more money, some of the creditors were 'pressing their claims', summer wages would have to be paid and there was no prospect of any notable income before the next home game in September. Audley signed off by saying, 'To the few hundreds of loyal supporters, I tender my best thanks for their support and I join in their regrets that sufficient financial support could not be found to continue the club.'

It is ironic that, after years of financial struggle, the original Port Vale club finally went under at the end of a season in which they had attracted easily their highest overall average home crowd since their formation and their second-largest average league home attendance ever. The statistics suggest that the policy of signing outside players to attract more supporters was working and it is natural to wonder why the directors did not persist with it, to see if the club could have been made into a going concern, instead of just throwing in the towel.

In the circumstances, the heart says that more time should have been given to find out whether the club could turn the corner and get within range of breaking even, if not become a profitable concern. Perhaps, if Audley, Gleaves et al. had not acted with undue haste, Burslem Port Vale could have been saved and gone on to greater things.

However, it is easy to be optimistic on the outside, not facing the potential prospect of one's hard-earned cash endlessly disappearing down the proverbial black hole. The fact of the matter is that Vale had struggled financially most of the time since they had become professional in 1885 and Robert Audley had resorted to a number of expedients to prop up the club during the ten years he had been in the chair, not least including putting his hand in his own pocket when all else had failed. It can be argued that, without his financial fixes and personal generosity, Vale would have ceased to exist years before and it may have been that he, Gleaves and the other directors had reached the end of their tether by 1907, worn down by endlessly putting their fingers in the dyke to prevent the dam from bursting.

From their perspective, it may well be that one swallow did not make a summer and they thought that the improved attendances during the 1906-1907 season were a flash in the pan. Having said that, the evidence shows Vale's average home crowds had improved significantly for the fourth year in a row, with the overall gates more than doubling over the period and the league attendances becoming almost twice as large.

Nevertheless, it appears that the directors were not blamed for the demise of the club, but that, on the contrary, it was considered that they had fought a valiant battle for a long time to keep Vale afloat. The *Sentinel* perhaps summed up the prevailing mood, with the eulogistic comment, 'How bravely they have stuck to a very unenviable task is well known.'

Indeed, it is very difficult to see how the club could have persuaded their bank to have extended their overdraft for a business that was primarily loss making. Even had the bank proved to be gullible, it is hard to imagine Vale's benefactors repeating such an elementary mistake when the next financial crisis loomed, as it very probably would have done, sooner rather than later. Also, alternative sources of large sums of money were less available at that time than they are now because the finance industry was much more conservative and, as the club's credit worthiness was frowned upon by their supporting bank, the situation cannot have endeared Vale to other banks.

Maybe Robert Audley would have once more made up the money deficit from his own funds, but the prospect of him doing so was obviously minimised by the pressure the club was under from creditors at that point. By pressing their claims at a time when the club was so vulnerable, they effectively brought it to extinction, in a situation that is far from unknown to professional football clubs in the early twenty-first century. Furthermore, there was the payment of summer wages to players under contract to consider, which again was something that was very difficult to avoid.

It might have been that, had only one or even maybe two of the financial hammer blows occurred at that time, the hearts of the Vale directors would have persuaded them to have produced the cash (if indeed they possessed it) to keep the club going. However, as chance had it, the virtually insurmountable financial crisis struck at the very time that a silver lining had appeared.

Perhaps in 1907 the club was on the verge of a new, more profitable and successful era or maybe the endless struggle to survive would have continued, with its inevitable collapse coming not long after the curtain actually fell. It is hard to ignore the evidence of Vale's longer history, which showed a pretty consistent pattern of financial problems, but the consistent rise of attendances over the club's final four-year period cannot be dismissed as a fluke. Interest had clearly grown significantly, but we will never know whether it would have been maintained or continued to rise had Vale ploughed on beyond 1907. It could be that the original club was doomed to die, but that its spirit was so vibrant that it had to live on. In a sense, the latter must be true because a new Port Vale rose like a phoenix out of the ashes of its predecessor and still holds a passionate place today in the hearts and minds of many thousands of folk in North Staffordshire and beyond.

When Robert Audley thanked 'the few hundreds' of Vale fans for their loyal support, he was minimising the actual interest in the club, perhaps because it would not have looked quite so justifiable to have had it wound up if he had admitted that the number of supporters attending the matches actually ran into thousands. The average known overall home attendance in the 1906-1907 campaign was over 4,763, whilst that in the league was more than 4,147. In addition, two gates of 10,000 were recorded in the F.A. Cup, for the visits of Northamptonshire League Irthlingborough Town and First Division Notts County. These statistics alone seem to confirm that Vale had significant potential support, which had rarely been tapped, but could have been in the future.

Many, and probably most, of the spectators who had attended Vale's matches would very likely have been sad, if not devastated, that the club had ceased to exist and they may well have wondered what they would do on Saturday afternoons during the forthcoming season and beyond. A void would probably have loomed large for a good number of them because football passion aroused is not easily destroyed and rarely transferred. They would still have been Vale supporters at heart and so there existed the potential for someone, who could engage their interest and thereby induce them to part with their money, to create a profitable enterprise, providing the cost of doing so was limited.

While Burslem Port Vale were competing for the final time in the Football League in the 1906-1907 campaign, Cobridge Church were achieving the championship and cup double in the lowly North Staffordshire Church League for the first time in its history. They lost only two of their twenty league games and won the cup at Vale's Athletic Ground on 20 April 1907. There was absolutely no connection between the two clubs nor, until the end of the season, could anyone possibly have imagined that their paths would meet in the very near future.

Boosted by their comprehensive success, the church team decided to try their luck at a higher level and applied to join the North Staffordshire Federation League for the following campaign. They were accepted and became members of what still amounted to a very minor competition. Whilst Cobridge Church were anticipating the excitement of their new challenge, Vale were going through the process of being wound up. The traumatic demise of the Valeites had not gone unnoticed by the joint-secretaries of the Cobridge club, Mr Millward and E. C. Brundrett, and they moved decisively to take advantage of an opportunity that had presented itself. Under their direction, the committee of the church team took a big risk and negotiated the takeover of the Athletic Ground from the liquidating club in the hope that the move would help to put them on the map. As the church itself (Christ Church, in Church Terrace) overlooked the stadium, the arrangement was very apt and homely.

For a local church side to take on effectively a Football League ground was a quantum move that, on the surface, seemed to be one step from madness, not least because of the maintenance costs that would be incurred. However, Cobridge Church had a big advantage over Burslem Port Vale in that they were not saddled with debts. Messrs Millward and Brundrett had spotted the chance to put their club in the relative big time and they had done their homework extremely well. There was very little chance that a side named Cobridge Church would attract anywhere near the numbers of spectators to justify owning such a grand ground – but a team named Port Vale was an entirely different matter!

The joint-secretaries realised that the ground could be obtained for a knockdown price from the old club desperately trying to sell off its assets to meet its creditors and that thousands of football fans in the vicinity no longer had a team to support. They could be accommodated at the Athletic Ground, as they had been until the end of the previous season, and the way to get them there was to change the name of the Cobridge Church first team to Port Vale, which is exactly what the committee did. The likelihood was that money would then roll into their club on an unprecedented scale at the turnstiles. The *Sentinel* commented that, 'The plucky management has embarked on a big undertaking.' With their eyes clearly focused on the future, Millward and Brundrett went to the trouble of getting the permission of the Football Association for the adoption of their new name. By not using the "Burslem" prefix, it was clear that Cobridge Church were not claiming to be the old club, which was still in existence and in the process of liquidating. So the original Port Vale name came back into being and has, of course, remained so ever since, although their reserve side initially continued to be called Cobridge Church.

The new Port Vale team was comprised mainly of the successful Cobridge Church players of the previous campaign and began the 1907-1908 season by trouncing Newchapel United 6-0 at home in their first league game on 14 September in front of 'a fair crowd indeed for a junior football match'. What proportion of the spectators had until very recently been Burslem Port Vale fans can easily be imagined. The team won the following two matches as well, the second of which, at home to Longton Hall, attracted 600 spectators, a remarkable number for the North Staffordshire Federation League. Apart from the vastly inferior quality of their opponents, it must have seemed to the increasingly returning Vale supporters that they had never been away! It is very doubtful whether many cared that the new club had absolutely no connection with the old one and that it was being run by an entirely different group of people. The name of the team and the continuation of the ground would have been virtually everything to them.

After their inspirational start, the new Vale team went off the boil and won only one of their next six league games. Ironically, while the new Port Vale were struggling, the old club came good at the death. On 22 November, an extraordinary meeting was held at the Queen's Hotel, in Cobridge, to make the necessary arrangements to wind up Burslem Port Vale voluntarily. All the club's remaining assets were put on sale, to try to clear the outstanding £1,000 liabilities, and, in due course, netted a surplus of £108 6s. 4d. Remarkably, after all the years of financial struggle, at the very end of the road the shareholders received a small payback!

The new Port Vale finished the season fifth out of nine sides in the league, but only three points adrift of the champions, Florence Colliery. The committee were sufficiently encouraged, not least by the amount of support that they were getting, to move up a further grade for the following campaign and membership of the North Staffordshire & District League, the top junior competition in the area, was secured. As well as the natural urge for the team to do as well as possible, it is not hard to imagine the committee anticipating that better opponents would bring in more spectators and thereby more funds to the club.

In anticipation of the impending challenge, the club signed a number of new players and the season tickets consequently sold well. Unfortunately, the side were not able to rise to the occasion, gaining just four points from their first twelve league matches and, by the end of December 1908, finding themselves eliminated from all the four cup competitions they had entered! This time, the committee had bitten off more than they could chew, not only because the team were being humiliated on the field, but also because the financial pressure had correspondingly mounted as the attendances, not surprisingly, also suffered. The master plan of Messrs Millward and Brundrett appeared to be in ruins and it seemed more than possible that the new Port Vale might go the way of the old one, but a lot more quickly.

A quick fix was needed to prevent the season becoming a catastrophe, but it seemed to be beyond the capabilities of the committee to achieve it, especially because they lacked the necessary wherewithal. The resurrection of Port Vale had been rapid, but the desire for success was clearly greater than the resources of the club to enable it to happen. Cobridge Church had undertaken a major gamble by taking on the Athletic Ground, but the provision, in addition, of sufficient funds to attract quality local players appeared to be beyond them. The prospects were grim and the committee at that point must have been pondering their boldness, and perhaps rashness, in pushing upwards so rapidly.

Remarkably, as chance had it, it turned out to be exactly then, just when Vale urgently needed saving from disaster for the second time in eighteen months, that a group of knights in shining armour charged in to their rescue! The problems being experienced by the Cobridge Church committee provided the opportunity for a consortium of Burslem Port Vale stalwarts, led by their former team manager, Sam Bennion, to buy their way into the new club. With Bennion as the chairman and Harry Myatt as his deputy, the old guard thenceforth effectively controlled the new Port Vale, although E. C. Brundrett remained as the secretary. The newcomers quickly stabilised the situation, so that their arrival proved to be a turning point and the club then went from strength to strength.

It is easy to imagine the bemusement of the old Burslem Port Vale officials, with their attention focused on their dying club in 1907, when Cobridge Church made their audacious move in occupying the Athletic Ground and changing the name of their first team to Port Vale. As the new club took shape, the old guard were initially forced to sit on the sidelines, but, when the moment presented itself, they acted decisively and effectively took over the new Port Vale. In reality, aside from the change of chairman and secretary, the considerably lower grade of football being played and a financial headache on a much smaller scale, things must have seemed not greatly different from how they had been before the old club's demise.

The new management team rapidly signed a series of former players and other talented footballers, which led to an amazing transformation in the side's fortunes. Nine league games in a row were won, with 37 goals being scored in the process, as Vale marched up the table to finish a creditable eighth out of fourteen teams.

The new side were so powerful that only one new signing of note was made for the 1909-1910 season and the team started like a rocket, gaining 27 points from their first 14 matches. The crowd for the opening home match, against Stoke Reserves on 11 September, was an excellent 3,500, which was 500 more than the old Burslem club had attracted to their final Football League match against Blackpool on 27 April 1907! Amazingly, the attendance doubled for the third league home game, against Fegg Hayes, on 9 October and interest remained high throughout the whole of the campaign. On 5 March 1910, the prestigious Staffordshire Junior Cup was won at Stoke's Victoria Ground, in front of a magnificent gate of 12,500, when Chillington Rangers were beaten 3-2. Vale would have won the North Staffordshire & District League championship as well had the deciding match at Stoke Reserves, on 23 April, not been abandoned after a pitch invasion, with the visitors 2-0 ahead. In the event, the wrangle about the affair went on for so long that the game was never replayed and the championship was declared void!

Inspired by the level of support they were getting, the directors spent £250 on having a 1,800-capacity grandstand built in time for the start of the 1910-1911 season. Unfortunately, though, that summer Vale became victims of their own success because their star strikers, Joe Brough and Billy Cavenor, both signed for Football League clubs and the club were unable to replace them with players of similar quality. The outcome was that no trophies were won, although the team finished a respectable fourth in the table and the league attendance and receipts records were smashed on 8 October 1910 when 9,000 fans generated £120 for the visit of Stoke Reserves, who triumphed 3-0.

Plans were afoot for the Football League to form a new Third Division. The Vale directors believed that the club were potential members because of their substantial ground and sizable support and so they called a public meeting at Burslem Town Hall on 2 June 1911. There was a 'large and enthusiastic gathering' and a number of former Burslem Port Vale officials were instrumental in the adoption of a plan to form a limited liability company, which was considered necessary to enable the club to survive in the Football League. The existing directors were willing to hand over the reins to the new company and £500 capital had been promised by the end of the meeting.

A second meeting took place at the town hall on 21 July, as a result of which the new company bought the club for £330, with the blessing of Sam Bennion, and 4,000 five-shilling shares were issued. Unfortunately, by then, the Football League had decided that it was impossible to put together the proposed Third Division in time for the new season, but a new Central League was formed by Football League reserve sides from the Northwest and a few other strong teams. Vale applied for membership and were admitted on a trial basis for one season, which effectively put them within range of the Football League once again. The new directors tried to bring back the name of Burslem Port Vale for the club, but they were prevented from doing so by the registrar of joint-stock companies, so the team remained without its old prefix.

The start of the new campaign was only 6½ weeks away and the Vale officials really pulled out the stops to sign a profusion of players with Football League experience, to help meet the standard required, in time for the first match. The enthusiastic gamble to set up the new company proved well vindicated because the team finished the season as runners-up and won the Staffordshire Cup to boot. The opening home gate, against Oldham Athletic Reserves on 4 September, was an encouraging 8,000 and over 9,000 attended the 1912 New Year's Day game at Cobridge against Liverpool Reserves, but the average known league crowd was a disappointing 5,346, although that was more than a thousand higher than Burslem Port Vale had attracted in their final Football League season. Much encouraged, the directors decided to apply for a place in the Football League and, hopefully, regain their elite status only five years after the original club had folded. Although it remained to be seen whether they would be successful, the transformation of Vale's fortunes over such a short period was quite remarkable.

Having said that, a key question which can be asked is whether the resurgence of Port Vale was inevitable after the sad demise of the old club. A study of Football League clubs, which resigned or were not re-elected up to 1907 and then folded, strongly suggests that Vale's comeback was far from predetermined and, instead, was most unlikely:

In 1893, Accrington, founder members of the league, resigned and folded in 1896. The club did not re-form and had no connection to the later Accrington Stanley and the current Football League team of the same name.

The following year, Middlesbrough Ironopolis resigned from the Football League and disbanded. The club was not resurrected and had no association with the current league side, Middlesbrough, who were in existence at the same time.

Just two years later, Rotherham Town finished in penultimate position in the Second Division and did not apply for re-election. They then folded and did not re-form. Also, they had no connection to the current Football League team, Rotherham United, or any other club from the same town.

In 1900, Loughborough (who were commonly known as Loughborough Town) finished bottom of the Second Division, with just eight points from 34 matches. They were not re-elected and became defunct soon afterwards. They never re-formed and had no association with any other club from the town.

The next year, New Brighton Tower finished fourth in the Second Division, just six points adrift of a promotion place, but the cost of running the club proved prohibitive, so they resigned from the Football League and disbanded. They were not resurrected and they had no connection with the later club from the town, which was a member of the league from 1923 to 1951.

Finally, in 1907, Burton United ended up bottom of the Second Division and were not re-elected. They folded in 1910, were never re-established and had no association with any other club from the town, including the current Football League side, Burton Albion.

Technically, and certainly legally, the same fate befell Burslem Port Vale because the new club was really Cobridge Church under another name and had entirely different owners. Although the new Port Vale took over the Athletic Ground from the old club, that did not mean that the two organisations were one and therefore the argument as to whether the current outfit were founded in 1876 or not is in reality superfluous because the date in question was actually 1907. However, the immediate surge in the size of the gates of the renamed Cobridge Church clearly indicates that most, if not all, of the Burslem Port Vale supporters regarded the new outfit as at least the inheritor of their favourites and perhaps in effect the same club. Because there was no gap between the performances of the two clubs, it meant that the fans were able to watch Vale play their final home game of the 1906-1907 season and their first of the following campaign and that would have given a very strong sense of continuity.

Nevertheless, for around eighteen months, there were two Port Vales in existence. At the time that the old Burslem Port Vale stalwarts under the leadership of Sam Bennion took control of the new club in December 1908, the original organisation still existed! The meeting which finally wound up the old club was held at the Queen's Hotel on 15 January 1909 and even after then there were remaining payments that had to be made.

While the key decisions and arrangements for the dissolution of the original club still needed to be made, the Burslem Port Vale officials were in no position to consider setting up a new organisation of approximately the same name. Indeed, they were the people least likely to do so because they had decided to pull the plug on the outfit that they controlled. The last thing that would have been on their minds was to launch themselves into potentially even more of the same problems.

No doubt the vast majority, if not all, of the old club's supporters did not want Vale to collapse, but it is doubtful whether many of them had the wherewithal to fund a new outfit, even on the modest scale of a local junior football team. If they had had the necessary assets to do that, then they would probably already have been beneficiaries and officials of the Burslem club. The prospect of funding the maintenance of the Athletic Ground would have been a daunting prospect, especially for those without any experience of running a football club. Also, unlike in the early twenty-first century, there was no tradition of fans setting up their own clubs from new and it probably was that most of the long-standing supporters were resigned to the fate of their beloved Vale.

Therefore, it seems highly unlikely that Port Vale would have been resurrected had it not been for Cobridge Church. It is possible that down the line an attempt would have been made by a group of dispirited former supporters to create a new Port Vale, but it is doubtful whether the Athletic Ground would have been taken on. However, without it, it would have been difficult to have taken gate money, so the prospect of Vale rising like a phoenix would have been remote. In any case, each year that passed would have seen the prospect recede. Without someone grabbing the bull by the horns, after three or four years, Port Vale would almost certainly have become no more than a rose-tinted fading memory.

It may have been that another enterprising club would have seen the opportunity that had presented itself had Messrs Millward and Brundrett, of Cobridge Church, not done so in the summer of 1907. However, the time available to put a new Port Vale together and take over the Athletic Ground before the start of the next season was so short that Millward and Brundrett must have been on the case almost immediately. Even then, Cobridge Church took a big risk in buying the Athletic Ground, which was potentially a huge liability. The fact is that, in hardly any time at all, a vision of the future was created and the necessary action carried out in order to bring it about. Cobridge Church took a dangerous calculated gamble, which could easily have gone awry (and perhaps did within eighteen months) and it is not hard to admire their perceptiveness and courage in establishing the new Port Vale.

It is possible that the church club beat other contenders to the draw in effectively re-establishing Vale, but successful great schemes are rarely envisaged by many and far fewer have the nerve to carry them through. If there had been other clubs vying to take on the Port Vale name, they would have had even less time than Cobridge Church to do so in readiness for the following campaign and therefore may well have missed the boat. Had that been the case, it would then have been sensible to have waited till the following close season to launch the new club, but by then the old Burslem Port Vale supporters would have found something else to do with their time on Saturday afternoons, so it would have been more difficult to have persuaded them to revert to their former behaviour. Therefore, a year on may have been a year too late.

Although Cobridge Church saved Vale from oblivion, as has been seen, there was a limit as to how far they were able to take the club forward. When the team were struggling out of their depth in the North Staffordshire & District League during the first half of the 1908-1909 season and the club had developed financial problems, the future hung in the balance. Without the rescue charge by the old Burslem Port Vale stalwarts in December 1908, it may have been that the new club was itself on the way to collapse. Whether the situation would have become that serious is unknown, but the committee would almost certainly have had to have cut costs. It is well possible that the Athletic Ground would have had to have been abandoned, although selling it would very likely have presented a major headache, not least because the other junior clubs (the only likely interested parties) would have clearly seen from Cobridge Church's experience that the ground was a potential liability in local football.

Without Sam Bennion and co. and the necessary funds to attract better players, it is most likely that Vale would have finished the 1908-1909 campaign well adrift at the bottom of the table and a spiral downwards may well have followed. No doubt the crowds watching the almost perpetually losing side would have plummeted and Vale would have become an increasingly unattractive club for good local players to join. The following season could well have been spent in the much weaker North Staffordshire Federation League again and perhaps Vale would have stabilised at that level, being destined to become just a sorry remnant of a once vibrant Football League club. Even worse, it is not impossible that Cobridge Church would have abandoned the great Port Vale experiment, reverted to their former name, rejoined the North Staffordshire Church League and played their home games in Cobridge Park, to the future notice of hardly anyone except themselves.

However, the old Burslem Port Vale stalwarts came to the rescue very quickly once they realised that the new club was in trouble and that there was the opportunity for them to take it forward. The hard work had already been done by Cobridge Church in resurrecting the club and their committee had amply illustrated what could be done with imagination and nerve. They had set the example for others to follow and the move that Sam Bennion et al. made was their logical course of action. To them, to save Port Vale and become associated with the club again was simply a no-brainer. Indeed, they may well previously have been sitting on the sidelines, kicking themselves that they had been outthought by Cobridge Church and champing at the bit, as long-standing supporters, to get involved with the club. Even had Bennion not been alive by then or not been interested in the project, the same, or a very similar, outcome would almost certainly have resulted because he was only the foremost individual in a passionate consortium. Therefore, if history was rerun, it is extremely likely that the result would be virtually the same.

The formation of the limited liability company in the summer of 1911 seemed to be simply a natural progression. Vale had become a fair force in local football by then, but, to try to take the club up to the next level, a more solid business structure was required. In the world of football, hope springs eternal and it is therefore not surprising that the Vale directors wanted to progress the club back into the Football League, where they felt it belonged. To do that, the formation of a proper company was needed. The fact that the Football League were touting the foundation of a Third Division undoubtedly whetted the appetites of all the Vale stalwarts and was probably instrumental in the timing of the creation of the new company. However, it is exceedingly likely that the move would have been made before long anyhow because the Football League dream could not be extinguished.

As it turned out, there were Vale supporters with more financial clout than Sam Bennion and they were able to take the club forward to a higher level. Because Bennion and the existing directors were first and foremost Vale supporters, they willingly gave their blessing to the new company. In any case, with the strength of the tide for further improvement, it is doubtful whether they could realistically have succeeded in standing in the way. However, had they resisted the change, instead of being the catalyst of it, the existence of Port Vale would still not have been in doubt, although the team would almost certainly have continued to play at a lower level than the Central League, which they subsequently joined. Even in that case, it would probably only have been a matter of time before the directors changed their minds or were replaced (perhaps through natural evolution) by others with more ambition and the Football League dream would then no doubt have been advanced.

In conclusion, after the sad demise of the original club, Vale made a remarkable comeback in progressing from the local church league to a step away from the Football League in only four years. Perhaps even more importantly, they had become a limited liability company, which put the structure in place for the achievement of yet higher things. None of this would have been possible without the brilliant Messrs Millward and Brundrett and it may well have been that, in their absence, Port Vale would have ceased to have existed altogether. In that case, the current Vale supporters would no doubt be twiddling their thumbs on Saturday afternoons or having to go to the Britannia Stadium to watch Stoke City's amazing success in the Premier League and Europe. Thank God For Cobridge Church!

6 Leeds City Luck

At the end of their highly successful 1911-1912 season, Vale had hoped to apply for election to the Football League, but, unfortunately, their existing competition, the Central League, informed them that the club would have to decide by 27 April if they were retaining their membership. As that date preceded the Football League's annual meeting, the club were in a quandary because their resignation from the Central League would risk them having no competition to play in the following season. As the champions, Lincoln City clearly had a better case for admission to the Football League, Vale decided to play safe and stayed put in the Central League, whilst the "Imps" duly regained their place in the sun.

The Vale defence had proved to be easily the best in the league in the 1911-1912 campaign, but just three sides had scored fewer goals. Therefore, to bolster their chances of topping the table the following season, the club signed a number of new forwards. The immediate outcome was a 5-0 trouncing at Stalybridge Celtic in the opening match on 3 September, but the team soon settled down and lost only three of their following sixteen league games. For the penultimate match of the run, a fine crowd of 9,000 assembled to see Vale beat Crewe Alexandra 2-1 at home on Christmas Day 1912. By then, they had fought their way through three rounds of the F.A. Cup, scoring thirteen goals in the process, and been eliminated from the competition!

Unfortunately, Vale were having trouble with their pitch, which was sinking because of mining subsidence, but the problem proved to be a blessing in disguise. Hanley was keen to have a Football League club and a consortium of businessmen from the bustling town, led by Frank Huntbach, proposed that Vale should relocate there in return for the input of 'a large sum of money'. This was a very attractive proposition, particularly because the club was running at a significant loss and therefore was not in a position to improve the Cobridge pitch, even if such was possible. Consequently, the proposal was unanimously accepted and the Hanley men were given equal representation on the board. Thus Vale acquired a new ground and fresh funding, both of which were very important in their quest to return to the Football League.

The season finished disappointingly, with three consecutive league defeats, but Vale still ended up a creditable fourth in the table. The lack of a higher finish was to some extent compensated for by the winning of the Birmingham Cup, by 1-0 in the replayed final against Wolverhampton Wanderers Reserves, at Stoke's Victoria Ground, on 21 April, although the competition was by then not as prestigious as it had once been.

The new stadium was constructed at a cost of £3,000 on the site of the Kent Street Recreation Ground, close to Hanley town centre, apparently with accommodation for 35,000 spectators, although it is doubtful whether anywhere near that number could actually have crammed inside. Even allowing for the extra interest from the Hanley public, the expectation of such large crowds seemed rather optimistic because Vale's record home attendance up till then was only 15,000. So it proved as the largest ever official gate at what became known as the Old Recreation Ground was recorded as only 22,697, although the directors' ambition was no bad thing if Vale were to achieve their objective of returning to the Football League.

A Central League record 18,000 paying customers packed into the new ground on 1 September 1913 to see Vale draw their opening match of the season 3-3 with Blackburn Rovers Reserves and an estimated 2,000 more people got in free through uncompleted entrances! The phenomenal degree of interest augured very well for Vale's future and the next two league home games also attracted very large crowds, of 14,000 and 12,000. Although, inevitably, the attendances could not be maintained at those levels, they remained relatively high throughout the campaign as Vale made a strong challenge for the championship, even though they tailed off to finish fourth. Nevertheless, the average known home gate was a new club record 9,348, a seventy per cent increase on that of the previous season!

The team also had considerable success in the F.A. Cup, fighting their way through five preliminary and qualifying rounds, scoring an amazing 25 goals in the process, before they were eliminated in the first round proper. Also, they annihilated Wednesbury Old Athletic 12-1 and Darlaston 9-1 on the way to reaching the final of the Birmingham Cup, where they lost 2-1 at Stoke in a replay on 20 April 1914. In addition, the club had found a most potent strike force in Chris Young and Joe Brough, who scored 37 and 35 league and cup goals in 40 and 44 matches respectively!

In the close season, the club felt sufficiently confident to apply for election to the Football League. However, one of their competitors for a place were Stoke, who had dropped out of the premier league in 1908. Instead of the two clubs potentially ruining each other's chances, Vale agreed to step down in favour of their Potteries rivals, whom it was believed had the stronger case, on the understanding that Stoke would reciprocate the favour in the future. As it turned out, Stoke did not get elected and therefore, probably, neither would Vale have done.

Despite the loss of players to fight in the Great War, the club strengthened the squad for the 1914-1915 season and had fair confidence that they could at last win the Central League championship. The team began well and lost only two of their opening fourteen league matches, but the attendances fell away through the shortage of time and money because of the war effort. However, the club were helped out by the players, who agreed to accept a twenty per cent cut in their wages. On 21 September, Vale recorded their biggest ever victory in a competition when they annihilated Burton Rangers 14-1 at home in the first round of the Birmingham Cup, with Chris Young scoring an all-time club record seven goals! In the next round, on 2 October, the team did almost as well, in trouncing Brierley Hill Alliance 10-1, after banging in eight goals in the first half and then easing up!

On 9 November, Vale went to the top of the table and then equalled the Central League record score in beating Blackpool Reserves 9-2 at Hanley on 2 January 1915. Unfortunately, by then the club, like many others, was struggling financially to keep going and had to resort to public appeals for money. Also, the side's championship challenge petered out and they finished in third position, but they did win the charity competition, the North Staffordshire Infirmary Cup. Chris Young ended up with an even more sensational goal tally than he had the previous campaign – 40 in an identical number of league and cup appearances, although he managed only two successful strikes after the end of January!

Vale's relative success that season would have meant that an application to rejoin the Football League would have been well within order, but this time they were victims of the war. The league put their normal programme into abeyance 'in the hope that every eligible young man will find in the service of the nation a higher call than playing the game of football'. Thus Vale were thwarted once again in their quest to regain a place in the premier league and decided not to play in a competition in the 1915-1916 campaign as 'the war was pressing for the services of all our available lads'.

With their ground standing idle and a lack of income to maintain it, the Vale directors decided to copy the example of numerous other teams and get back into competitive action, in the 1916-1917 season. The club fortunately gained temporary election to the Football League, which was operating regional competitions, and joined the Lancashire Regional Section, to make up the numbers. This meant Vale could gain experience and extra revenue by playing against some of the top clubs in England and presented the opportunity to improve their claim for permanent membership after the war was over, especially if they impressed. Although a number of former Vale players were available, assembling a side proved difficult and the club placed much reliance on guest footballers.

Unfortunately, as expected, the team struggled at the higher standard and finished fifteenth out of sixteen clubs, but, amazingly, they did achieve their all-time record highest league score in annihilating Blackpool 11-1 at home on 18 November 1916! Also, victories were gained against Oldham Athletic, Blackburn Rovers, Bolton Wanderers and Manchester United, all of whom were members of the First Division of the Football League, which cannot have harmed Vale's prospects of a return to the fold. In addition, the season was a resounding success financially, as the club made a profit of £692 9s. 2½d., mainly because the players were only paid their expenses. The war was therefore proving to be a boom time for the Vale!

Despite several of their regular players being conscripted before the start of the 1917-1918 campaign, Vale performed much better at the second time of asking (except for a 7-0 trouncing at Everton) and finished a highly respectable eleventh. This time, the team beat five First Division clubs: Burnley (by 5-2), Oldham Athletic, Bolton Wanderers, Preston North End and Blackburn Rovers, which again would likely have improved their credentials.

By the beginning of the 1918-1919 season, forty of Vale's pre-war and wartime players had been conscripted, so getting a side out was more difficult than ever. Therefore, the team's final position of twelfth in the league was highly satisfactory and there were victories over Burnley, Manchester United, Bolton Wanderers, Oldham Athletic and Blackburn Rovers and a double against Preston North End to savour.

Because of the club's success, there was much excitement about the Football League's decision to add four new sides to an expanded competition when normality resumed, after the war, the following August. Vale seemed to be in a good position to get the call, being former members and one of only five non-Football League teams to have taken part in their wartime competitions. In anticipation of a new challenge, the club appointed as their secretary-manager Joe Schofield, Stoke's long-serving ex-player, secretary and director. However,

Vale were in for a great shock at the league's meeting on 10 March 1919 when they gained 27 votes, but failed by just one to force a second ballot in their bid to gain election to the Second Division. The successful clubs were Stoke, West Ham United, South Shields, Rotherham County and Coventry City, whilst Glossop failed to gain re-election and neither Rochdale nor Southport Vulcan, who had both finished higher than Vale in the final Lancashire regional league, gained admittance.

Therefore, the club continued to operate in the Central League, with a golden opportunity having been lost and no closer to their much-cherished Football League goal. It seemed most unlikely that anywhere near as good a chance to get back in the premier league would come along in the near future and Vale's apparently endless failure to achieve their target must have seemed to their more pessimistic supporters like a jinx.

Nevertheless, the club assembled an extremely strong team for the 1919-1920 season, in an attempt finally to win the Central League championship. Amongst their new signings were the experienced Rangers players Willie Aitken, a right-sided forward, and Peter Pursell, a left-sided, ex-Scotland international defender. Although they initially arrived without a transfer fee, Vale eventually had to pay Rangers a combined total of £500 for their services. The team started like a rocket, playing 'exhilarating' football and taking eleven points from their opening six league matches, to put themselves firmly at the top of the table.

Vale tasted defeat for the first time on 27 September when they lost 3-2 at Manchester United Reserves, but the following week there was a sensation because Leeds City were charged with making illegal payments to players during the Great War and consequently suspended from the Football League whilst an investigation took place. Because they refused to hand over the relevant books and papers, there was much discussion about their possible expulsion from the league and their replacement by a new club. As Vale had come so close to regaining admission to the league in March, they were clearly in pole position if such a scenario occurred.

Leeds City had been founded in 1904 and elected to the Football League the following year. Their whole league existence had been spent in the Second Division, where they had generally performed soundly, achieving a highest position of fourth in 1914, although they had finished in penultimate place in 1912. As the required documents were not in the event produced, they were indeed expelled from the league, on 13 October 1919, and forcibly wound-up by the Football Association, with five of their officials being banned for life from involvement in football activities! Four days later, their assets were sold off at an auction at the Metropole Hotel in Leeds and sixteen of their players were bought by nine other clubs for a total of £9,250. Although City had never been particularly well supported, being in a strong Rugby area, the size of the population in their catchment area clearly justified there being a Football League club and soon there was to be another. Leeds United were formed on the very same afternoon as the City auction took place, became managed by the ex-Vale left back, Dick Ray, and gained admission to the league the following year.

As expected, Vale's luck was finally in and they were elected to take Leeds City's place in the Second Division, beating off an audacious late bid from Tranmere Rovers. After the misfortune of their previous attempts to regain their league status, justice was finally done with Vale's return to the fold and their reserve team took over their Central League fixtures. Therefore, Port Vale had achieved an amazing comeback and risen like a rocket from the North Staffordshire Church League to the Football League in just twelve years!

Vale received numerous telegrams from other clubs congratulating them on their success and the team fortunately inherited Leeds City's playing record, which gave them ten points from eight games, through four victories and two draws. As they found it tough to adjust to the required standard, the points already in the bag acted as a useful buffer against failure.

It was common knowledge that football clubs had made illegal payments to players during the war and therefore Leeds City were extremely unlucky in experiencing such a dramatic fate, although in a sense they brought the outcome upon themselves. The issue arose through a dispute over wages between the club and Charlie Copeland, one of their full-backs, who was then given a free transfer. Copeland had threatened to report the club to the Football Association if he did not get his way and so that was exactly what he did. Clearly, had City reached an agreement with Copeland or the latter not acted in such a vindictive way, the issue would never have come to light. Once the matter was before the F.A., a considerably lesser punishment may well have resulted had the club simply handed over the documents. By refusing to do so, the City officials were obviously flouting the authority of the F.A., who were effectively left with no choice except to come down hard on the recalcitrant club and make an example of them. So Leeds effectively, and quite unnecessarily, handed their Football League place on a plate to Vale. It is obvious that the Hanley club struck extremely lucky with the unexpected turn of events, but it could be argued that the fates had been against them since they had been in the Central League and that the recent circumstances had balanced out their fortune.

If City had not been expelled from the Football League and had continued to produce results in the Second Division at the same level of consistency, they would have gained 52 or 53 points in total, which would have meant that they would have finished a highly creditable fourth, but twelve points adrift of promotion. As far as the city of Leeds was concerned, the expulsion of their Football League club made very little difference except in the very short term because within a year United, their new club, had gained election to the Second Division. They finished their first season, 1920-1921, in fourteenth place out of 22 teams, achieving roughly the kind of success that was not untypical of Leeds City. The following campaign, they moved up to ninth and in 1922-1923 to seventh. Then the next season they won the championship and promotion to the First Division. So it took them just four years to achieve what Leeds City had failed to do in eleven campaigns, although it could be argued that the latter were finally on the up when they were expelled. Perhaps United's achievement was because they were a more robust club or it could have been that success for the only league team in a city the size of Leeds was well overdue. How Leeds City would have performed over the years until the present day can only be the subject of speculation, but, as the size of a team's supporter base is a strong indicator of their likely degree of accomplishment, it may well have been that City overall would not have produced outcomes dissimilar to those of United.

Of course, had Leeds City managed to avoid expulsion from the Football

League, the future of Port Vale too would have been different. The Valiants, as they were starting to be nicknamed, would no doubt have pressed on with their attempt to win the Central League championship in the first post-war season. By the time they were elected into the Football League, they had lost a second match, by 2-1 at Blackburn Rovers Reserves on 11 October. It could be argued that the players' minds were not fully on the job by then, with a possible transfer to the Football League looming, but it was far from inevitable that Vale would be stepping up a grade. In any case, it was possible that another win would have strengthened the club's premier league claim, so the team certainly had something to play for.

By the time the Valiants replaced Leeds City in the Second Division, they had dropped to fourth in the Central League, but were only one point behind the leaders with a match in hand. They had accumulated eleven points from their opening eight games, which was an average of 1.375 points per match, a ratio that would normally give only an outside chance of winning a championship if repeated on average throughout the rest of a season. However, such success over a whole campaign would usually result in the runners-up spot being achieved. As it turned out, Blackpool Reserves won the Central League that season with 58 points and, had Vale's first team proceeded to pick up points at their 1.375 per game ratio, they would have gained 57.75 points in total. As only whole points are awarded, rounding off would therefore have given them 58 points and the Valiants would have won the championship by virtue of having a 0.407 superior goal average. Any way round, judging by their performances in their initial eight games, it seems that Vale would have had a relatively successful season in the Central League and that conclusion is substantiated by their achievement in gaining 30 points from the 34 matches they played in the Second Division, at a considerably higher standard.

Even by 1920, only seven of the 44 teams in the Football League were located south of Coventry and so an attempt was made to redress the balance by the creation a new Third Division for the 1920-1921 campaign, comprised mainly of teams from the Southern League. Had Leeds City not been expelled from the Football League the previous year and the Valiants therefore not gained admission to the Second Division, the latter might well have considered themselves to have been eligible candidates for the new combination. However, the only members of the Third Division north of Luton were Northampton Town, Norwich City and Grimsby Town, and the last named alone were located north of Hanley. Even then, Grimsby were only lumped in with the former Southern League clubs because they had been relegated from the Second Division. It is therefore doubtful that the Football League would have seen Vale as strong contenders for inclusion because the league was extended for a particular purpose, into which Vale did not fit. By absorbing the best teams of the Southern League, a strong rival competition was effectively eliminated and the addition of the new clubs added considerably to the strength and authority of the Football League.

However, having expanded their membership by a third in one fell swoop and relegated the Southern League to obscurity, the Football League decided to cream off the eighteen clubs with apparently the most potential from several strong leagues in the North and the Midlands to form a new Third Division

(North) for the following season. Amongst the successful applicants were Vale's old Central League rivals, Crewe Alexandra, Southport, Rochdale, Stalybridge Celtic and Lincoln City, and it is very difficult to imagine how the Valiants, having come within a whisker of re-election in March 1919, could have failed to have become founder members of the new division.

So, had Leeds City behaved more properly and not been expelled from the Football League, it is extremely likely that Vale would have regained their place in the competition by 1921 at the latest anyway. However, their election in 1919 had a big advantage because they began playing in the Second Division, whereas, if they had rejoined the league in 1920 or 1921, they would have had to compete in the Third Division (South) or Third Division (North). The problem with the latter outcome was that there was only one promotion place available in each of the new divisions per year and therefore nothing less than winning the championship of one or the other could have lifted the Valiants back to their former status in the second tier. Therefore, they would have been placed at quite a disadvantage.

No-one will ever know in this instance how Vale would have fared, but an examination of the performances of the promoted teams from the Third Divisions, in their first season in the higher flight, relative to those of the Valiants, might give an idea, albeit a very imprecise one. For example, Crystal Palace, the first champions of the Third Division in 1921, finished fourteenth in the second tier the following year, four places above Vale and three points better off.

The winners of the two regional Third Divisions in 1922 were Southampton and Stockport County. The next campaign, the former ended up eleventh in the Second Division, six positions higher and with five points more than Vale, but the latter finished three places lower and with a point less than the Valiants.

At the end of the 1923-1924 season, the two promoted clubs of the previous campaign, Bristol City and Nelson, were both relegated. The former finished bottom, six positions below the Valiants and with nine fewer points, whilst the latter ended up in penultimate place, five points adrift of the Hanley club.

Vale improved considerably in the 1924-1925 season and climbed from their previous year's sixteenth place to eighth. However, the two newly-promoted teams, Portsmouth and Wolverhampton Wanderers, did better still, ending up fourth and sixth, with six and four more points, respectively, than the Valiants.

The following year, Vale dropped two places to tenth and finished five positions below Swansea City, the 1924-1925 Third Division (South) champions, with five fewer points. However, the Valiants ended up five places above the Third Division (North) winners, Darlington, with six more points.

In the 1926-1927 campaign, Vale improved their position to eighth and finished well above the two previous season's promoted teams, Reading and Grimsby Town, who ended up six and nine places below them, with five and eleven points fewer, respectively.

The Valiants performed well the following year too and secured ninth place, three positions above the 1926-1927 campaign's Third Division (South) champions, Bristol City, and with five points more than them. However, Vale could not match the success of their arch-rivals, Stoke City, the previous season's Third Division (North) winners, who finished fifth, with eight points more than the Hanley club.

At the end of the 1928-1929 campaign, Vale ended up second to the bottom, with only 34 points, and were relegated. They were well adrift of the two promoted teams, Millwall and Bradford Park Avenue, who finished fourteenth and third, with five and fourteen more points, respectively.

In total, in the eight seasons in the 1920s in which promoted Third Division sides competed with Vale in the second tier, the Valiants finished above seven of them and below eight. The statistics show that the Hanley club performed somewhat better in relation to the Third Division (North) champions than they did against those from the south, ending up above four of the former and three of the latter and below three from the north and five from the south.

In conclusion, it may have been that Vale would not have spent very long in either of the new Third Divisions before they would have been promoted, but it appears that their chances of success would have been greater in the northern section than its southern counterpart, as the latter seems to have been the stronger competition. Having said that, it must be emphasised that an examination of the performances of teams the season after they have won championships is a somewhat inexact measure of how good they were when they were promoted.

A further point to consider in how Vale might have fared in the Third Divisions, had Leeds City not been expelled from the league in 1919, is how the Valiants actually fared in the northern section in the 1929-1930 season after they had finally been relegated. As it turned out, they won the championship at the first attempt, four points clear of the runners-up, Stockport County, and a massive seventeen points in front of Darlington, who were third. With 103 goals scored and only 37 conceded, Vale completely outclassed every team in the division except County. An indication of the degree of the Valiants' success is that the 67 points they gained were the largest number attained in the Third Division (North) until they were equalled by Barnsley in 1939 and then beaten by Doncaster Rovers (with 72) in 1947.

So a combination of guesstimation and study of a later real situation indicate that Vale would quickly, if not immediately, have been a force in the Third Division (North) had they become founder members in 1921. It is likely that they would also have done well in the southern counterpart a year earlier, even though they would probably have found it a tougher proposition. Fortunately, as events turned out, and most specifically because of the obstructive attitude of the Leeds City officials in 1919, the Valiants did not need to worry about the Third Division until 1929 and instead enjoyed one of the best periods of their history in the Second Division in the 1920s.

Thanks to Leeds City, Vale finally regained their place in the Second Division on 13 October 1919, to the great joy of their supporters. The team's first league match was at South Shields the following Saturday and they had just four days to prepare for it. Five of their regular players were ineligible to play in the Football League, whilst a gruelling nine-hour journey had to be made to the Northeast the day before the game. Predictably, under the circumstances, Vale lost, but rather unluckily and only by 2-0. Nine days later, their first league home game, against Tottenham Hotspur, the undefeated leaders and eventual champions, attracted a splendid crowd of 16,000, over three times as many as had attended Vale's final Central League match. Unfortunately, the outcome was another defeat, by 1-0.

The team were finding the step-up in standard hard to adjust to and they won only three of their first fifteen league games. However, they eventually settled down and improved in the second half of the season, much inspired by the shooting ability of their new centre-forward, Bob Blood. Vale finished a respectable thirteenth, out of 22 sides, and Blood hit 24 goals in only 28 appearances! Also, the campaign was a triumph with regard to the Valiants' home crowds and their league average of over 11,247 was easily a then club record.

In the 1920-1921 season, Vale were holding their own in middle of the table until February when Bob Blood was sold to West Bromwich Albion for £4,000, a then record fee for both clubs. After his departure, only two of the remaining sixteen league matches were won, with a mere six goals being scored as the Valiants tumbled to finish sixth from the bottom. However, the Blood transfer had solved the club's immediate financial problems and a profit of £1,187 3s. 11d. was made on the campaign, not least because the average league home attendance had risen still further to more than 14,143.

Unfortunately, Vale failed to solve their goalscoring problem and won only five league matches in the 1921-1922 season up to the end of January. By then, they were bottom of the table and the *Sentinel* was driven to ask the question, 'Is the position hopeless?' Just as relegation was looking almost inevitable, the team produced a remarkable reversal of form, for no apparent reason, so that 22 points were gained from the final seventeen games. The outcome was that they finished in eighteenth place, three points clear of the drop zone.

There was an even greater shortage of goals scored in the following campaign. The Valiants limped along to end up sixth from the bottom of the table, just two points above the relegation places, having found the net only 39 times.

In the summer of 1923 occurred an episode remarkably reminiscent of the Leeds City affair, although the outcome was very different. The matter started when Billy Barr, Vale's ex-trainer, informed the Football League that the club had made numerous illegal bonus payments to players in the 1921-1922 campaign. The following investigation found the Valiants to be guilty and they were fined £100. The chairman, Sampson Walker, was charged an equivalent amount; Joe Schofield, who was still the secretary-manager, had to pay £25; three other officials had to stump up £150 in total and seventeen players were fined £1 each. There was no other punishment and, in the context of Leeds City's fate, it might be considered that Vale got off lightly, although they appear to have co-operated with the league's inquiry, which may well have proved decisive in their lenient treatment. History could well have repeated itself otherwise and a chapter in this book might then have examined how the Valiants could possibly have avoided expulsion from the league and what their fate might have been thereafter!

The 1923-1924 season was a struggle until halfway through February because of the team's continuing lack of firepower and, sadly, the most notable event of the period was the death of the team's inside-left, Tom Butler, on 11 November 1923. Eight days earlier, Butler had been outstanding in Vale's 1-1 draw in the league at Clapton Orient and scored the equaliser, but had then suffered a compound fracture of his left arm near the end of the game. Unfortunately, he developed septic poisoning and died from lockjaw. It is tempting to think that, had Leeds City not been expelled from the Football League, the complex combinations of alternative events would have meant that Vale would not have played that particular fixture at Clapton that day, if at all that campaign, and therefore Butler would not have sustained his injury and thus would not have died. Such is chance!

On 9 February 1924, the Valiants lost 2-0 at home to Bristol City, the bottom side in the division, and stood only one place above the relegation zone. However, as the worst was feared, the team finally got into their stride and secured seventeen points from their final fifteen matches to finish sixteenth, five points clear of the drop zone. The significant improvement was largely the result of the switching of Billy Briscoe from left-half to inside-left and Wilf Kirkham from inside-right to centre-forward and the two players scored sixteen goals between them, to the end of the season, after they had been moved.

Kirkham and Briscoe were also well on cue during the 1924-1925 campaign, which heralded the start of a mini-golden age for Vale that lasted for four years. Kirkham, who was described by an Aston Villa fan as 'a dashing centre-forward with brains', hit 33 goals in 44 league and F.A. Cup appearances, whilst Briscoe managed 12 in his 24 games at inside-left. They were much responsible for the Valiants' fine finish in eighth position in the league and their F.A. Cup trouncings of Boston (by 6-1 at home) and Alfreton (by a club competition record 8-2 away) in the final qualifying rounds. The team's marvellous success was duly capped by the announcement that the club had made a then record £4,469 13s. 11d. profit on the season. A big advantage of that was that the directors decided to buy the Old Recreation Ground from Stoke-on-Trent Corporation, instead of continuing to rent it, and made the first payment, of £2,250.

A new offside rule, to the advantage of the attacking team, was brought in for the start of the 1925-1926 campaign, as a result of which Wilf Kirkham set his scoring target as two goals a game! He proved to be rather overoptimistic, but still struck 35 times in 40 appearances as Vale mounted a serious promotion challenge. On 2 April 1926, they were fourth and just four points adrift of Derby County in second place, but the Valiants won none of their final seven matches and ended up eighth again. Once more, the club made a profit on a highly satisfactory season, this time of £1,950 12s. 10d., although it was essentially due to the sale of Tom Cooper, their excellent right-back and a future England international, to Derby for £2,500.

Wilf Kirkham surpassed himself the following campaign and netted an all-time club record 38 league goals, as well as three in the F.A. Cup, in a total of 45 appearances. However, he was the only player to score with any degree of regularity until Harry Anstiss, a bustling inside-forward, was signed from Sheffield Wednesday in February 1927 and struck eleven times in fifteen matches to the end of the season. Their exploits were instrumental in Vale finishing eighth in the table yet again, but this time with 45 points, one more than the previous year.

Although the Valiants started the 1927-1928 league campaign with four defeats and a draw in their opening five games, they quickly reversed their fortunes by gaining 23 points from the following 15 matches to rise to sixth place on Christmas Eve, just three points off the promotion pace. By then, Wilf Kirkham had scored eleven times, but he managed only two more goals in the rest of the season and five consecutive defeats put Vale back down amongst the also-rans. Endless changes to the forward line failed to find a consistent goalscoring blend, but the Valiants still finished a highly creditable ninth, with only one point less than they had gained the previous year.

However, the Valiants' short-lived golden age was over and they were relegated the following season for the first time in their history, finishing in penultimate place with 34 points. Their defence proved to be the equal worst in the division, with 86 goals conceded, and only five points were gained away from home all year. The team were thrashed 7-1 at Preston North End and 6-0 at Barnsley, but, remarkably, they annihilated West Bromwich Albion 8-1 at home on 9 March 1929! Then, in front of a paltry home crowd of 3,307, the *Sentinel* noted that Vale made a 'spectacular descent to the Third Division' on 4 May by trouncing Bristol City 5-0 in their final game!

It was truly the end of an era and the Valiants' ten-year stay in the Second Division, which had begun courtesy of Leeds City, was over. However, as the Vale supporters pondered the future amidst rumours of the closure of the club because of pressing financial problems, there was further extremely bad news. Their talisman centre-forward, Wilf Kirkham, who had once more finished as the leading scorer, was transferred to their arch-rivals, Stoke City, albeit for £2,800, the second-highest fee that the club had ever received. Without him, though, a lengthy stay in the Third Division seemed likely.

7 Missing The Dribble Wizard

It is stating the obvious to say that Sir Stanley Matthews is widely renowned as one of the greatest legends that football has ever known. He made 697 Football League and 54 full England international appearances (despite losing seven years of his career to the Second World War). He twice became the Football Writers' Association Footballer of the Year and once the European Footballer of the Year. He received an F.A. Cup winner's and two runners-up medals. He twice gained a Second Division championship medal and one as a First Division runner-up. He became the oldest footballer ever to play for England and in the First Division. He was awarded a CBE in 1957, was knighted in 1965 and retired as a professional player at the age of fifty! But he had humble beginnings.

On 25 January 1915, Vale and Stoke clashed in a semi-final of the North Staffordshire Infirmary Cup, a new competition arranged to raise funds for the hospital. At the time, Vale were second in the Central League, just a point behind the leaders with two games in hand, whilst Stoke were ten points clear at the top of the Second Division of the Southern League. The match was played at Vale's Old Recreation Ground, in Hanley, in front of a crowd of only something over 3,000, with the Great War having taken its toll on attendances at football games. With local pride to play for, both clubs selected strong line-ups, but the home team overwhelmed Stoke and secured a splendid 3-0 victory, thereby becoming the first side that season to put three past them.

Exactly one week later, on 1 February, a third son, named Stanley, was born to Jack Matthews, the "Fighting Barber", who was a highly successful featherweight boxer. The Matthews family lived at 89 Seymour Street, a terraced house in Hanley, just over half a mile away from the Port Vale stadium, but approaching two miles from Stoke's Victoria Ground. The young Stanley was fast and agile and took to a football like a duck to water, spending endless hours practising dribbling. His father wanted Stanley to follow in his footsteps and become a pugilist, but his son was obsessed with football and determined to follow his path in the working man's ballet. He later said, 'I had only one thing on my mind – to become a footballer.'

Although he was initially a centre-half, Matthews was guided to outside-right at his school in nearby Wellington Road and this positional change proved the making of him. As well as playing, Matthews was also a football fan and naturally supported his home town club, Port Vale, like many people in Hanley did. Although the origins of the Valiants had been in the valley of ports to the west of Burslem, the club's move to the largest and most bustling of the six towns of Stoke-on-Trent in 1913 had opened up a whole new area of support for them and squeezed that of Stoke to the south.

At first, Matthews used to get to Vale's ground about half an hour before the end of their games and wait for the gates to be opened so that early leavers could depart. He would then sneak in and watch the end of the matches!

As well as the proximity of his home to the Old Recreation Ground, there was also a very specific reason why Matthews became a fan of the Valiants, as he later recalled: 'Most of the players used to come to have a shave and haircut at my dad's barber's shop at 7 Market Street [which was later renamed Huntbach

Street], so, of course, I supported Vale and I worshipped Bob Connelly, their centre-half.'

At the beginning of the 1920s, when Matthews was old enough to take notice of what was going on around him, both Vale and Stoke were in the Second Division of the Football League. In 1920, the latter finished tenth, just two points and three places above Vale, who had taken over the expelled Leeds City's fixtures. The following season, both teams struggled, with Stoke ending up third from the bottom and avoiding relegation only on goal average, whilst the Hanley side were three positions, but just a single point, better off. In a remarkable reversal of fortune, Stoke finished the 1921-1922 campaign as the runners-up and were thereby promoted to the mighty First Division. However, Vale only secured the same number of points as they had the previous season, dropped one place and kept clear of the relegation zone by just three points.

Unfortunately for Stoke, they were unable to meet the standard required in the First Division and finished their initial campaign there in penultimate position, above the bottom team, Oldham Athletic, only on goal average. As usual, Vale had a difficult time the same year, but rose a place in the table, although they ended up a point closer to relegation. By then, Matthews was eight and both he and his father were aware of the main events surrounding the two main Potteries clubs and their respective degrees of success.

Stoke finished the 1923-1924 season as the top team in Stoke-on-Trent for the third year running by ending up sixth in the Second Division, whilst Vale were down their normal end of the table, although they climbed up a position, with a more comfortable safety margin of five points from the drop zone. The following year, Vale were back in the ascendancy, beginning one of the most successful periods in their history, and finished a creditable eighth. Stoke, however, had a real struggle and ended up third from the bottom, a single point above the relegation zone. Their respective performances in the 1925-1926 campaign differed little in specific achievement from the previous year as Vale secured the same position, with just two points more, and Stoke (who had added the suffix of "City" to their name) dropped one place and gained three fewer points than they had the season before. However, that was sufficient to relegate them in penultimate place to the Third Division. By that time, Matthews was eleven and his favourite team had become the pride of the Potteries.

As football was an extremely popular sport and had long been the national game of England, the country was full of young boys longing to become professional footballers when they grew up, especially those from the working class, who hoped to escape from the future drudgery of manual labour. Matthews was just one of them, but living in an even more uninspiring city than most. It was obvious even by then that he was a rare young footballing talent, but there was still a long way to go before he could compete with experienced players in the grown man's game. Therefore, although Matthews was aware that there were two professional clubs in his home city, whose fortunes were varying in comparison with one another, he was realistically nowhere near ready to decide which of them would have the pleasure of his services should he continue his successful development. That turned out to be fortunate for Stoke at the end of the 1925-1926 season as they ignominiously plunged into the depths of the Third Division for the first time in their history.

The following year, as Matthews was continuing to mature, City came back with a vengeance as they comfortably won the Third Division (North) championship, with 63 points from 42 games. However, Vale too did very well and again held eighth place in the Second Division. Stoke resumed their position as the top dogs in the Potteries in the 1927-1928 season, finishing an excellent fifth in the second tier, just five points adrift of the second promotion place. Their Hanley rivals maintained their remarkable consistency, dropping just a single position to ninth and with only one point less than they had gained the previous campaign.

By 1929, Matthews was becoming a junior football force and made his debut as an England schoolboy international, at the age of fourteen, in a 4-1 win against Wales at Dean Court, Bournemouth. It was becoming clear that he was an exceptionally gifted player and extremely likely to have a very successful professional career. Unfortunately, just at the time that Vale needed to prove a real role model to their talented young fan, if they wanted to try to secure his signature in due course, they managed to get themselves relegated, in penultimate place, from the Second Division at the end of the 1928-1929 season! Stoke, however, their main rivals for Matthews' services, finished the campaign in the upper reaches of the table once more, this time securing sixth position, and were not a million miles away from membership of the coveted First Division.

Determined to regain their status at the first attempt, the Vale directors made five major new signings before the beginning of the 1929-1930 campaign. Thus bolstered, the team started off like an express, winning their opening five league matches and in the process scoring fifteen goals and conceding just two. By 21 December, they had accumulated 33 points from their 19 games played and were eight points in front at the top of the table. On 1 February 1930, they were in the middle of a six-match winning run and hammered Carlisle United 4-0 at home to lead the division by five points. By then, Sam Jennings, their tall new centre-forward, had scored 15 goals in 16 games, whilst Albert Pynegar, their inside-right, had hit the net 14 times in 19 matches. The vast majority of the 9,279 spectators who saw Vale's convincing win against Carlisle were, of course, cock-a-hoop. What all, except for possibly very few, of them did not know was that that very day, on his fifteenth birthday, Stanley Matthews had joined Stoke City's staff as an office boy for a pound a week wages. Nor is it likely that, if they had known, they would have cared, but, as it turned out, it was a monumental event in the history of Port Vale as well as Stoke City.

Matthews had gained quite a reputation by then as a devastating junior right-winger, with a tremendous burst of speed, who could dribble, shoot and cross the ball, and apparently Aston Villa, Birmingham, West Bromwich Albion and Wolverhampton Wanderers were also all very interested in securing his services. However, Stoke's manager, Tom Mather, had his wits about him and got his man (or youth, more accurately), although at the time the Potters' boss cannot possibly have realised what an exceptionally fine decision he had made. Neither can the other clubs, including Port Vale, have possibly understood what a wonderful opportunity they had let slip through their fingers. Only with hindsight is it possible to reflect on the full implications of Stoke's signing of the now legendary Sir Stanley Matthews from right under the noses of their Hanley neighbours.

Although Vale were in pole position to land the impending star from their own town, who was one of their supporters, they contrived to lose out to their greatest rivals. It was not that they did not try to sign him because, as Matthews later said, 'Certainly Port Vale asked my father for an option on my services.' So why did they not succeed?

Stoke, of course, had the better pedigree. They had been formed between eleven and sixteen years earlier than Vale and had become founder members of the Football League. They had spent eighteen seasons in the First Division, whilst the Hanley club had managed none at all in the top flight. Also, the Potters had reached the semi-finals of the F.A. Cup in 1899, whereas the Valiants had never progressed beyond the fifth round. In addition, Stoke had produced seventeen international players, while Vale had groomed just three. Finally, the Potters almost invariably attracted higher attendances than their Hanley counterparts and bigger crowds meant larger payments and/or incentives for players, irrespective of the existence of the official maximum wage for footballers. It is likely that most, if not all, these facts went through the mind of Jack Matthews, who was persuaded by the persistent Tom Mather to let Stoke take his son.

Nevertheless, since the Great War, there had not been a lot to choose between the success of the two local sides. In ten full seasons between the end of the war and Matthews signing for the Potters, Stoke had finished higher in the league on six occasions and Vale on four. Also, in 1929-1930, while the Valiants were flying high and on their way to winning the Third Division (North) championship, the Potters were having a mediocre season in the Second Division and eventually finished with two more defeats than victories. In addition, neither team had done a great deal in the F.A. Cup in the 1920s, except for Stoke in the 1927-1928 season when they reached the quarter-finals, with Vale having been eliminated the round before. Therefore, on recent history, it was far from a formality that City would necessarily be able to lure the young Matthews away from signing for his boyhood favourites.

Although on balance, Stoke were the more attractive of the two local clubs for Matthews to have joined, they were not really decisively so, especially when counterbalanced by the emotional pull on his heart by his home town team. Therefore, was it possible that Vale could have beaten their rivals to the draw and secured Matthews' signature if they had made a strenuous effort to do so?

It would appear so because Matthews later said: 'I was always a Vale supporter, even when I signed on for Stoke as an apprentice at fifteen. I still supported Vale and it was only when I played my first reserve game for Stoke that I didn't support Vale any more. It was a thrill for me when I joined Stoke to get a little booklet which gave me admission to any ground in England. So, when I was fifteen, if I had a free Saturday, I used to go up to Vale with my ticket and watch them play. That was a great thrill.'

As Matthews remained a Vale fan after he had joined Stoke and even at that stage enjoyed little more than watching the Valiants perform, it is obvious that he would have been over the moon to have signed for them. The implication clearly is that Vale did not make sufficient effort to get him on board. They made an approach to his father, but then appear to have given up.

However, the reality was that the decision on which club to join was not Matthews' alone to take and perhaps was not in his hands at all. He later proved that when saying, 'My father was instrumental in me signing for Stoke because in those days if your father told you to jump in the river, you had to do it or you'd get a clip around the ear!' So Jack Matthews had to be courted and that is exactly what Stoke's Tom Mather did. However, as Jack knew the pleasure of the faces and heads of most of the Vale players and Stanley was a big fan of the club, the Valiants ought to have got Matthews on their books. His signature would clearly not have been in the bag had they matched Mather's determination, but it was probably Vale's to lose.

Undoubtedly, the Valiants' main focus in the 1929-1930 campaign was on regaining their Second Division status and they were unable to relax their efforts throughout the season because they were run close by Stockport County in their successful championship bid. Also, Vale's eyes must have been further distracted from Matthews by the death of their team manager, Joe Schofield, on 29 September 1929. Schofield was highly respected and the *Sentinel's* assessment of him was that he had 'discovered many promising players and then brought them on'. Unfortunately, his replacement, Tom Morgan, the reserve team manager, never gained the same reputation for spotting and grooming young footballers, even though he steered the Valiants to the Third Division (North) championship in 1930 and their highest ever league finish (fifth in the Second Division) the following campaign.

Therefore, it is at least possible that had Joe Schofield lived for four more months, or a bit longer, he would have been successful in signing Matthews. But fate took Schofield at just 58 and Matthews signed for Stoke. The world of football is full of missed opportunities and, in due course, the Valiants were left to rue their failure to get their ultimately most famous fan on board. However, the scale of the loss took some time to become apparent.

Stoke finished a respectable eleventh in the Second Division in the 1930-1931 season and were not assisted in doing so at all by Matthews, who played for their reserves. Because Vale ended up only seven points adrift of the runners-up, West Bromwich Albion, in their finest ever league performance, it is doubtful whether Matthews would have appeared in their first team either that campaign.

The young winger continued his presence in Stoke's second string the following season and signed for them as a full-time professional on his seventeenth birthday, thereby ensuring that he had eluded the attention of the Valiants. He finally made his first-team debut for the Potters in a 1-0 victory at Bury on 19 March 1932, but appeared just once more that campaign, in a 2-0 home win against Barnsley a week later, and therefore made a minor contribution to Stoke's success in finishing in third place, three points clear of Plymouth Argyle, Bury and Bradford Park Avenue. Nevertheless, the Potters were clearly well on the up before young Matthews got to exhibit his talents with them.

That same campaign, Vale had a remarkable escape from the drop. They looked doomed in penultimate position with two games to play, being three points and goal average adrift of safety. However, they won both their remaining matches, the final one by 2-0 at already-promoted Leeds United, on 7 May 1932, to finish with a 0.05 better goal average than Barnsley, who were relegated. Obviously, had the Valiants signed Matthews and played him in the first team, it would have made no difference to which division they would have been competing in the following season, unless, of course, he had put in worse performances than Dickie York, James Henshall, Tom Tippett and Roger Jones, who shared the outside-right position that season.

Stoke continued their progress in the 1932-1933 campaign and finished as the Second Division champions a point ahead of the runners-up, Tottenham Hotspur, and six points clear of the third-placed side, Fulham. Matthews made fifteen league appearances for the Potters and scored one goal, ironically in a 3-1 victory at Vale on 4 March 1933. His involvement was sufficient to gain him a championship medal, but, having appeared in less than half of Stoke's games, it cannot reasonably be argued that they were promoted because they had him in their team. On the contrary, City performed better when he was not playing, gaining 37 points from 27 matches, compared with 19 from the 15 games in which he was present!

Unfortunately, the Valiants struggled in the shadow of their local rivals and finished the season sixth from the bottom, albeit safe from relegation by four points and goal average. Consequently, had Matthews been a Vale player then, his blossoming skills would have been immaterial as to their destination for the next campaign.

Stoke settled into the First Division comfortably enough and ended up twelfth in the 1933-1934 campaign, with 41 points from 42 games. Newcastle United, who were relegated in penultimate place, gained seven fewer points than the Potters and normally the inclusion or absence of a single player would not make a difference of nine positions to a side in a 22-team league, unless the individual was Diego Maradona or Pelé – or, perhaps, Stanley Matthews. That season, the "Wizard of the Dribble" really came into his own, scoring eleven goals in 29 First Division matches and four in the same number of F.A. Cup games as Stoke reached the quarter-finals. Even excluding the endless crosses he put into the opponents' goalmouth, his contribution was clearly outstanding because his scoring rate was exemplary for a right-winger. Therefore, it is not impossible that, without him in the side, seven league points could have been lost and the Potters' campaign instead have turned into a battle against relegation, although the team performed almost as well when he wasn't present, securing twelve points from thirteen matches.

Vale had no such problems that year and finished eighth in the Second Division, seven points behind the runners-up, Preston North End. Whether having Matthews in the side would have enabled the deficit to have been made up can only be the subject of speculation, but it is reasonable to assume that he would have performed better in the lower standard of the second tier than he did in the first. In that case, it is not beyond the realms of possibility that the flying outside-right would have scored a goal every other game on average and put the ball on the head of the Valiants' centre-forward, Tom Nolan, more frequently still. As Nolan notched 22 goals in 32 league appearances as it was, his tally in that eventuality might have been quite marvellous. The only problem could have been that Nolan's forte was power shooting and that would not have made him a natural partner for Matthews, who liked to get the ball into the penalty box.

The "Magician" made his debut for England in a 4-0 hammering of Wales at Ninian Park, Cardiff, on 29 September 1934, so Stoke had a new international on their books. The Potters finished the 1934-1935 campaign tenth in the First Division, with the same number of points as matches. They were sixteen points adrift of the champions, Arsenal, and nine clear of Leicester City, who ended up in penultimate position. Although Matthews continued to develop his game as a goal provider and scored ten league goals, his ratio of successful strikes to appearances declined to 1 in 3.6. That was a fine achievement nevertheless, but City would have had to have performed particularly badly without him in order to have been relegated.

By that time, Vale were in decline and ended up fifth from the bottom of the Second Division, although they finished eight points above the relegation zone. Therefore, it does not appear possible that the inclusion of Matthews in their team would have made any difference as to outcome of their league status.

In the 1935-1936 season, Stoke performed extremely well and finished fourth in the first tier, their highest ever position. However, they were nine points adrift of the champions, Sunderland, and had a vastly inferior goal average. Nevertheless, Matthews again bagged ten league goals and struck up a developing partnership with the Potters' exciting young centre-forward, Freddie Steele, who later twice became Vale's manager.

The campaign was a calamity for the Valiants, who were relegated from the Second Division in penultimate position and it was eighteen years before they regained their status. Had they earlier snapped up the teenage Stanley Matthews, as they might have done, it would seem to have been well within his power to have prevented them from dropping down a level. The team ended up just a single point behind third from the bottom Barnsley, although with a vastly inferior goal average. Therefore, it would have required Matthews to have been able to make a two-point difference to Vale's finishing total to have made a crucial difference at a time when he was well capable of turning a game on its head in a flash. That season in the league, the Valiants tried no fewer than eight players at outside-right, in what was a problem position for most of the time: Frank Ryder, Cliff Birks, George Stabb, Luke Dean, Roy Burns, George Shenton, Arthur Caldwell and Henry Pinkerton. Had that motley crew been replaced by Matthews the maestro, it is hard to believe that Vale would not have been saved from relegation.

In addition, had the Magician then been with his boyhood favourites, he would very probably have played in one of the Valiants' most famous F.A. Cup victories, on 13 January 1936, when the First Division leaders, Sunderland, were despatched by 2-0 in a third round replay in Hanley. Vale's actual right-winger that historic day was Clifford Johnson, whose only previous appearance for the club in that position was in the first match, two days earlier, on Wearside! It is, of course, exceedingly unlikely that Matthews would have performed so much worse than his inexperienced counterpart that it would have made a difference of three goals to have enabled Sunderland to have triumphed.

Stoke slipped back into midtable in the First Division in the 1936-1937 season, finishing tenth, with 42 points from the same number of matches. They were fifteen points adrift of the champions, Manchester City, but ten points above the relegation zone. Matthews played forty times, but only scored seven goals, although he was vital as a provider for Freddie Steele, who netted 33 times in 35 league appearances! Without the Magician, it is difficult to believe that Steele would have been anywhere as near as successful, but the probability is that the Potters would have preserved their First Division status anyway.

Vale performed reasonably in their first season in the Third Division (North), finishing eleventh, with 44 points from 42 matches. However, they were sixteen points adrift of the champions, Stockport County, and therefore with no realistic chance of promotion, even had they had the Wizard of the Dribble in their side. However, the team fought their way to the semi-finals of the division's Northern Section Cup before losing 3-0 at Chester on 10 April 1937. The *Sentinel* noted the failure of Vale's forwards in the game and not least of all that of the reserve right-winger, Jack Harrison, who was making only his second appearance in the first team. Had Matthews played in his stead, it would still have been extremely difficult for the Valiants to have changed a three-goal deficit into a victory, but the maestro did almost that when, aged 38, he inspired Blackpool to an amazing 4-3 win against Bolton Wanderers in the 1953 F.A. Cup final after they had trailed 3-1 with only 22 minutes remaining! If Matthews had produced his wizardry for Vale in the much lower quality Northern Section Cup game, they might well have won the competition, although the Earth would probably not have shifted off its axis at the scale of the achievement!

Stoke found the 1937-1938 season a struggle, even with Matthews on their books, and finished sixth from the bottom of the First Division, just two points clear of Manchester City in penultimate place and with an inferior goal average to them. As the Magician played in 38 of the Potters' 42 league matches and scored six goals, had they had a lesser outside-right, Stoke would very likely have been relegated.

In their respective division, the Valiants performed just as poorly as their Potteries rivals that campaign, ending up with the same number of points as them, but had six points in hand on Barrow in penultimate position. Therefore, had they had their most famous fan on the right wing, their Football League status would undoubtedly have been the same the following year.

Stoke made a significant improvement in the 1938-1939 season, the last one before the Second World War, and ended up seventh in the First Division, with 46 points, 13 adrift of the champions, Everton. Matthews played in 36 of the Potters' 42 league games and consequently they could not have won the title, even had he managed to be ever present and put on his greatest all-time performances. That year, he scored just twice and his transformation from a darting right wing marksman to a great goal provider was complete and he never again managed to notch more than four league goals in any single campaign.

For that final inter-war campaign, Vale were transferred to the Third Division (South) for geographical reasons and found the competition harder. They finished fifth from the bottom and avoided a re-election plea with just three points to spare because of their inferior goal average to Walsall in penultimate place. However, as they survived in the Football League and were 18 points behind the champions, Newport County, it is inconceivable that, had they had Matthews in the team, it would have made any difference to their destination for the following season, when it eventually arrived.

With the outbreak of the Second World War in September 1939, the Football League programme proper was abandoned in favour of area competitions and so the situation remained for the duration of the conflict. When normality was resumed in 1946, Stoke had got a fine side at their disposal and missed winning the First Division championship by a whisker at the end of the season. By then, the Wizard of the Dribble had fallen out with the City manager, Bob McGrory, and ceased to be an automatic choice in the team, so he asked for a transfer to Blackpool, where he lived! With just three games remaining and the title in the balance, amazingly the club accepted his request and pocketed £11,500 from the deal on 10 May 1947. Uproar amongst the supporters resulted, but the Potters remained in real contention to win the championship. The outcome came down to the final match, at Sheffield United on 14 June, which Stoke needed to win to take the title, but they lost 2-1 and finished fourth.

Obviously, it is one of the great Potteries football might-have-beens to consider whether the league would have been won for the only time in City's history had the Magician been in their team that day. The Potters' great centre-half, Neil Franklin, a regular in their side that season, had no doubts: 'Stan was the best player I ever played with. If he had not been sold, I am sure Stoke would have won the First Division championship.' However, of course, that would have depended on him having been selected by McGrory, the manager responsible for Matthews' departure from Stoke.

Had the maestro been with Vale that campaign, it seems very likely that he would have had a much quieter time. The team improved their league form and finished tenth in the Third Division (South), but 23 points behind the champions, Cardiff City, who were duly promoted. It is, of course, unimaginable that Matthews exhibiting his finest form in all 42 league matches would have succeeded in overturning such a huge deficit and so the Valiants would almost certainly have continued to play in the third tier for yet another year, just as they did in the real world.

The various speculated alternative eventualities for Vale with Matthews on board have all consisted of possibilities purely resulting from his own individual contributions. However, the longer the Valiants had had him in their team, the greater the likelihood that other footballers of high quality would have been attracted to play alongside him and been interested in joining the club. Quality attracts quality and it may have been that, so supplemented, Vale would have become a force in the Second Division and possibly gained promotion to the first tier for the (so far) only time in their history. Having said that, it is arguable whether the Valiants could have afforded to pay big-name players even the limited maximum wage on offer at the time, although it is tantamount to certain that the club's attendances would have blossomed with prize assets on show. So it may have been that careful speculation would have paid dividends and a new era in Vale's history would have consequently opened up.

The Port Vale possibilities outlined over the various seasons would have depended on Matthews remaining their player for as long as he did Stoke's and that is unlikely. To start with, the Magician almost left the Potters in February 1938 when he requested a transfer, but, on that occasion, City had the sound sense to turn it down. At that time, football clubs virtually owned footballers and there was nothing that Matthews could do about Stoke's response to him.

For most of their history, Vale have been more strapped for cash than their Potteries rivals and the 1930s was no exception. By 1933, Matthews was becoming a hot property as an established member of Stoke's First Division team and clearly, had he signed for his home town club instead, he would have been likewise for them too, especially as they were playing in the division below City. The 1933-1934 season was a financial disaster for the Valiants, with a loss of

£2,771 being announced, which was blamed on a lack of support. Consequently, to cut costs, fifteen players were released. They included Billy Tabram, the regular centre-half, who was sold to Hull City for a large fee, whilst Brentford paid £1,550 for left-back George Poyser and Vale also received payment for the versatile Fred Mills from Leeds United. In such circumstances, it is very difficult to see that the Valiants would have rejected any reasonable offer for the highly desirable nineteen-year-old Stanley Matthews had he then been one of their players. It is, of course, not unlikely that Stoke would have been eager to have coughed up the money to sign the exceptionally promising outside-right. Then perhaps thereafter history would have repeated itself, except that Vale might well have been several thousand pounds better off and the Potters the same amount poorer!

In December 1934, with further financial problems mounting, the Valiants sold their right-winger and leading scorer, Jack Friar, to Preston North End. Had the Wizard of the Dribble still been on Vale's books, it is very doubtful whether they would have signed Friar the previous July and it is likely that Matthews would have been sold instead, perhaps to Preston, if they could have afforded him.

Despite the transfer of Friar, Vale remained in such financial difficulties that they sold their centre-forward, Tom Nolan, to Bradford Park Avenue in July 1935. Nolan had scored 16 goals in 39 league appearances the previous season and was the only player they had who was capable of finding the net with any degree of regularity. As they had finished fifth from the bottom of the Second Division with him in the team, they were taking a big risk with their status in the following campaign. However, such were their money problems that the directors sanctioned Nolan's sale and Vale were duly relegated. Had Matthews still been with the club and an offer come in for him instead, there can be little doubt that he would have been sold.

Inevitably, the home attendances declined considerably during the relegation campaign, which led to a financial crisis. An extraordinary shareholders' meeting was held at the Grand Hotel, in Hanley, on 27 March 1936, where it was revealed that the club's average weekly income was just £181! The directors announced that £2,000 was needed to prevent the club from folding. Had the Magician still been in their ranks, it is obvious that the Valiants would have tried to sell him because the survival of the club was at stake. As it turned out, sufficient funds were raised through a public appeal and a benefit match with Stoke for Vale to continue.

As most of Vale's supporters know today, their financial problems have not gone away and there were plenty of further occasions when a bid for Matthews would almost inevitably have been accepted. Therefore, it is exceedingly likely that the Wizard of the Dribble would have been sold by the Valiants sooner rather than later.

It is possible that the importance of Matthews to the teams he played in has been exaggerated because in his 33-year professional career, he only won a single F.A Cup winner's medal and two Second Division championship ones. In addition, not every footballer who played with Matthews was desperate to do so and some thought that, as the Wizard of the Dribble, he was a liability at times, rather than an asset. One such player was the England inside-forward, Raich Carter, who said: 'He was so much of the star individualist that he was really not a good footballer. When he got the ball on the wing, you didn't know when it was coming back. He was an extraordinarily difficult winger to play alongside.'

Another England star frustrated with Matthews was the centre-forward, Tommy Lawton, who said, 'We all had our moments when were exasperated with Stan because he'd take the ball off down the wing as if he was playing on his own.' Despite Lawton's criticisms, there cannot have been many footballers who would have been reluctant to have nonchalantly let slip in a pub the comment, 'Stan Matthews? Oh, I played with him!'

One of the innumerable fans of the Wizard of the Dribble was John Charles, the legendary Welsh centre-forward and centre-half. Of Matthews, he said, 'He was the best crosser I've ever seen – and he had to contend with the old heavy ball.'

More accolades have been given by Johnny Giles, the ex-Republic of Ireland midfielder and manager, who only saw Matthews first hand towards the end of the latter's career. Nevertheless, Giles said, 'He had everything – good close control, great dribbling ability and he was lightning quick.'

As well as assessing Matthews' impact on football clubs he played for and might have done, a further question that can be examined is what the effect would have been on his career had he initially signed for Vale instead of Stoke. The Valiants won the Third Division (North) championship at the end of the season in which he joined Stoke as an apprentice and finished six places higher in the Second Division than the Potters the following campaign, so it may at first have appeared that he (or his father) had made the wrong choice of club. However, City ended up third in the season that he made his first-team debut for them and then they won the championship the following year after he had played in a substantial number of their games. So Matthews clearly joined a club already on the up and his timing was therefore (almost certainly accidentally) immaculate. In the five Second Division campaigns from 1931-1932, Vale finished in the top half just once and were eventually relegated. It then took them eighteen years to regain their status. Therefore Matthews (or his father) most likely made a good decision in avoiding the Hanley club.

Having said that, it is almost inconceivable that the Magician would have remained with the Valiants as long as he did with Stoke unless the team had gone on to have significant success, not least at or near the top of the Second Division, one would have thought. Indeed, as has already been suggested, it is extremely likely that he would have been sold to a bigger, and most probably a First Division, club before long, in which case his career would almost certainly have taken off similarly to how it actually did. The main difference might have been that he would have served a slightly longer apprenticeship outside the top flight.

After all has been considered, there has only ever been one legendary Sir Stanley Matthews during the whole time that there have existed innumerable incidental football clubs, such as Port Vale and even Stoke City for that matter, although the Valiants might really have appeared on the map for a short while had the Wizard of the Dribble initially signed for them instead of their Potteries rivals.

8 Homeless In Hanley

Having only saved themselves from a re-election plea in the Third Division (South) in their penultimate match of the 1938-1939 season, ominously Vale decided to rely on youth seeing them through the following campaign. The reason for that essentially was that the club had made a £1,723 0s. 1d. loss, despite having achieved a £659 increase in gate receipts from the previous year. Indeed, financial catastrophe had only been avoided through a £1,455 surplus in the transfer market. Therefore, the club's expenditure needed to be cut back. The bleak picture was presented at the annual meeting on 19 June, but not a single question was asked by any of the shareholders present, so that the whole proceedings were over in five minutes!

The new season began much as might have been anticipated, with Vale bottom of the division after the opening two games, having gained just one point and scored no goals. However, the day after (3 September), Britain declared war on Germany, thus starting the Second World War, and the Football League programme was abandoned. For a while, there was chaos as the government initially banned all sports gatherings, but then a week later decided to permit the playing of organised football in 'neutral and reception areas', which included the Potteries. While the Football League decided how to proceed, the Valiants arranged a series of friendly matches, which were played in front of small crowds.

Eventually, the League decided to hold area competitions and Vale were put in the Western Regional Tournament, with eleven other sides. The opening game was on 21 October and the Valiants exhibited fine form to trounce Crewe Alexandra 6-1 at home, but only in front of 2,100 spectators, which turned out to be one of their largest attendances of the season!

The make-up of the team soon bore little resemblance to that which had begun the campaign, as different players were conscripted, forced to work on Saturday afternoons and left the area in search of employment, whilst others returned to the district. The side generally performed fairly well, apart from 8-1, 8-3 and 7-0 annihilations by Manchester United, Liverpool and Manchester City respectively. However, the crowds did not pick up and only 1,000 spectators turned out at Everton (their lowest ever first-team attendance) on 9 December to watch the home team beat Vale 3-1.

The club were already struggling to make ends meet, especially as they were paying their players the permitted thirty shillings per match, but the Football League had arranged a dearth of fixtures for December. The Valiants consequently organised four friendly games to fill the gap, but managed to lose money on them and then inclement weather brought a series of postponements in January and February 1940.

Under pressure from its clubs, the League set up a cup competition, to try to stimulate interest from the public and provide a lifeline in the struggle for financial solvency. Unfortunately, Vale managed to get themselves knocked out of this Football League (War) Cup in the preliminary round in a replay at Walsall on 15 April in front of just 883 spectators. The team did well to finish the season in eighth place in the league, with 22 points from the same number of matches, but the campaign proved a financial disaster, with a £2,261 loss being recorded.

The directors then decided that the cost of continuing to operate a professional side the following campaign was prohibitive and instead resolved to run just an amateur junior side, Port Vale "A", in the North Staffordshire League, so as to keep the club ticking along. As it turned out, the juniors did very well and won the locally-prestigious Sentinel Cup and shared the North Staffordshire League Cup. Even better, the team operated at a profit, but bank overdraft charges and depreciation of Vale's assets (mainly the ground) meant that the season recorded a total loss of £794 14s. 1d.

The Valiants continued with the same setup in the 1941-1942 campaign and the "A" team again proved to be a credit to the club, retaining the Sentinel Cup and winning the North Staffordshire League championship. The following season, they surpassed themselves, again topping the league and being victorious in the Haywood Hospital Cup and the Fenton Nursing Cup, as well as finishing as the runners-up in the locally-acclaimed Staffordshire Junior Cup. Again the team generated useful funds, but the campaign ran at an overall loss of £972 9s. 4d. because of further depreciation of the assets and overdraft charges, and the forced payment of income tax and war damage contributions. Vale's financial position was thus extremely precarious.

Unfortunately, as fate had it, the Valiants were then struck by a hammer blow as their president, Major William M. Huntbach, had died on 8 May 1942 and his £3,000 of debentures with the club had been called in. Not surprisingly, with a lack of income to compensate for the loss, a financial crisis resulted, which, by a year later, had left Vale 'in a very grave position', as the *Sentinel* put it. In a desperate attempt to solve the problem, the remaining directors then implored the Football Association to give them financial help. When their pleas failed, they made a public appeal for £3,000 to plug the gap, but sadly it fell on deaf ears, no doubt not least of all because of the uncertainty of the war situation.

The club was on the brink of collapse and the directors felt that they had no option except to try to negotiate the sale of their Old Recreation Ground to Stoke-on-Trent Corporation, the previous owners, who held the first option on it. Fortunately for Vale, the council were willing to undertake the deal and, in June 1943, a price of £13,500 was agreed, which was £4,000 beneath its value in the balance sheet of the annual accounts. The club then applied to the council to rent the stadium from them, but the corporation refused the request, not least because they had plans to use it as a sports ground themselves.

Consequently, there was uproar at Vale's annual meeting on 26 July, despite there being only five shareholders present. There was criticism of the directors for not arranging a special meeting before deciding to sell the stadium and it was also argued that the sale should not have proceeded without the agreement of the council that the team could continue to play there. The chairman, Tom Flint, responded by stating that, 'The directors have been pushed into this position and are in no way responsible.' He went on to say that the ground had become a major liability, with considerable damage having been done to it by children, and that it would be too costly to undertake the necessary repairs. Flint concluded with the ominous comment that the directors were determined to keep the club in existence, if it was possible to do so! Despite his assurances, Vale had reached the desperate position of having become a football club without a ground and any professional players.

More in hope than judgement, Vale began the 1943-1944 season with the amateur "A" team playing as usual because the ground was not scheduled to pass into the ownership of the corporation till 31 October. At the beginning of that month, the council decided to allow the Valiants to use the stadium until the end of April 1944, which enabled the juniors to complete their campaign, though they did so this time without winning any trophies.

Despite the reprieve of the ground, the Vale directors searched for alternative accommodation, but without success. Consequently, a meeting was held to discuss the future of the club, at Hanley Town Hall on 20 March 1944, and it was decided to ask the council if the Valiants could use the stadium temporarily for two or three seasons after the end of the war. On 29 June, Vale's request was more or less granted because the corporation agreed that they could rent it for three years at a total cost of £1,200.

Although the club had effectively been saved from extinction, at least in the short term, finding a new ground was the club's priority because there seemed every chance they would become homeless in 1947. In due course, a suitable site for a new stadium was discovered off Hamil Road, in Burslem, which was some rough land that had been used as a tip, and negotiations for its purchase from its owners, the Brownhills Estates Company, then began. Of course, it seemed incongruous that, having lost their home for the sake of £3,000, the club could even contemplate the construction of a completely new ground, but the directors managed to offset the majority of the land purchase cost by selling part of it on to a colliery firm! Also, as the Supporters' Club enthusiastically launched a New Ground Appeal Fund, with the aim of raising £30,000, the board virtually took a leap in the dark and forged ahead.

Inevitably, there was the distinct possibility that Vale would not be able to raise sufficient money for the scheme, in which case the existence of the club would be in real jeopardy, especially as costs would be accumulated along the way. Also, the proposed relocation in Burslem was a very risky plan because one of the main reasons why the Valiants had moved to bustling Hanley (where they had squeezed Stoke's fan base) in 1913 was the lack of support from the north of the city when they had been based in Cobridge.

Following the successful 6 June D-day landings in Normandy, it appeared likely that the war would be won and, so encouraged about the future, but also in urgent need of funds for the new ground, Vale resumed professional football and joined the 54-team Football League North for the 1944-1945 campaign. The first match, at home against Birmingham, on 26 August, was won 3-0 by a rapidly-assembled side in front of a very encouraging gate of 8,768. The crowd was only 1,268 short of that which had assembled for the opening Third Division (South) home game of the 1938-1939 season; it was 5,268 more than that which had turned up for the final match of that campaign in Hanley and was 3,666 greater than that which had gathered for the first home fixture in the aborted 1939-1940 season. Although it was only a single instance to go on, the turnout can only have spurred on the directors with their plan to return Vale to Burslem and the contract for the purchase of the land was signed in the middle of September.

By then, the recent ground beggars had come up with the most grandiose scheme of constructing a 70,000-capacity stadium on their new 13½-acre site, with parking available for a thousand cars! However, reality dictated that building was only to begin when a ground licence and sufficient funds became available.

Perhaps unsurprisingly, after a four-year absence, Vale found it difficult to get into their footballing stride and finished 45th in the Football League North, 54th out of sixty teams in the League's Second Championship, played after Christmas, and 48th out of sixty sides in the Football League Cup, Qualifying Competition, as well as progressing no further than the Qualifying Tournament of the Midland Cup. However, a highly satisfactory profit of £1,262 0s. 9d. was made on the season, whilst the Valiants' average home league attendance was only 572 below that in their final pre-war Football League campaign. Not surprisingly, the directors were very pleased with the situation, although the Supporters' Club had only raised something over £300 towards the cost of the new ground.

Vale competed in the Third Division (South) North Region in the 1945-1946 season, which consisted of the eleven teams of the pre-war division that were located north of the River Thames. As the war ended, the Valiants had a more settled side and finished third, as well as reaching the third round of the revived F.A. Cup, although they could only manage eighth position in the North Region Cup. However, once again, the most important matter was the club's finances and a further profit was made, of £1,265 2s. There was more good news because the council agreed to extend the lease on the Old Recreation Ground to 24 June 1950, although it was Vale's intention to have moved to their new stadium by then. In the meantime, the plans had been revised to accommodate 80,000 spectators, which seemed a tad excessive, especially as the 1945-1946 league campaign's crowds had averaged only 7,212!

The Football League competitions proper resumed in the 1946-1947 season and Vale returned to action in the Third Division (South). Their first home game, against Exeter City (which was lost 2-1) attracted a fine crowd of 14,490, their highest league gate since 1934. Indeed, the attendances held up so well, despite the side winning only two of their initial ten matches, that the directors paid a then club record fee for Blackpool's 'terrier type' half-back, Jimmy Todd. The team finished a respectable tenth in the league and fought their way to the fourth round of the F.A. Cup, but the highlight of the campaign was a new club record profit of £4,133 2s. 5d. that was made. Fortunately, as spectators flooded back to football following the end of the war, Vale's average home attendance increased to 10,582, their highest for nineteen years, and their gross gate receipts rose by nearly fifty per cent to £20,872 0s.7d. The club's unusually healthy financial position therefore rather luckily enabled significant progress to be made on the construction of the new ground and thirty miles of terracing was being planned.

The following season, Vale improved to eighth in the league, but obtained only the same number of points as they had in the previous campaign and were nowhere near to promotion. Nevertheless, the average home crowd increased to 13,569, the second largest in the whole of their history up to that point, and the gross gate receipts rocketed to £26,666 18s. 11d. However, a financial loss of £1,292 14s. was made, primarily because the club had become rather blasé about their new-found wealth, which had led to a considerable net transfer debit. As a result, a £100 life membership scheme was set up to raise funds for the new ground, the work on which had already cost £13,000. In addition, the then most expensive ever pitch in Britain was being laid for £100.

Despite the financial loss and the continuing drain of funding work on the new ground, the anticipation of even more money flowing in through the turnstiles encouraged the directors to spend a new club record fee of £10,000 on Liverpool's left-sided forwards, Stan Polk and Mick Hulligan, in a determined effort to try to gain promotion to the Second Division. There was a great demand for season tickets, which was of potential help in financing building work on the new ground and splendid crowds of 17,394 and 18,497 witnessed the opening two home league games of the 1948-1949 campaign as the team began strongly. However, the side's performances and consequently the size of the gates fell away. That did not help the financing of the ground and the 100 Club had still only signed up fifty members by January 1949. Consequently, the directors decided to complete the new stadium in stages, with the short-term capacity being cut by half to a more realistic 40,000.

Immediate payments for ground work were helped by an £8,000 grant from the Football Association and more money was raised by the sale of Billy Pointon, a goalscoring forward, to Queen's Park Rangers for a then club record five-figure fee and left-back Harry Hubbick to Rochdale for approaching £1,000. As all ideas of promotion were abandoned in the chase for still-needed funds, offers were then invited for Vale's other relatively attractive players.

Although the team finished a disappointing thirteenth in the league and only six points clear of the re-election zone, the annual accounts revealed a then club record £7,120 9s. 5d. gross profit, which therefore produced vital money to help complete the new ground. However, this financial success was primarily achieved at the expense of the team through player sales and the overall position was worrying because the average league home attendance had dropped by 1,500 and the gross gate receipts had consequently declined by £835 8s. 5d., whilst wages had rocketed by £2,447 7s. 5d.

By then, Vale had got into a vicious circle, whereby the completion of the new ground, and quite possibly the club's survival, had become dependent on the sale of players, which, of course, had the effect of weakening the team and in turn producing poorer results, thereby eroding the support and reducing the income at the gates. In addition, as the team had dropped to within range of having to seek re-election, any further transfers of the club's best footballers threatened to put the Valiants out of the Football League altogether, which would essentially defeat the whole object of having a grand new stadium. Also, with only a year to go to the end of the lease on the Old Recreation Ground, the raising of funds to finish the new ground was becoming a race against time. The reality was that the club was little further out of the mire than it had been in 1943 and the situation was precarious in the extreme. If insufficient further funds could be found to complete the Burslem ground in the forthcoming year, the club really would be facing the abyss.

A herculean effort was therefore needed to get Vale over the finishing line before catastrophe struck and the Burslem section of the Supporters' Club got the ball rolling by donating £600 to the cause, whilst the directors issued 22,000 new five-shilling shares in an attempt to keep the stadium move on schedule. By then, the Old Recreation Ground was becoming dilapidated and the Valiants' newly-signed goalkeeper, Ray King, described it as looking like 'some shanty town way out west'!

Unfortunately, on 27 October 1949, the corporation decided to turn down

Vale's application to transfer the seats and two of the stands from their existing ground to the new stadium, which created a new financial problem because the club had been banking on saving money through their use. The board then launched a 100,000 Shillings Fund in yet another attempt to keep the project afloat. There was even worse news at the beginning of December when the Ministry of Works refused to issue a licence for Vale's use of the new ground, without specifying why! Eventually, permission to proceed was given, which was a relief, but only 17,738 shillings (just under £887) had been raised by the new fund by the middle of February 1950, which was nowhere near enough.

The Valiants briefly stood face to face with disaster, but, on 2 March, the new ground move was salvaged, and the club perhaps saved, by the sale of their prized asset, the sharpshooting Ronnie Allen, to West Bromwich Albion for an amazing £20,000, by far the largest transfer fee Vale had ever received! Although Allen was a player of rare quality, the money was tantamount to a gift from heaven at such a crucial point and most of it, not surprisingly, was ploughed into securing the ground move. At the time, the team were sixth and still in with a slender chance of winning the championship and promotion. However, they won only three of their remaining thirteen matches after Allen's departure and finished thirteenth once more.

The opening of the new ground had been scheduled for Easter Monday 1950 when Vale were due to play at home against the league leaders, Notts County, but just two weeks beforehand the board decided, on the advice of the architect, that it would not be ready in time! Also, there were still no arrangements for any cover for the spectators at the stadium and so the club made a further appeal to the council, this time for the removal of just the Swan Passage Stand and they were finally given permission to take the steel stanchions and the roof!

The Ronnie Allen sale fortunately enabled a new club record gross profit of £10,671 to be made on the season, which finally confirmed that the move to the new stadium would go ahead. However, the Ministry of Works struck again and refused Vale permission to transfer the stand from the Old Recreation Ground, which ensured that the new 40,000-capacity arena would be entirely open air!

At last, on 2 August, the public were allowed into the new stadium at an open night and an impressive crowd of 12,000 people turned up in persistent rain to examine the "Wembley of the North". The ground was still some way from completion by the time of the first home game, on 24 August against Newport County, even though £50,000 had already been spent on it. The playing area was huge at 115 yards by 83 yards and the *Sentinel* said that, 'There is full scope for the strategist and the enterprising winger.' A banquet luncheon for dignitaries was held on the day at the Queen's Hall, in Burslem, and the club chairman, William Holdcroft, announced to the assembled host that the stadium was to be named Vale Park. A new club record home crowd of 30,196 gathered to watch the match in the rain and were rewarded with a 1-0 victory, thanks to a goal scored by the inside-right, Walter Aveyard.

So, after seven years of struggle, the Valiants finally transferred their operations from the Old Recreation Ground to Vale Park and from Hanley to Burslem, back to their roots. Today, the move of home seems little more than an interesting episode in the club's long history, but it begs a series of questions to be answered, not least of all as to whether it was inevitable or even necessary in the first place.

The creation of the stadium planned as the grandiose "Wembley of the North" ironically resulted from a financial crisis that brought the club to its knees and came perilously close to destroying it. The search for a new ground was born of desperation and the development of pie in the sky ideas of an 80,000-capacity stadium were perhaps the result of fantasies stemming from the endless strain to keep the club alive and produce funds virtually out of nothing. The whole episode is remarkable in that for the sake of a deficit of just £3,000 in 1943, £50,000 had to be found by 1950 to finance a still unfinished new stadium! The Vale directors' performance over that period could in no way be said to have constituted a classic example of prudent housekeeping. On the contrary!

So was the move from Hanley to Burslem actually necessary? It was most unfortunate for Vale that their president, William Huntbach, died whilst propping up the club to the tune of £3,000, but the loss of such a relatively small sum of money should not have threatened the Valiants' very existence or forced them to fund a vastly more expensive new ground. There is an element of "for want of a nail" about the whole situation.

Had Huntbach not died in the middle of the Second World War, but at a more normal time, it may well have been that Vale could have covered the £3,000 loss, most obviously by the sale of a player or players, as was their common remedy to their financial problems, which endlessly occurred. For example, in 1938, with just their routine money difficulties, the club made a profit of £2,900 on player transfers and, in 1939, they achieved a favourable balance of £1,455 on their transfer transactions. However, in 1943, the Valiants were not operating as a professional football club. They were ticking along as an amateur outfit, waiting for the war to end so that they could then resume their normal activities. Hence they had very little regular income at the very time that they needed it.

In peace time, the directors might have dealt with the immediate £3,000 deficit by extending their overdraft, providing their bank had been willing to let them do so. Probably the bank would have done because they would have made more money, at Vale's expense, providing the bankers felt that the club had enough assets to stay in business. With their ownership of the ground and the players at their disposal, in normal times the club would easily have had enough collateral to have covered a £3,000 loan in the event of defaulting on it. However, in wartime, finance is very insecure and the bank cannot really be blamed for running scared because Vale no longer had players for sale as they had ceased to be a professional club. In any case, transfers of footballers had been suspended for the duration of the war. In the event of the club's collapse, the bank and other creditors would essentially have ended up with the value of the ground at their disposal minus the costs of liquidation. In that case, there would extremely likely have only been one potential buyer, the corporation. As the council agreed in June 1943 to pay Vale £13,500 for the stadium, it may well have been that they would have offered a similar sum, or not as much, had the club gone to the wall and so the preferential creditors would perhaps have had around that amount, or something less, to split between them. So the reality was that, even during the war, the bank would probably not have been taking a great risk by extending the club's overdraft, but it seems that a climate of fear prevailed and so the obvious solution was not undertaken.

However, in retrospect, the sale of the ground seems to have been undertaken in a rather hasty manner, which may well have been unnecessary. The deal was not completed until 31 October 1943 and therefore Vale had survived that long without the apparently desperately-needed sale income. As the Supporters' Club ultimately launched a fund to raise £30,000 for the new Burslem stadium, the directors could have taken the time to explore with them whether the fans could realistically hope to raise just the required ten per cent of that amount, the £3,000 or thereabouts to plug the hole in Vale's finances, and thereby enable them to continue their ownership of the Hanley ground. Although the Supporters' Club in the event took a year to drum up just £300 for the new venture, presumably an appeal to save the club from extinction would have met with a somewhat better response than the one of collecting funds for a magnificent new stadium did, even in the uncertain climate of 1943. In addition to the fans' efforts, the club could have made an emotional direct public appeal for money and courted Stoke City for help, not least through a benefit match. As the Potters had helped Vale out on quite a number of occasions previously, it is difficult to believe that, not least for shame, they would not have assisted their old rivals at their hour of most need.

In addition, despite seemingly being on the brink of extinction by July 1943 and desperately struggling for money thereafter, Vale returned to being a professional football club within a year! As it turned out, it was a good move because the public had become eager to watch matches again and a profit of £1,262 0s. 9d. was made on the 1944-1945 season, £1,265 2s. the year after and £4,133 2s. 5d. in the 1946-1947 campaign. Although returning to professionalism was risky, the directors were willing to take the plunge in 1944, so obviously they could have done so the year before, with the objective of contributing towards filling the £3,000 hole.

Even had the Vale directors remained calm in the face of adversity and taken the time to fully explore these various fundraising options, they may well have concluded that none of them would prove to be the answer. However, the various possibilities combined might well have solved the problem or at least put the club within range of a solution. In addition, when it came to finding funds for the new ground, the board proved to be masters of the art, so that £50,000 had appeared by 1950. Therefore, it seems that, had they made even the most cursory efforts to produce £3,000 (or the remaining balance that was required) in 1943, they probably would have been successful and Vale would have stayed at Hanley.

Any way round, the very last option that the directors should have contemplated was selling their ground, without an alternative waiting in the wings, because it put the very existence of the club in jeopardy. The argument that was put forward by shareholders at the annual meeting in July 1943, that the directors should have arranged a special meeting before deciding to sell the ground, can only be regarded as entirely reasonable. Had there been such a meeting, a brake on the board's rush to dispense with the stadium might well have been applied. Furthermore, it is little short of incredible that the directors agreed the sale with the corporation without having had any reassurances that the club could continue to function at the Old Recreation Ground.

Although it is probably a conspiracy theory too far, it is just possible that the directors had had enough of putting their fingers in the dyke to prop up the ailing Hanley ground and wanted a fresh start at a prestigious new state-of-the-art stadium, in which case the withdrawal of the Huntbach debentures created a convenient situation whereby funds could be much more easily obtained than they normally would have been. However, it is altogether more likely that the board panicked because the members were stricken with anxiety that they would have to find £3,000 from their own pockets had the deficit not been made up by other means.

The problem with the timing of Huntbach's death in turn begs the question of whether there was anything inevitable about the occurrence of the Second World War, which was the cause of the abnormal conditions that Vale found themselves in. Traditionally, Nazi Germany and, more specifically, Adolf Hitler, have been blamed for causing the war, but in sober reality there is a dearth of evidence that suggests any of the major participants or their leaders actually wanted a world war. Blame can be attributed for actions which led to the war, but, like many complex international events, it seems that the outcome was largely the unexpected result of the struggle of wills and the failure of communications between the key statesmen involved.

That Adolf Hitler's Germany was expansionist cannot be denied, but the territories that were directly taken in the second half of the 1930s were all either lands lost in the Great War or German-speaking areas, both of which were argued as being justified. As a result, Britain especially and France adopted a policy of appeasement to Germany on the notion that Hitler was fundamentally a reasonable man and a clever, but traditional, diplomat, who had limited goals and would settle down under the long-held conventions of the European great powers once his arguably fair territorial claims had been met. Indeed, Britain's almost complete misunderstanding of Hitler is amply illustrated by the infamous image of the prime minister, Neville Chamberlain, waving a piece of paper in his right hand at Heston on 30 September 1938, prior to delivering his 'Peace for our time' speech after returning from Munich. Chamberlain's utter naivety was brutally exposed on the following 15 March when German troops marched into Czechoslovakia, dismantled the state and replaced the western part of it with their own Protectorate of Bohemia and Moravia.

Britain and France belatedly woke up as a result of this latest German territorial expansion and determined to resist any further attempts at expansion by Hitler. However, the latter did not appreciate the Anglo-French volte-face that had been undertaken and presumed that his previous international behaviour remained acceptable. Unfortunately, for all concerned, from then on he was under a complete illusion regarding the consequences of his actions. Therefore, after Hitler demanded lost German territories from Poland and invaded on 1 September 1939 when he did not get them, he was incredulous when Britain and France subsequently declared war. Thus the Second World War was not least caused by the vacillating policies of Britain and France in the face of Germany's endless expansionism, with catastrophic results for all concerned. Not for the first time, the war appears to have been one that nobody wanted, but which resulted from the muddle-minded policies of the initial participants. The outcome of that, in turn, for Port Vale Football Club, was the creation of a crisis which fundamentally changed the club's future.

Further to illustrate the chaotic nature of history, the probably avoidable Second World War in many ways resulted from the almost definitely avoidable First World War and the harsh treaties which followed it. The essence of Hitler's argument in the 1930s was that Germany had been unfairly treated at the Treaty of Versailles, following the Great War, in 1919 and that he was only trying to reclaim lands which had unfairly been taken away. For a while, his argument was quite convincing, or at least Chamberlain thought it was.

The causes of the Great War itself were a classic case of how bluff and counter-bluff and an unwillingness to lose face led to the one outcome that none of the great powers wanted – a long, extremely destructive and financially disastrous war of attrition. Even worse, the devastating consequences of the conflict were blamed almost entirely on Germany by the victorious Allies, especially through the war-guilt clause, and the punitive terms imposed bore little relation to those on which the Germans had surrendered. The effect was the unnecessary creation of bitter resentment in Germany, which Hitler so cleverly (for a while) exploited.

Therefore, the predicament that Port Vale found themselves in in 1943 was much the result of the shambolic behaviour and actions of a small number of the world's most powerful men. The Valiants could not have avoided the death of their president, William Huntbach, nor probably the consequent recalling of his monies in the club, but, had those events occurred during a time of peace, there almost certainly would not have resulted a financial problem on the scale of that which actually occurred and it may have been that the club would essentially have ridden out the storm. In that sense, Vale were extremely unlucky to have been presented with such a sticky situation, but how it was dealt with was largely in the hands of the custodians of the club.

It appears that the Valiants' future would have been significantly different if history had been rerun and consequently the Great War and/or the Second World War had been avoided; if William Huntbach had not died in wartime and if the Vale directors had pursued alternative options open to them during the ensuing financial crisis. To start with, the club would have remained at the Old Recreation Ground, in Hanley, and found £3,000 to deal with their latest financial problem instead of spending £50,000 on an entirely new stadium in the "Mother Town". Then, presumably, they would have been able to stumble on much as normal instead of embarking upon seven years of upheaval and worry.

As it turned out, the move to Vale Park initially seemed a great success in terms of attracting crowds to the team's matches because football was at its most popular as a live spectator sport in England in the post-war period and the new stadium could accommodate many more supporters than the old one. The highest crowd ever recorded at the cramped Old Recreation Ground was 22,697, way back in 1920, and that was trounced out of sight by the opening gate of 30,196 at Vale Park. In consecutive seasons, from 1953-1954 to 1955-1956, the Valiants exceeded the 40,000 mark at Burslem and, in 1960, recorded their largest ever home attendance, of 49,768. Therefore, these figures suggested that the efforts of the directors to move the Vale home had been well and truly vindicated.

However, from 1955, the trend was inexorably downwards and the average league gate at Vale Park dwindled from 20,869 in the 1954-1955 campaign to just 2,738 twenty-six years later. The latter figure was lower than any average recorded during the whole 37 years that the Valiants spent in Hanley, except for the first season of the Second World War, spent mainly in the distinctly unattractive Western Regional Tournament. Also, remarkably, the average league attendance in the very first campaign in Burslem was 2,151 less than it had been in the final one at the Old Recreation Ground, which was an alarming 16.6 per cent drop! Furthermore, at no point since 1957 have the average league and overall crowds at Vale Park reached the figure which was achieved in the Valiants' final season in Hanley!

As Vale improved their league position slightly from thirteenth out of 22 sides in their last campaign at the Old Recreation ground to twelfth out of 24 in their first at Burslem, the playing fortunes of the team seem to have had little or no bearing on the decline in attendances. However, Hanley was undoubtedly more conveniently positioned to attract spectators than was Burslem, being centrally located within the Potteries. Also, as Hanley was the main retail centre, shopping and watching a match could easily be done on the same trip, often as a family, with women largely taking care of the former, while mainly men indulged in the latter. Once Vale had returned to Burslem, though, the two pursuits needed to be done on separate occasions and could no longer be part of a combined family outing.

In addition, the Old Recreation Ground had long been regarded as Vale's home and the move to another stadium in a different town changed the specific habits of their supporters and broke up their old communities on the terraces. Some of the fans simply did not relish the change and others found a fortnightly trip to a near-characterless and entirely uncovered new ground a third of a mile outside Burslem town centre to be rather inconvenient and, in wet weather, absolutely dismal.

Indeed, the five seasons when Vale Park attracted the club's highest ever overall average home attendances were those that ran consecutively from 1952-1953 to 1956-1957 when the Valiants had an outstanding side in the Third Division (North) and then rivalled Stoke in the Second Division. Once the team's fortunes ebbed, the crowds rapidly dwindled and so the splendid gates of the fifties had little or nothing to do with the fact that Vale were playing at the still unfinished "Wembley of the North".

The fact of the matter is that the Valiants' relocation to Burslem was a retrograde move because they already had most of the support from the northern part of the city anyway, but they abandoned the core area of Hanley. The bustling big town had lost its football club and the support for Vale from Hanley declined thereafter. Even worse, by withdrawing from the hub of the Potteries, the Valiants allowed Stoke to squeeze their support in the future "city centre" and they returned to their traditional role as a small town club. Today, Vale seem to have no connection with Hanley at all, whereas the Potters have taken advantage of the Valiants' absence from the town to claim that they are the club of the city, not least by having a retail shop in the prestigious Potteries Shopping Centre, unlike their rivals.

Furthermore, the Old Recreation Ground was a tight little stadium, with much atmosphere, where plenty of noise could be generated in support of the team and to intimidate the opponents. Although by 1943 it had become somewhat run down, that was essentially because the directors had made very little effort to develop it. In reality, it was the right-sized ground for a club of the Valiants' stature, unlike the white elephant that Vale Park quickly became, with its vast unoccupied terraces and seemingly feeble sounds from the home supporters drifting into the heavens.

There is also the matter of Ronnie Allen, who found fame as a result of his transfer to West Bromwich Albion in 1950, which was vital in securing the funds to enable the Valiants' move to Vale Park to be completed. After his departure in March 1950, the team lost eight of their remaining thirteen league matches to tumble from promotion outsiders into the bottom half of the table. The following two seasons, Vale finished fairly comfortably in midtable, but well adrift of promotion and therefore it is extremely unlikely that Allen's presence would have significantly altered the situation.

However, at the end of the 1952-1953 season, the Valiants missed out on the Third Division (North) championship and promotion by a single point. Allen generally played at outside-right and in that campaign the position was occupied by Mick Hulligan. No-one can say whether swapping Hulligan for Allen would have been worth an extra point or more, but it probably would because the latter had a more distinguished career. Also, during his time with Vale, Hulligan averaged a goal every 9.09 games, whereas Allen was much more prolific, achieving a ratio of one in 3.9. Because goals win games and there were 23 league matches in which the Valiants could have secured the extra point they needed by scoring just once more, the odds are that, had Ronnie Allen been in the 1952-1953 team, Vale would have won the championship. However, there is no certainty that, as an outstanding individual, he would have fitted into the workmanlike ethos that was the essence of the side at that time.

However, even if the Vale directors had been stupid enough to have turned down West Brom's offer in 1950, it is highly likely that Allen would have been sold before 1953. Also, the Valiants waltzed to the Third Division (North) championship in 1954 and so, even without Allen, promotion only took one year longer than it might have done.

As far as Allen's future was concerned, cream tends to rise to the top, even in football. It is unimaginable that a player with his talents would have played out his career at Vale. If he had not signed for the "Baggies", he would surely have joined another top First Division club. In the event, he was converted to a centre-forward and scored 208 goals in 415 league games for Albion, all of them in the First Division. He gained an F.A. Cup winner's medal with West Brom in 1954 and was a regular member of their side which finished as the First Division runners-up that same campaign. He then played for four more seasons for Crystal Palace before embarking on a long career as a manager and a coach. Not the least of his achievements was that he became an England international and was capped five times. Had he remained at Vale, he would very probably have achieved none of that success.

In summary of the main developments, the unnecessary Great War was instrumental in causing the Second World War, which in turn created a financial crisis for the Valiants with the death of their president in 1943. The outcome of that was that the Vale directors unfortunately decided to spend a huge amount of money they did not have on building a vast new stadium in Burslem, which since has proved to be far too large for its purpose. Had the club continued to be based in Hanley, the home matches would have remained far more atmospheric and the supporters much closer to the action.

Far more importantly, Vale would have been sitting on a gold mine, whose value would have inexorably risen as it became a prime site for development in the rapidly-expanding city centre town of Hanley. Many readers will know that today the site of the Old Recreation Ground is occupied by part of the Potteries Shopping Centre (the major retail development in North Staffordshire) and its car parks. The sensational plans for it as a new, flagship, purpose-built 'multi-million pound' retail centre, which were published by the *Sentinel* on 12 November 1979, could so easily have announced that the shoppers' paradise would be constructed partly on the site of Vale's run-down Old Recreation Ground. No doubt the developers would have offered to buy the land from the club for a price they could not refuse and additionally agreed to build the Valiants a brand new, state-of-the-art stadium to boot. Of course, it is to be expected that the Vale chairman at the time, Arthur McPherson, would have driven the hardest bargain possible, secured the club's foreseeable future, poured funds into promotion-potential player purchases and insisted on the construction of a sensibly-sized stadium, with ample car parks and excellent road access, on the site of the former Shelton Bar steelworks, which later became known as Festival Park. Alternatively, had he and the rest of the board been completely outmanoeuvred by the council and the developers, the Valiants might have ended up with a typical tiny, modern, featureless, concrete ground in a location peripheral to the main population of North Staffordshire, perhaps close to Freeport in Talke or at Chatterley Whitfield!

In conclusion, had Vale remained at the Old Recreation Ground, in Hanley, and forgotten all about the future Vale Park, their history since 1943 would have been radically different and quite possibly more rosy in the long term. The struggle to survive in recent times may never have happened and the club would not have gone into administration in 2002 for want of a stand too far at Vale Park. Perhaps the Valiants would eventually have gone on to finer things, but, more likely, they would have continued to find life difficult, although not to the same extent as of late. But, for want of £3,000, or perhaps the proverbial nail, in 1943, Vale would have had a very different future.

1. THE DEATH OF KING HAROLD GODWINESSON at the Battle of Hastings in 1066, as depicted by the Bayeux Tapestry. Could it be that the arrow, which apparently by chance struck the king in his right eye, led to the foundation of Port Vale Football Club?

2. A CANAL WHARF IN PORT VALE. Can the existence of such a location prove that the traditional story of the origin of Vale's name is wrong?

3. A RUSH BY ENGLAND ON THE SCOTLAND GOAL in their international match at Kennington Oval, in London, on 5 April 1879. Can Vale's meteoric rise be attributed to their rejection of such primitive tactics in favour of the revolutionary idea of passing the ball?

HD 214334

Certified Copy of an Entry of Death
Pursuant to the Births and Deaths Registration Act 1953

Registration District Wolstanton

1892. Death in the Sub-district of Burslem in the County of Stafford

Columns: -	1	2	3	4	5	6	7	8	9
No.	When and where died	Name and surname	Sex	Age	Occupation	Cause of death	Signature, description, and residence of informant	When registered	Signature of registrar
180	Twenty Fifth June 1892 74 Pitt Street USD	Francis McGinnes	Male	23 years	Professional Footballer	Nephritis (Dropsy) Vomiting Exhaustion Certified by A. Lindsay MD	+ The mark of Eliza Kerrigan Present at the death 74 Pitt Street Burslem	Twenty Seventh June 1892	HC Powell Registrar.

Certified to be a true copy of an entry in a register in my custody.

LC Haywood Deputy Superintendent Registrar

2/11/2011 Date

4. THE DEATH CERTIFICATE OF Vale's legendary goalscorer, FRANK McGINNES. Would Vale have been promoted to the First Division of the Football League had he lived longer?

5. CHRIST CHURCH, in Church Terrace, Cobridge. What might have happened if the church had not saved Vale from extinction in 1907?

6. LEEDS CITY football team, 1917-1918. Would Vale have returned to the Football League without the inadvertent help of the Leeds club?

7. STANLEY MATTHEWS. What heights might the "Wizard of the Dribble" have inspired Vale to had they signed him in 1930, as they should have done?

8. THE OLD RECREATION GROUND, in Hanley. How might Vale have remained at their city centre stadium, instead of moving to Vale Park, and would they have made a fortune by doing so?

9. THE PENALTY THAT NEVER WAS, in Vale's F.A. Cup semi-final against West Bromwich Albion at Villa Park on 27 March 1954. Would Vale have won the cup had the fateful decision to award it to their opponents not been given?

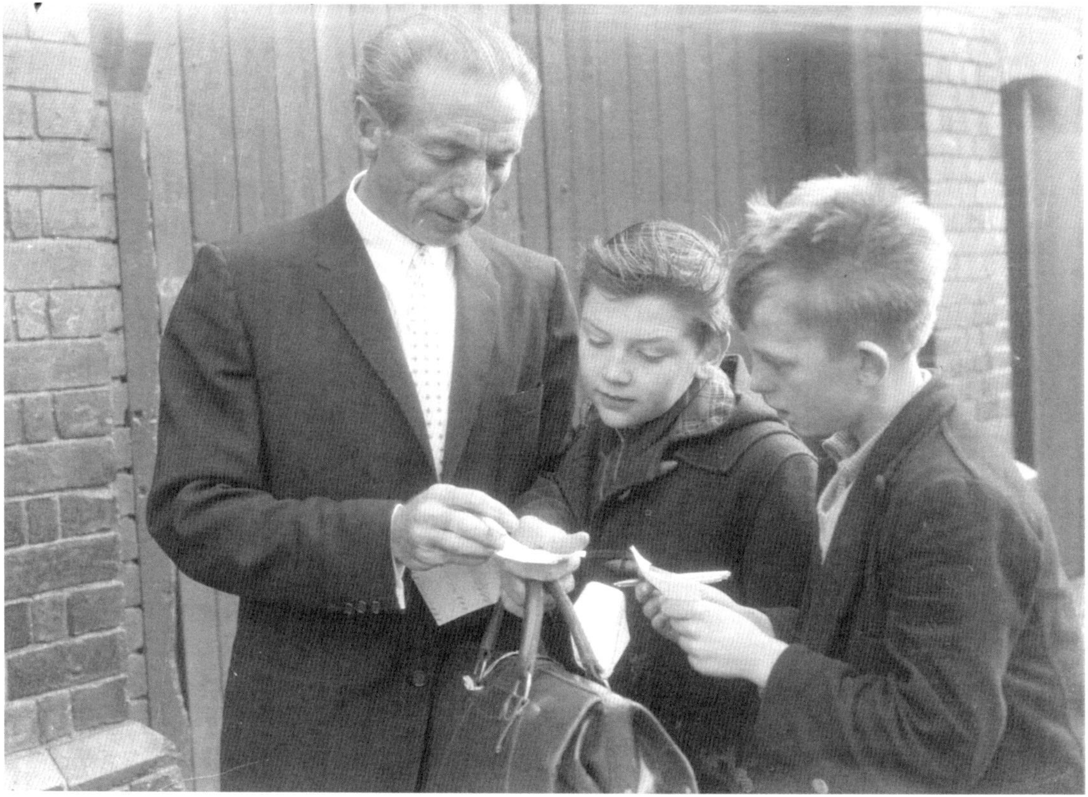

10. STANLEY MATTHEWS near the end of his fabulous football career. How could Vale's fortunes have been transformed had they signed him as a player in 1959 or 1961 and not as a manager in 1965?

11. JOHN McGRATH AT VALE PARK. Would Vale have remained a laughing stock had he not become their manager in 1979 and could his dismissal in 1983 have been avoided?

12. JOHN RUDGE OUTSIDE HIS OFFICE AT VALE PARK IN 1983. Might he never have become Vale's manager and how different would Vale's history have been had he not?

13. THE PARTIALLY-COMPLETED LORNE STREET STAND. How fabulous a future would Vale have had if the construction of the stand too far had never been undertaken?

14. BILL BRATT and MICKY ADAMS. How might events at Vale have turned out differently had they and others acted in different ways?

9 When We Won The Cup!

At the end of October 1946, Gordon Hodgson was appointed as the new manager at Vale. He was an ex-goalscoring inside-right, who had had a highly successful career with Liverpool, Aston Villa and Leeds United and had been capped by England. He had had no previous managerial experience, but had been the youth team coach at Leeds.

Just over a week before Hodgson arrived in Hanley, Vale were languishing third from the bottom of the Third Division (South), but, despite being managerless, the team succeeded in winning their next two matches! In Hodgson's first game in charge, on 2 November, the Valiants produced their best display thus far in the season in trouncing seventh-placed Reading 5-1. They then fought their way to the fourth round of the F.A. Cup and went ten matches undefeated in December and January 1947, which moved them up to eighth position in the league. The transformation in the team's fortunes was ascribed to Hodgson's coaching and planning abilities and a pivot of the rejuvenated side was the tough centre-half, Tom Cheadle, whom the manager installed as his first-choice stopper half-back. However, Hodgson had other irons in his fire and also organised trials for hundreds of local youngsters in an attempt to develop a successful youth policy.

In the spring, the side went off the boil and finished in tenth place, 23 points behind the champions, which encouraged Hodgson to start to wheel and deal, but he was severely handicapped because the club were ploughing most of their available funds into financing the new stadium they were constructing in Burslem. Thus the ground was Vale's priority and Hodgson was obliged to do the best he could, in the circumstances, with the first team while he waited for his youth policy to bear fruit.

In spite of the trying situation, Hodgson managed to steer the senior side up two places in the league the following campaign, to eighth, although once more they were well adrift of promotion. However, during the season, he installed two talented youngsters into the side, Bill McGarry, an aggressive and busy right-half, and the tough Basil Hayward, who was brought in at centre-half when Tom Cheadle was successfully moved to centre-forward, which had become a problem position.

Although in August 1948, the club chairman, William Holdcroft, confidently announced, 'We are going out for the Second Division,' Vale finished the campaign a very disappointing thirteenth, 23 points behind the champions and only six clear of the relegation zone. However, because money was still draining away into the new ground project, it might be considered that Hodgson was doing a sterling job in keeping the team out of serious danger. One thing for certain, the manager handed Reg Potts, a young and skilful left-back, his Football League debut during the season and then picked him regularly from January 1949.

In May, Hodgson signed a promising new 6' 2" goalkeeper, Ray King, from Ashington, and put him straight into the first team. Both moves proved to be astute because King went down in history as one of Vale's finest ever keepers and became an England "B" international.

Although the Valiants gained two more points in the 1949-1950 season than they had the year before, they again finished thirteenth and so no real progress had been made towards regaining their long-lost Second Division status. On the contrary, the team had been seriously weakened in March 1950 by the sale of the star forward, Ronnie Allen, to West Bromwich Albion for a then club record fee of £20,000, primarily to ensure that the ground move went ahead. However, Hodgson had given two more promising youngsters their first-team debuts during the campaign, the talented outside-right, Colin Askey, and Ken Griffiths, a skilful inside-forward.

Despite the razzmatazz surrounding the club's move to Vale Park in the summer of 1950, the side performed little better in the 1950-1951 season and ended up just one place higher than the previous year, although two more teams had joined the competition. Finishing 25 points behind the champions, the Valiants seemed no nearer to promotion than when Gordon Hodgson had arrived at the club, but four more promising young players had been blooded in the first team during the campaign. They were Roy Sproson, a commanding left-sided defender, who went on to become a Vale legend; Stan Turner, a tough-tackling right-back; Albert Leake, a versatile half-back and inside-forward; and John ("Dickie") Cunliffe, a tricky left-winger.

Therefore, by 1951, all except one of the first-choice players of the legendary 1953-1954 side had been assembled at Vale, although at that point their emergence into the "Steele Curtain" team could obviously not have been envisaged. Only two of the blossoming footballers had preceded Hodgson's time at the club: Reg Potts, who had appeared in four wartime matches for the team before being called up for national service, and Tom Cheadle, who had not been a regular in the side until Hodgson had arrived. However, all of them were groomed and developed as players by Hodgson and Colin Askey later said, 'He must take hell of a lot of credit for the 1953-1954 side.' Nevertheless, only Tom Cheadle of the ten future heroes played over thirty league games for Vale in the 1950-1951 season and he managed just 32 appearances, whilst six of those players made ten starts or under. It is therefore clear that, although he must take much of the credit for their development, Hodgson had not seen the potential of those specific footballers to gel into a formidable team. That was still to come.

In 1951 much work remained to be done on the new Vale Park ground and there were major problems with the surface drainage of the pitch, both of which required funding, whilst a sizable loss was looming on the annual accounts, so the club took the opportunity to land £12,000 from the sale of Bill McGarry to Huddersfield Town on 10 March. The "Terriers" therefore got their hands on a future England international and the Valiants made money from the sale of one of Hodgson's starlets, which they could put towards offsetting their trading loss and the completion of a ground that they had barely been able to afford in the first place. Although one can only speculate as to whether McGarry would have improved the remarkable 1953-1954 team had he remained with Vale, he seemed to be the type of industrious player who would have fitted into the side and undoubtedly he would have been a big asset to the squad. However, it is likely that a footballer of the class of McGarry would have moved on from the Valiants anyway, even if the Huddersfield offer had not come in at that time, and his transfer to another club within the next two years would appear to have been likely, not least because Vale remained beggars. Nevertheless, as it turned out, the Steele Curtain side hardly needed him.

Sadly, with his work only partly done, Gordon Hodgson died of cancer on 14 June 1951, aged just 47. On the surface, little progress had been made during his five campaigns as the manager of the Valiants as the team had remained virtually static in midtable, with a highest finish of eighth and a lowest of thirteenth. However, in that time, the club had achieved a near-financial miracle in funding the new Vale Park stadium, although Hodgson's best players and others besides had had to be sold to provide essential monies for it. Also, although the full fruit of his labours were as yet unknown and remained to be realised, he had developed almost an entire side that would soon prove to be at least the equals of two of the finest teams in the whole country. There is also the irrefutable point that Hodgson remained well respected as the manager by his employers, despite there having been no visible sign of progress on the playing front in five years, which illustrated a most unusual degree of loyalty, even in that age of greater director patience. A fitting tribute was given by one of his starlets, Roy Sproson, who said, 'Everybody liked and respected him and his loss was so sad.'

Hodgson's real worth was quickly laid bare for all to see following the appointment of his successor, Ivor Powell, an ex-Wales international half-back. Unfortunately, he 'tried to rule by fear,' according to Ray King, and rapidly undid much of Hodgson's good work. The team were a goal down within thirty seconds of their opening match of the 1951-1952 season, at home to Reading, and only two victories were gained in their first nineteen games! As the results gradually got worse, Powell endlessly resorted to shuffling the side in the hope of finding the right blend, to no avail. The atmosphere was not helped by the transfer of the popular and versatile Alan Martin to Stoke City in the middle of September, in exchange for Albert Mullard, an inside-forward, and £10,000. However, this was not Powell's fault because money was desperately needed to pay for expensive drainage improvements, as well as to try to finish the work on the ground. Also, Mullard was to prove the final piece in the jigsaw of the great team shortly to come. However, although all eleven players of the future Steele Curtain side were now at Vale, Powell only selected five of them with any degree of regularity and clearly did not see how the precious gems could be assembled into a virtually unbeatable machine.

After a 2-0 defeat at Leyton Orient on 17 November, with the Valiants rock bottom in the division, the directors lost patience with Powell and he was sacked. Nevertheless, he went on to guide Carlisle United to promotion from the Fourth Division in 1962 and, decades later, entered the *Guinness Book of World Records* as the oldest working football coach, retaining his title until he retired at the age of 93 in 2010!

Ray King said that there was 'complete relief' in the dressing room after Powell had departed, but the managerless team still only won one of their following five games, which included a first round F.A. Cup exit at Colchester United. However, on Christmas Eve 1951, the directors appointed the near-legendary, ex-Stoke City and England international centre-forward, Freddie Steele, as their new player-manager, although they had to pay Mansfield Town a four-figure fee in compensation for his services. He took command at the end of December and said, 'I think we have enough material at hand to pull out to safety,' but his reign started with two defeats, which included the team's thirteenth consecutive loss on the road! After that, the team could do little wrong and they lost only four of their remaining twenty league matches to the end of the season to finish thirteenth. Amazingly, the transformation was achieved without the recruitment of any new players, although Steele's seven goals in fourteen appearances were very helpful. However, the future Steele Curtain players increasingly emerged, with six of them appearing in the final five or more games, whilst two others played in the bulk of the matches after the new manager had arrived.

Vale were transferred to the Third Division (North) for the 1952-1953 campaign and Steele was so confident about their prospects that he made no significant new signings, preferring to stick with the young players who had emerged and one or two old hands. Eight of the following season's heroes were picked for the opening game at Bradford City and, although it was lost 1-0, the Valiants quickly got into their stride. The manager put a great deal of emphasis on fitness and teamwork and the side became very difficult to beat or even score against, as they became serious championship contenders.

In March 1953, with Vale third in the table, Steele spoke at a sports forum in Stone and revealed the secret of his success when he said, 'In present-day football, the players must think together, play together and try to get results by striving together.' Although there would be nothing out of the ordinary in that today, at the time his comments were revolutionary. The basic system of play had been 2-3-5 since the 1880s and rarely did any British club deviate from the accepted formula. However, on 25 November 1953 (over eight months *after* Steele's ground-breaking statement), the England international team, still steeped in the traditional tactics, were completely outthought and trounced 6-3 at Wembley by Hungary, the masters of innovation, in one of the most definitive matches in British history. Colin Askey said: 'Tactics weren't talked about in those days. There were a goalkeeper, two full-backs, three half-backs and five forwards, but Freddie had us all operating as one and he was ahead of his time.'

At the end of March, the Valiants were just a single point behind the division leaders, Oldham Athletic, and remained undefeated in their remaining nine games to the end of the season, but were unable to find the extra elusive point to put them level, to become the champions on goal average. Although it was not known at that point, the decisive moment occurred four minutes from time on 4 April when the "Latics" broke away to equalise in a 1-1 draw at Burslem. Although the overall outcome was disappointing, almost all the preparation had been completed for the record-breaking campaign that was to follow and nine members of the Steele Curtain side were by then regulars in the team: Colin Askey, Tom Cheadle, Ken Griffiths, Basil Hayward, Albert Leake, Albert Mullard, Reg Potts, Roy Sproson and Stan Turner.

Individualism had been sacrificed in favour of a combined effort, according to Steele's novel principles and the side had conceded just 35 goals all season, ten fewer than the next lowest total in the division and only two more than Huddersfield Town, who had the best defensive record in the whole Football League. A major reason for this success was that the manager had the whole team defending, which was practically unheard of. Thus the defensive duties started with the centre-forward, Basil Hayward, and Steele had his wingers doubling up to assist the full-backs, whereas at other clubs they rarely set foot in their own half.

Colin Askey summarised the position when he said, 'Gordon Hodgson developed us as players, but Freddie Steele made us into a team and finished the job that Gordon had started.' The 1953-1954 campaign was about to confirm that and Vale began with a run of seven league matches without defeat. From the outset, Ray King was preferred in goal to Ray Hancock, who had made 45 league and F.A Cup appearances the previous season, and, after only two games at outside-left, Mick Hulligan gave way to Dickie Cunliffe. The Steele Curtain side was then in place and, aside from injuries, more or less picked itself every week.

After losing 1-0 at Gateshead on 12 September, the team embarked on an all-time club record 22 league and F.A. Cup matches without defeat, which stretched to 16 January 1954. By the beginning of the new year, Vale were nine points clear at the top, with a game in hand, and had amassed an amazing 43 points from 25 games! They had also fought their way to the third round of the cup, by winning 3-1 at Darlington and then overcoming Southport 2-0 after a replay. A 1-0 win in the third round at Queen's Park Rangers was followed by a tough tie at First Division Cardiff City on 30 January, but the teamwork of the Valiants was too good for their high-flying opponents, who offered a blank cheque for Askey's services!

In the fifth round, Vale drew the cup holders, Blackpool, at home and the prospect of seeing the legendary "Wizard of the Dribble", other stars of the "Matthews Final" and the club's seven internationals led to the selling out of all the 42,000 available tickets for the match on 20 February! It finally looked as though the Valiants' number was up, but they astonished the football world by sweeping aside the First Division aristocrats 2-0. The players' instructions were to stop Blackpool from playing and they did so with ruthless efficiency, helped by a near-waterlogged pitch. The *Sentinel* reported that Vale's 'hard-fighting, quick-on-the-ball play smothered Blackpool's intricate approach work' and the result once more was 'a triumph of teamwork'.

Eight special trains helped to carry 8,000 of the Valiants' supporters to the sixth round tie at Third Division (South) Leyton Orient and they cheered the team on to a 1-0 victory, secured mainly by another impressive defensive performance. So Vale became only the second Third Division side to reach the F.A. Cup semi-finals. A tough tie against the First Division leaders, West Bromwich Albion, beckoned and the interest in the Potteries was so great that 40,000 fans queued up for the 25,000 tickets that were on sale at a reserve game against Mossley on 20 March, the attendance at which was a staggering 30,000!

A week later, a hundred coaches and fourteen special trains ferried Vale supporters to Villa Park for the showdown against Albion, who were the highest scorers in the whole Football League. A crowd of 68,221 paid £20,086 12s. to see the battle between the country's finest attack and defence, which was also a veritable David against Goliath clash that ensured it captured the public imagination. The Valiants were confident that they could win the day, but they had a problem in that their playmaker, Ken Griffiths, was missing with a knee injury and Derek Tomkinson was brought in from the reserves to replace him. Albion, however, were at full strength. Vale's line-up that afternoon, in the traditionally-stated order of play, was: Ray King, Stan Turner, Reg Potts, Albert Mullard, Tom Cheadle, Roy Sproson, Colin Askey, Albert Leake, Basil Hayward,

Derek Tomkinson and Dickie Cunliffe.

From the start of the match, Vale clamped down on their opponents and made sure that the "Baggies" couldn't get their usual constructive play going. Then, in the fortieth minute, Leake forced the ball home to give the Valiants the lead. Once Vale were in front in a game, the Steele Curtain would become even more difficult to penetrate as the team were dab hands at protecting leads. Roy Sproson later said: 'At half-time we seriously thought the game was as good as over. The confidence was such that we never entertained the thought of being beaten and West Brom gave us few problems.' Also, Colin Askey later said that Albion's right-half, Jimmy Dudley, had told him, 'Our dressing room was silent at half-time because we hadn't got a clue how to break you down.'

In the second half, the Baggies gave up their usual flowing style and, in desperation, relied on long lobs down the middle of the pitch, hoping to beat Vale in the air, with little effect. However, in the 62nd minute, Albion equalised from a seemingly harmless slow lob from Dudley, which drifted into the net. The film evidence shows Cheadle shape to head the ball out, but then fall backwards as the ex-Valiants star, Ronnie Allen, ran in next to him with a foot up. Whether there was any physical contact, with the West Brom centre-forward committing a foul, is not clear, but the *Sentinel* report said that Cheadle was 'bustled' off the ball. Although 'bustle' was a rather vague term, the body contact it suggested would probably have been legitimately within the rules, as applied at that time, in the much more physical game that existed then.

In addition, in his book, *Hands, Feet and Balls*, Ray King said that, 'The ball struck the back of his [Cheadle's] head and was diverted into the corner of the net.' Any way round, the upshot of the centre-half failing to clear the ball was that King had insufficient time to adjust his position in time to save the day. As he was initially well positioned in relation to the incoming ball, had Cheadle not attempted to head it and/or Allen not rushed in to challenge, the film suggests that the keeper would have had absolutely no trouble in making an easy save. The footage also reveals that, after the ball had entered the net, Allen paused and looked across the pitch, seemingly towards the linesman to check whether the goal had been allowed, before wheeling away with joy. Of course, it can be regarded as common sense that he wanted to confirm the position before becoming too excited or it may have been that he knew a reason why the goal should have been disallowed.

That, at the very least, luck had been against the Valiants regarding the goal was confirmed by Charles Richards, who reported in *The Birmingham Mail* that day that the ball 'was either deflected or spun' after Dudley had lobbed it so that, 'The goalkeeper [King] was completely deceived by the movement of the ball.'

Just eight minutes later, Albion's outside-left, George Lee, was put through on goal, but the unfortunate Cheadle put in a tackle outside the penalty area, as is clearly shown on the film. Whether or not the Vale captain intended to bring Lee down, he did not connect with the ball and therefore undoubtedly committed a foul. As the film suggests that the left-winger was otherwise clean through, it might well have been that, had today's more stringent rules then applied, Cheadle would have been sent off and the Valiants forced to play the remaining twenty minutes with ten men. However, the rules were what they were at the time and, of course, were accepted by both clubs before the game took place. So Cheadle remained on the pitch and had apparently saved Vale from conceding for a second time, as the film indicates that the foul was committed two feet or more outside the area. Astonishingly, though, the referee, Mr H. Webb, pointed to the penalty spot, perhaps having been deceived by the distance inside the area that Lee had ended up from the impetus of his speed and the tackle. Interestingly, the footage then shows a forlorn Cheadle trying to attract the attention of the referee and pointing to a groove in the pitch made by one of his boots after the tackle, whilst other Vale players protested that the Albion outside-left had handled the ball before the incident. The film indicates that the boot mark was not there beforehand and that it started approximately where the initial contact was made, clearly outside the penalty area.

In addition, Charles Richards made a revealing comment in *The Birmingham Mail* about the legitimacy of the Baggies' build-up to the foul tackle incident, which supported the Vale players' protests: 'I must say I felt sure Lee elbowed the ball past Turner before being brought down.' In other words, the journalist stated that he was convinced that West Brom's outside-left had committed a foul *before* the Cheadle challenge occurred. If that was the case, then the question of whether a penalty should have been awarded or not is irrelevant. Also, although it is not possible to prove whether Richards was right or wrong, it is highly unlikely that he was favouring the Valiants in his report, not least because there would have been numerous Albion fans in the newspaper's circulation area.

Although the visual evidence makes it virtually indisputable that the penalty was mistakenly awarded, the referee's decision was, of course, final and, ironically, it was Allen who duly converted the spot kick. Although King got close to saving it, the penalty was perfectly struck, low and hard into the left corner of the net.

However, the match was still not over and Vale went in search of an equaliser, which they thought they had obtained four minutes from the end when Leake converted a cross to score what was described by Colin Askey as 'a tremendous goal'. Unfortunately, as the Valiants' luck that day had it, it was disallowed for offside, although Roy Sproson later said that the players were 'stunned' by the decision.

Thus ended Vale's most valiant attempt to become the only Third Division side ever to get to the F.A. Cup final and it was little consolation that the West Brom goalkeeper, Norman Heath, said, 'You had all the bad luck.' Nevertheless, all of the three controversial events in the match went against Vale and, by any standards, it can be considered that chance was well and truly against them that day. Had only one of the three been in their favour, they would have gained a draw and lived to fight another day against the First Division's top team, in the titanic battle to get to Wembley.

An analysis of the key events of the game shows that things might easily have turned out so differently:

With regard to the first West Brom goal, had Cheadle decided not to try to head the ball, King very probably would have collected it with ease. Had Allen not put in a challenge, Vale's centre-half might have cleared the ball anyway. Had the referee decided Allen's challenge was unfair, the Valiants would have been awarded a free kick. Finally, had King ignored what was going on in front of him (which would have been a very fortuitous mistake) and even strolled to his near post, it is extremely likely that the ball would simply have bounced into his hands. If just one of those events had happened differently, it is very doubtful that the first goal would have been conceded.

As far as the winning goal is concerned, the referee made a serious error of judgement in awarding the penalty, which clearly should have been a direct free kick to Albion instead. The officials should have got the decision right, but, as can be seen even today, especially with modern replay technology, human error still plays its part. Having immediately thought that he should award a penalty, the referee could still have taken time to consider the matter and examined Cheadle's groove in relation to where Lee had fallen, but he chose not to. Perhaps the absolute certainty and speed with which he made his erroneous decision was worse than the mistake itself, especially with such much riding on the outcome. The more so was the case because in those days, with the old, heavy case ball, it was far more difficult to score from free kicks than it is now and so it is unlikely that the Baggies would have pierced the Steele Curtain had the right award been made. Alternatively, the referee might have, correctly or incorrectly, upheld the Vale players' protests and given a free kick against Lee for handling the ball before the fateful tackle had been made.

Finally, regarding Leake's disallowed goal, close offside decisions are notoriously difficult to call and even today the very best officials cannot help but get a proportion of them wrong. If in doubt, the rule of thumb is to favour the defending side and it may be that at Villa Park that was what happened. Any way round, however, it was most unfortunate for the Valiants in 1954 that the call went against them.

Had just one of the many numerous instances outlined above occurred differently, Vale would have drawn the match and still been in with a strong shout of becoming the only Third Division team ever to win the F.A. Cup. However, had a single instance in two of the controversial key situations of the match gone in the Valiants' favour, they would have won the tie and, had they had the good fortune to have had all three of the events fall their way, they would have triumphed by 2-0.

In addition, had Vale not sold Ronnie Allen to the Baggies in 1950, he almost certainly would not have been playing for them that day and therefore his decisive contributions would not have occurred. In that case, the odds on the Valiants winning through would have shortened considerably.

Furthermore, suppose Ken Griffiths had been fit for the semi-final. What effect might that have had? Because injuries are so much a part of football, it could be argued that Vale did well to have only one member of their Steele Curtain side missing for the big match. However, it was often stated that Griffiths made the forwards tick and so his absence was a notable loss. Perhaps if he had played, it would have made a sufficient difference for the balance to have swung decisively in the Burslem team's favour.

All in all, Vale came within a whisker of reaching the F.A. Cup final that day and, if the mix of the numerous ingredients in the melting pot had been altered slightly, as it so easily could have been, the outcome may have been very different. Such was the remarkably slender margin of success and failure.

Had they won through to the final at Wembley, either in the original match or through a replay, the Valiants would have faced another First Division side,

Preston North End, on 1 May. Had they overcome the mighty Albion, Vale would certainly have fancied their chances of lifting the cup, as indeed the Baggies did in the real match, winning 3-2, thanks not least to a brace of goals from Ronnie Allen. Although the result was close, Preston were not the same force as were West Brom. They had finished eleventh in the league, ten points adrift of Albion, who had done the double over them that season. Also, the Baggies team which beat them in the final had really gone off the boil since their success against the Valiants, having gained only three points from their final seven league matches, and finished as the runners-up, four points behind their arch-rivals, Wolverhampton Wanderers. Therefore, as an out-of-form West Brom beat Preston, Vale would have been in with a good chance of winning the much-coveted prize.

As it turned out, the Valiants had no time to bemoan their luck because ahead lay twelve league fixtures, to be played in the next 32 days, and their lead at the top of the division had been reduced to three points, although they had three games in hand. Like true champions, they remained undefeated right to the end of the season and trounced Stockport County 7-0 at home on 10 April. Vale finished their remarkable campaign with 69 points, eleven ahead of the runners-up, and had conceded only 21 goals, with just five of them at home. Thus they created a new Football League defensive record over 46 matches, which stood until 1996. Also, they let in an amazing 29 fewer league goals than the next-best defence in the whole four divisions of the league in the 1953-1954 campaign and lost only three games.

Not surprisingly, during the close season, there were no significant player departures from the club, who intended to rely on their record-breaking team to tackle the new challenge in the Second Division. A solid start was made to the 1954-1955 campaign, with seven points being gained from the first six matches, just one defeat being suffered and only three goals conceded. Then, on 16 September, there was a sensation as Vale lost 7-1 at Swansea Town, although Cheadle had to go off with a pulled muscle in the eighteenth minute and Turner was taken to hospital with concussion five minutes before half-time, with the score at 2-1. Nevertheless, the trouncing destroyed the reputation of the Steele Curtain and the Valiants conceded 31 goals in thirteen games from 25 September!

The main reason for the sudden flow of goals into the wrong net seemed to be a change of tactics by Freddie Steele, to try to end the early goal drought in the campaign. Thus, in September, he switched to 'a semi-continental style', heavily influenced by the tactics of the magnificent Magyars, who had destroyed England 7-1 in the return match in Budapest on 23 May. Steele explained that the objective was 'to build from the defence a striking force that can sustain penetrative counter-offensives'. Unfortunately, the effect was to expose the defence more and thereby undermine the main strength of the team, so he may well have done better to have stuck with his own novel Steele Curtain tactics.

Having realised that the new style was not working, in November Steele decided on a further change of tactics, to those which suited whoever was in the side! This new idea brought no success either and helped to lead to a 7-2 drubbing by Birmingham City on the 27th. By then, Vale were in relegation trouble and the rest of the season was a struggle to survive in the Second Division. In an attempt to stop the rot, Steele began to sign new players and this signalled the beginning of the end for the famous 1953-1954 team, with just six of its members appearing in the final match. Eventually, the Valiants did enough to stay up, but finished a very disappointing seventeenth, with only 35 points, and conceded 71 goals! At the end of the season, Derek Tomkinson, who had had an afternoon in the limelight in the fateful 1954 F.A. Cup semi-final, was released, having made a grand total of thirty appearances.

No new players of note were signed for the 1955-1956 campaign, but the great Steele Curtain side was soon creaking under the pressure of injuries and the challenge of promising reserves. Nevertheless, Vale began extremely well and gained fifteen points from their opening ten games, which (that season) was easily championship form. The main reason for the turnaround seemed to be the belated return to the successful Steele Curtain tactics because just five goals had been conceded. The journalist, Bernard Joy, explained "The Vale Plan" as he saw it, saying they 'treat the penalty area as a bastion which must be defended at all costs' and the forwards funnelled back to defend as soon as possession was lost.

However, nine matches without a victory followed, as injuries took their toll, and the Steele Curtain was torn to shreds at Blackburn Rovers on 12 November when the Valiants were trounced 7-1! The result was eight team changes for the next game at home to the bottom side, Hull City, but that was lost as well, by 1-0. However, as the injury list shortened, Vale's form improved and, to signify a real push for promotion, the ex-England international inside-forward, Eddie Baily, was signed from Tottenham Hotspur in the middle of January 1956 for a then club record fee of £7,000. Unfortunately, his presence was not enough and the Valiants finished the season twelfth, seven points adrift of the runners-up. Albert Mullard, who had made only six appearances, was then transferred to Northwich Victoria and thus became the first regular member of the 1953-1954 side to depart.

Although new signings were at a premium for the 1956-1957 campaign, the chairman, Fred Burgess, said, 'We have solid grounds for optimism.' At the end of September, he did not seem to be far wrong as the team had secured nine points from their opening nine games, but then Baily was transferred to Nottingham Forest for a money-recovering £7,000 because he was an individualist, who apparently confused the rest of the forwards. However, after his departure, Vale lost the next eight league matches, despite nine of the Steele Curtain side playing in half or more of them. Two victories in three games followed, but they proved to be a flash in the pan and the Valiants were in penultimate position on 15 January 1957 when Steele decided to resign. He said, 'I am quite prepared to accept the consequences.'

After he had left, if anything the team got worse and a debacle occurred at Burslem on 2 February when they slumped to an all-time Vale Park record 7-1 defeat by an Eddie Baily-inspired Nottingham Forest. A week later, the Valiants were hammered 6-3 at Fulham and saved from a complete rout only by a brilliant performance by Ray King.

On 18 February, the club appointed the ex-Norwich City and Workington manager, Norman Low, as the new team boss. He said: 'I know I have taken on a really tough job, but the present team has ability and with the right spirit, we shall get away from the bottom.' Unfortunately, it was not to be and Vale failed even to make a fight of staying in the Second Division, gaining just six points from their remaining fourteen league games. They finished bottom, with only 22 points, and had conceded a staggering 101 goals despite the fact that eight of the famous Steele Curtain side each had played in over half the matches! As the Valiants had, in the event, fared even worse under Low than they had when Steele had been in charge, arguably the club might just as well have urged the latter to stay!

Vale's relegation marked the end of an era. Freddie Steele and his remarkably successful defence had gone and the close season witnessed a clear out of players, including four from the marvellous 1953-1954 team. Ray King was sold for £2,500 to Boston United; Stan Turner and Reg Potts were transferred to Worcester City and Tom Cheadle joined Crewe Alexandra as their player-coach.

Only one of the members of the Steele Curtain side remained with Vale in the long term and that, of course, was the legendary Roy Sproson, who continued to ply his trade until his final appearance on 8 May 1972, at the age of 41! He made a staggering 836 competitive first-team starts for the club and scored 35 goals before becoming the coach and then the manager in January 1974. Unfortunately, his reign was not successful and saw a decline in the side's fortunes, which led to him being sacked in October 1977, with relegation from the Third Division looming. He turned down an offer from the club of a position dealing with the youth players, although the following month he offered to help Vale 'in any capacity', but in the event he never returned.

Of the remaining 1953-1954 heroes, Ken Griffiths was transferred to Mansfield Town for a four-figure fee in January 1958; Basil Hayward was sold to Portsmouth for 'a fair fee' in July 1958; Colin Askey departed to Walsall the same month for 'a fairly substantial' fee; Dickie Cunliffe left for Stoke City, along with £2,000, in September 1959 in exchange for Peter Ford and Harry Oscroft; and Albert Leake was transferred to Macclesfield Town in January 1961.

Wherever they were and wherever they went, the members of the famous Steele Curtain side were left to reflect upon the day when they almost achieved history by becoming the only Third Division team to reach the F.A. Cup final. Moreover, they could dream about how it so nearly came true that they could tell their grandchildren the story of "When we won the cup"!

10 The Sublime Skills Of Stanley

When Stan Matthews left Stoke City for Blackpool on 10 May 1947, at the age of 32, it was generally believed that his best years as a footballer were behind him and it was widely expected that he would see out his career with the "Seasiders". Incredibly, he amassed 379 appearances with them, all in the First Division, and was still a regular in their side in the 1960-1961 season in his mid-forties! Even more remarkably, he continued to be selected for England until 1957 when he became the oldest player ever to appear for them, at the age of 42! He ended up with 54 full caps and also played in 29 wartime internationals.

Fortunately for Matthews, the Blackpool manager, Joe Smith, was a big fan of his sublime talents. Smith did not want to restrict the brilliance of the "Wizard of the Dribble" and was happy for him to play how he saw fit, so that he entertained the crowds. Thus a second golden age beckoned for the maestro.

In the 1947-1948 campaign, Matthews made 33 league appearances for Blackpool, but he was unable to inspire them to glory because the Seasiders dropped four places in the First Division, to ninth. However, in the F.A. Cup, Blackpool were a different team altogether and reached the final, in which they were beaten 4-2 by Manchester United, despite twice being in the lead. Notably, Matthews played in every round and had the consolation of winning the inaugural Football Writers' Association Footballer of the Year award.

The following season, the "Magician" appeared 25 times in the league for the Seasiders, but they ended up seventh from the bottom and only clear of relegation by five points. This time, even with Matthews in the team, they only reached the fourth round of the cup, where they were despatched by Stoke after a replay, much to the delight of the Potters' fans.

However, in the 1949-1950 campaign, the Wizard of the Dribble played 31 First Division matches for Blackpool and inspired them to finish only four points adrift of the champions, Portsmouth, albeit in seventh position. The Seasiders also performed well in the cup, reaching the sixth round, with Matthews playing in three of their five games.

The next season, Blackpool improved still further in the league and finished third, albeit ten points behind the champions, Tottenham Hotspur. The Magician was once again a regular and appeared 36 times. The unfashionable Seasiders were becoming a force in English football and, for the second time in four years, fought their way to the F.A. Cup final, where they were beaten 2-0 by Newcastle United. Matthews played in all eight of their matches, but was unable to conjure up the brilliance to overcome their opponents.

However, in November 1951, he suffered an ankle injury, which limited him to only eighteen First Division appearances and Blackpool dropped to ninth. After their fine feat in the previous competition, the Seasiders were knocked out of the cup in the first round, even with the Wizard of the Dribble in their side.

Nevertheless, their finest hour came the following season. Although Matthews was out with a muscle injury for three months and made only twenty league appearances, he did enough to help Blackpool to finish seventh, seven points behind Arsenal, the champions. It is obviously a matter of conjecture as to whether the gap could have been closed successfully had the Magician been fit throughout the campaign. However, the best of the outside-right and the team were again reserved for the F.A. Cup, in which they reached the final once more. In total, the Seasiders played seven matches in the competition and Matthews appeared in all of them. In the final, they faced Bolton Wanderers and all seemed lost when they were 3-1 down with only 22 minutes remaining. However, the Wizard of the Dribble then conjured up a piece of magic with a perfect cross for centre-forward Stan Mortensen to pull a goal back. Mortensen equalised less than two minutes from time and, in one last effort, the 38-year-old Matthews crossed the ball once more, with just seconds remaining, for outside-left Bill Perry to snatch the winner and complete a sensational comeback. The "Matthews Final", as it became known, is still widely regarded as one of Wembley's greatest ever F.A. Cup finals.

Blackpool needed four replays to get through to the fifth round of the 1953-1954 competition, in which they were drawn away to Third Division (North) Port Vale. Although the Valiants were proving invincible at home, few people outside the Potteries gave the Burslem side the slightest hope of toppling the F.A. Cup holders, with the Wizard of the Dribble to boot, but that is exactly what they did, by 2-0. There remained the league for the Seasiders to concentrate on and, assisted by thirty appearances from Matthews, they improved their position to sixth.

The following season, the Magician played 34 league games and it was a good job he did because Blackpool finished only two places and three points clear of the drop zone. A third round exit from the cup completed an extremely poor year for the Seasiders and Matthews, by their recent standards.

Although Blackpool again exited from the cup at the first hurdle in the 1955-1956 competition, they surpassed themselves to finish runners-up in the league, ably assisted by their trusty right-winger, who made 36 appearances. Then there was greater glory for the Wizard of the Dribble, who became the first winner of the European Footballer of the Year award.

The Seasiders maintained their position as one of the First Division's best teams the following season when they ended up fourth, but injury restricted their talisman to only 25 starts. However, Matthews managed to play in all their four F.A. Cup matches, which took them to the fifth round.

Blackpool maintained their status amongst the elite in the 1957-1958 season as they finished seventh in the league, with the perennial Magician still managing 28 appearances. However, he could do nothing to prevent the Seasiders from exiting from the cup at the first hurdle through a 5-1 thrashing at Second Division West Ham United.

Unfortunately, time had caught up with Joe Smith and he resigned as Blackpool's manager in 1958 because of ill health. That was a disaster for the Wizard of the Dribble, not only because he had lost his mentor, but also because he was soon in dispute with Smith's replacement, Ron Suart, who wanted him always to stay out wide on the wing. That Matthews was not willing to do because he liked to come inside at times, to get more involved in the game, and so he ignored the new manager's instructions. The outcome was that the maestro became no longer an automatic choice in the team and, also with having a niggling knee injury, was limited to nineteen league appearances in the 1958-1959 campaign, although the Seasiders still managed to end up eighth. However, the Magician played in all Blackpool's six F.A. Cup games that season and inspired them to reach the sixth round.

When Matthews began the 1957-1958 season (his last as the Seasiders' automatic first-choice outside-right), Port Vale's manager, Norman Low, said the team would be fighting 'like hell' to get promoted from the Third Division (South). However, he also needed to be looking over his shoulder because all the sides finishing in the bottom half were to be relegated into a new Fourth Division. Nevertheless, Low was not a man of caution, as Roy Sproson later revealed: 'He would not tolerate defensive play and he told the players to go out and entertain the public. During Norman's stay, Vale played the best football known in my time.'

The team began well, taking 21 points from their opening sixteen games and went third in the table on 2 November. Unfortunately, they then went off the boil and won only six of their next 23 matches to sink into the bottom half. However, a 2-1 home win against Torquay United on 5 April 1958 put them in thirteenth place, a single point away from the safety zone. Unfortunately, Vale's efforts then petered out and they gained just two points from their final six games, to finish fifteenth. Thus the Valiants were relegated for the second successive season, into the basement division, just over two years after they had stood fifth in the second tier. They had experienced a spectacular decline by any standards.

Vale started the 1958-1959 Fourth Division campaign with only two new recruits in the team, but conceded a goal in the first minute of the opening game at home to Northampton Town, which they lost 4-1. Just two points were gained from the following four matches at Burslem and the first victory at Vale Park did not arrive until the Valiants' sixth game there! However, they were invincible away and suffered their first league defeat on the road only on 29 November! As their home form picked up and the ball kept flying into the opponents' net, Vale mounted a serious promotion challenge and went to the top of the table in early November. Their attack continued to score goals with almost effortless ease and the peak of their success was an 8-0 annihilation of Gateshead at Burslem on Boxing Day. The Valiants' fine form continued almost unabated until the end of the season and they ran out as the first ever Fourth Division champions, with 64 points. In the process, they scored an all-time club league record 110 goals, with five of their forwards reaching double figures: Stan Steele 22, Jack Wilkinson 21, Graham Barnett 20, Harry Poole 16 and Dickie Cunliffe 15. Also, Brian Jackson, their speedy and direct outside-right, who had been signed for £1,700 in July 1958, had weighed in with eight strikes.

Not surprisingly, Norman Low kept faith with the side for the challenge of the Third Division at the start of the 1959-1960 campaign. At first, this seemed wise as Vale won their opening two league games, but they gained just one point from their following six matches, in which an amazing 21 goals were conceded! After two matches into this sequence, Low decided that the attack needed pepping up and made a bid for 44-year-old Stan Matthews from Blackpool. By then, the Wizard of the Dribble was having to compete with two other right-wingers for a place in the Seasiders' first team and did not make an appearance at all until 15 October, so he looked surplus to requirements. Presumably, Low was thinking of playing him instead of Brian Jackson and the manager was convinced that the Magician would bring the crowds in. The impact of Matthews signing for Stoke

City two years later proved beyond doubt that Low was correct in his assessment. Unfortunately, Blackpool were not ready to part company with their man and so Vale, to their great cost, for a second time failed to sign the maestro.

Of course, it is often said that everything has its price and, presumably, had the Valiants been interested enough, they would have landed the Wizard of the Dribble. When the Seasiders transferred Matthews to Stoke two years later, they secured a fee of around £3,000 for him. Because he was two years younger in 1959 and Blackpool were not then ready to lose him, no doubt Vale would have had to have paid more than that for his services and perhaps £5,000 or a little over that figure does not seem unreasonable. As Brian Jackson was in good form at the time and the Valiants received £2,000 for him three years later, they might well have been able to have offset a fair amount of the Matthews cost by selling Jackson sooner rather than later. Also, the club had approximately the outstanding balance at hand because, a few days after their attempt to sign the Magician, they paid £2,000 to Stoke as part of a player part-exchange deal. Therefore, there can be little question that Vale could have afforded to have signed Matthews.

The Valiants continued to plug on unaided by the Wizard of the Dribble and finished the season in a respectable fourteenth place, with 46 points from the same number of games, with a 7-0 annihilation of Halifax Town and a 6-1 trouncing of Swindon Town the highlights of their league campaign. However, in the F.A. Cup, Vale were a different proposition altogether and fought their way to the fifth round, in which they were drawn at home to the Second Division leaders, Aston Villa. The team made a valiant effort to see off their powerful opponents, but eventually went down 2-1 in front of an all-time record home crowd of 49,768.

That same season, Matthews made only fifteen league and cup appearances for Blackpool, having become a bit-part player. For what use he had become to the Seasiders, they might as well have let him go to the Valiants and brought in a small fee. Instead of having a marginal impact on the fortunes of Blackpool, who finished eleventh in the First Division despite his frequent absence, the Wizard of the Dribble could have been a sensation at Vale and transformed the club, with huge crowds flocking in to see the sublime skills of the valiant veteran.

Nevertheless, Vale were starting to vie with Stoke City to be the footballing pride of the Potteries. Stoke finished the 1959-1960 campaign fifth from the bottom of the Second Division, only five points clear of the relegation zone, and drew in just 4,070 spectators to see their 2-1 home defeat by Ipswich Town on 30 March 1960. The upshot of City's struggle was that their manager, Frank Taylor, did not have his contract renewed at the end of the season and, on 3 June, he was replaced by Tony Waddington, whose main claim to fame at that point was that he had played as a wing-half for Crewe Alexandra.

Because the Potters were in financial trouble, the *Sentinel* said they had a 'huge problem' ahead the following season, in which relegation was considered to be a distinct possibility. In a sense, Waddington was successful because Stoke avoided the drop, but only by three points and goal average as they slumped to fifth from the bottom at the end of the campaign. The scale of the difficulty City faced was indicated by the size of the crowd that watched their final league home game against Liverpool on 3 May 1961 – just 4,463! Furthermore, their average league gate at the Victoria Ground had dropped to 9,569, which was 133 fewer people than Vale had pulled in a division lower, where there were less attractive teams to watch.

That season, the Valiants had made a fair degree of progress and finished seventh in the Third Division, with 49 points, scoring 96 goals in the process. Inside-right Cliff Portwood equalled Vale's post-war league and F.A. Cup goalscoring record, with 26 strikes, whilst centre-forward Bert Llewellyn notched twenty goals in only 28 league appearances after joining the Valiants for £7,000 from Crewe Alexandra in November 1960. With the attacking play on offer, it is no wonder that more spectators were interested in making their way to Vale Park than the Victoria Ground. The state of play was well and truly confirmed on 24 April 1961 when the Valiants achieved a 1-0 victory at Stoke in the deciding match of the Supporters' Clubs' Trophy that the two teams competed for.

Over at Blackpool, the 1960-1961 campaign proved to be something of a renaissance for the evergreen Stan Matthews, who made 27 First Division appearances. However, the Seasiders were not the team they had been and finished third from the bottom, a single point above relegated Newcastle United, and, at 45, the Wizard of the Dribble was no longer maestro enough to inspire them to do any better. Also, Matthews was a member of the side that was humiliated at Second Division Scunthorpe United in the third round of the F.A. Cup when they were trounced 6-2. Time at the top seemed to be running out for the Magician, the more so as he and his manager still did not see eye to eye and both of them believed that it would be better if he moved on.

By the summer of 1961, it seemed only a matter of time before the Valiants and Stoke swapped divisions and football supremacy in the Potteries swung decisively to Burslem. Although money was tight at Vale, a flurry of transfer activity prior to the 1961-1962 season led to the strengthening of the team (or so it was thought) at a net transfer debit of £8,000. Indeed, Norman Low was convinced that the side by then was 'capable of getting promotion'.

However, at Stoke, the situation seemed to be bleak. In anticipation of the campaign ahead, the *Sentinel* said: 'Stoke's problem is to arrest the alarming decline in support. After two depressing seasons, they face a most difficult task. Over recent years Stoke have become run-down and sorely need restoring to health.'

The start of the season did not go anything like according to expectations for Vale, who gained only one victory in their first six league matches. Brian Jackson remained on the right wing in what turned out to be his final campaign with the Valiants, but was dropped at the end of their opening six-game sequence. Although he regained his place, he was dropped again in April 1962 and sold three months later, being deemed surplus to requirements. Therefore, in early September, there appeared to be a place in the Vale team for an inspirational outside-right and there was one available, aged 46, languishing in Blackpool's reserves.

By then, Matthews was only being used by the Seasiders as a backup to Steve Hill on the right wing and did not appear in their first team until 30 September following an injury to his rival. Thus there was a golden opportunity for the Valiants finally to sign the Wizard of the Dribble and confirm that their outlook was very progressive. Although there was the risk that Matthews would no longer be able to cope with the physical demands of playing regular football in the Third Division, the size of the fee that Blackpool would have required for his services would very likely have paled virtually into insignificance alongside the vastly increased gate money that would almost certainly have come pouring in at the turnstiles. Indeed, so much was about to be proved, but not by Port Vale!

Having been rebuffed in his bold attempt to sign the Magician two years earlier, Norman Low did not repeat his bid. Had he been persistent during the season following his attempt, the Vale manager might well have landed his prize because Matthews was not a regular in the Blackpool side. The next campaign was probably not so conducive to such a bid because the Wizard of the Dribble often appeared on the Seasiders' right wing, but, by the start of the 1961-1962 season, the door appeared to be wide open again, not least because Matthews had a niggling knee injury.

However, the Valiants took eleven points from their six matches played from 9 to 30 September, which propelled them up to sixth place, just three points adrift of the second side. A promotion bid looked on the cards after all, but the time for securing the services of the Magician was running short. However, Low's focus was not on the ageing maestro, who returned to Blackpool's first team on 30 September because of an injury to Steve Hill and appeared in their 4-0 hammering of Chelsea. That should have alerted Vale's manager to the fact that Matthews was not a spent force, but it must have left the message that the Seasiders still required him, the more so because the Wizard of the Dribble also played in Blackpool's 3-0 defeat at Arsenal on 7 October.

Meanwhile, by 14 October, Stoke had won just three of their opening thirteen league games and were fourth from the bottom of the Second Division. Yet another battle against relegation looked on the cards and the attendance for the visit of struggling Preston North End that day fell to a mere 8,409. The *Sentinel* described the 1-1 draw as 'a sub-standard game', in which 'Stoke's performance had many flaws'. The Potters' average league crowd up to that point in the campaign was just 10,168, which compared unfavourably with Vale's average of 11,091 thus far. Therefore, the evidence still suggested that the two Potteries clubs were in the process of changing their status relative to one another.

In October, the Valiants' promotion bid went off the rails as they won only two of their eleven matches up to and including 9 December, by when they had slumped to thirteenth place. However, in the early stages of this unexpected poor run, on 18 October, there was a sensational development as Matthews signed for Stoke for a transfer fee of around £3,000. Tony Waddington had been alerted to the maestro's availability by Jackie Mudie, an ex-Blackpool team-mate and close friend of Matthews, and had had the vision to see what was possible. So, for a relatively small outlay, the City manager had struck gold, although it is doubtful whether even he had realised that the impact of his swoop would become such a phenomenon in the way that it did. Once more, Vale had been beaten to the draw by their Potteries rivals to exhibit the talents of the Wizard of the Dribble and for a second time the Valiants were left to rue their inertia, especially as the development fundamentally changed the future for both clubs.

On 28 October, Vale battled their way to a 1-1 draw at fourth from the bottom Lincoln City in front of a crowd of just 4,708. However, back in Stoke, where the excitement had been building for ten days, 35,974 people packed into the

Victoria Ground to see the return of the 46-year-old Magician over fourteen years after he had seemingly departed for ever. City's opponents that day were promotion-chasing Huddersfield Town and the unfortunate left-back who had to face the returning hero was the England international, Ray Wilson. The visitors seemed determined to keep the maestro quiet and put two, and sometimes three, men on him whenever he got the ball. Obviously, that left large gaps elsewhere and therefore, although Wilson later gained real renown as a member of England's only World Cup-wining team in 1966, he was unable to prevent Matthews inspiring the Potters to a 3-0 victory, albeit somewhat by default.

Stoke's following home match, against Walsall, drew in 24,869 fans and four more league crowds of over 20,000 were recorded at the Victoria Ground that season as the Wizard of the Dribble motivated the Potters into a revival which threatened to get them into the promotion race, although they eventually had to settle for a very respectable eighth place. In the scheme of things, the fact that City remained in the Second Division mattered little because the corner had been well and truly turned and an unstoppable force was gaining increasing impetus. Although the veteran winger could still do the business, he only made eighteen league appearances for the Potters that season, but his name had by then become much more important than his skills and so the crowds flocked to see him. The enormous increase in attendances brought a quantum leap in Stoke's income, and big money became available for the club to afford real quality players, who were attracted to play alongside the legendary Wizard of the Dribble. The first of these was the England international inside-forward, Dennis Viollet, who was bought from Manchester United for £23,500, but there were many others who followed in his footsteps.

The events at Stoke, and the huge public attention they brought to the Potters, were not at all what was required by Vale and, as the season progressed, Norman Low looked to sign a big name forward to produce a counterattraction to Matthews. Unfortunately, this was rather like trying to shut the stable door after the horse had bolted, the more so when a desperate attempt was made to sign Tom Finney, the Magician's former rival for the England outside-right spot. By then, Finney had retired from playing football and could not be persuaded to re-lace his boots. The Wales international inside-forward, Ivor Allchurch, also became a target, but nothing came of that development either and the Valiants were eventually forced to accept that they had been completely upstaged by their greatest rivals.

The 1961-1962 campaign turned out to be a disappointing one for Vale in the Third Division because they flirted with relegation before recovering to finish twelfth. However, at least they captured some of the limelight as they fought their way to the fourth round of the F.A. Cup, in which they performed heroics to draw 0-0 at Second Division Sunderland, on 27 January 1962, in front of a crowd of 49,468, despite being up against star striker Brian Clough and the "Roker Roar". The Valiants did better still in the replay four days later, beating their high-flying opponents 3-1, but were eliminated from the competition in the next round at First Division Fulham through a single goal in a match with two controversial and decisive incidents, both of which went against them.

At Stoke, the bandwagon rolled on in the 1962-1963 season, in which they completed their transformation and won the Second Division championship, which put them back in the top flight after a ten-year absence. The Potters' sustained promotion challenge led to their home crowds rocketing, to average 26,067 in the league, which brought in more money to add further high quality players to the side, especially the marvellous Northern Ireland inside-forward, Jimmy McIlroy, from Burnley for £25,000.

The Wizard of the Dribble made 31 league appearances, was once again inspirational and completed a fairytale story by scoring the goal which made City's promotion certain, in their final home game, against Luton Town, on 18 May 1963. He ran through the middle, dribbled the ball round the goalkeeper and tapped it into the net before being mobbed by his team-mates. According to the *Sentinel*, 'The crowd's standing ovation echoed and re-echoed around the ground with a din which must have been heard in nearly all the Six Towns.' For good measure, Matthews then received the FWA Footballer of the Year award for the second time, at the age of 48, in honour of his remarkable achievements that season.

Unfortunately for Vale, the same campaign proved to be a nearly year. The team were meandering about in the middle of the Third Division table when Norman Low resigned on 30 October because he was unable 'to see eye to eye with the board on their buying policy'. Even more surprisingly, Freddie Steele was brought back to try to kick-start the team's fortunes and the chairman, Joe Machin, said, 'We are sure he will take Vale back into the Second Division.' Machin was not far wrong because they came within four points of promotion, in finishing third in the Third Division, but in the event they were left in the shadow of their, by then, glorious neighbours.

Stoke found their first season (1963-1964) back in the First Division to be a struggle, although they successfully battled to avoid relegation and ended up seventeenth, with a ten-point cushion from the drop zone. Irrespective of their league position, the attendances were sensational and averaged 30,202, even though the Magician only played nine times. By then, it did not matter, though, because his job had been done. The Potters were amongst the elite and playing all the glamour clubs. Also, City had new stars for the crowds to flock to watch, not least Peter Dobing, a goalscoring inside-forward signed from Manchester City for £35,000, and a battering ram centre-forward, John Ritchie, who was destined to become Stoke's all-time top marksman. Perhaps the strongest indication of the phenomenal amount of progress the Potters had made in the 2½ years since Matthews had returned was that they finished as the runners-up in the League Cup, entirely without the services of the maestro.

Vale remained under pressure in the shadow of their illustrious neighbours and spent heavily in the summer of 1963 in a determined effort to achieve promotion. £30,000 was shelled out on the Everton and Northern Ireland outside-right, Billy Bingham, and the hard-shooting Albert Cheesebrough, from Leicester City, as the club chairman, Tom Talbot, said, 'We intend to spare no effort to put Vale on top.' Unfortunately, the money was not well spent and the new signings did not create the impact expected. Instead, Vale were only four points clear of the relegation zone in the middle of March, although a late revival saw them climb to finish twelfth. A saving grace was that once again the team had a good F.A. Cup run and put on a superb display at Liverpool, the First Division champions elect, to achieve a 0-0 draw in front of a crowd of 52,327 on 25 January 1964. The

Valiants came close to holding their high-flying opponents for a second time in the replay two days later, before losing 2-1 after extra time, and yet they gained just one point from their following seven league matches!

Overall, the 1963-1964 season proved a financial disaster for Vale, with a net loss of £42,650, largely because of a £45,567 deficit from transfer activity. The club's belated urgency to try to keep up with the Joneses (or the Matthewses) had cost them dearly. Therefore, there was little scope to improve the team for the following campaign and an almost endless series of dismal performances left the Valiants bottom of the table in the middle of February 1965. The outcome was that Freddie Steele departed 'by mutual consent' and Roy Sproson later said that, in this second spell as the Vale manager, Steele 'had not got the enthusiasm or drive as before'. Stan Matthews' former Stoke team-mate, Jackie Mudie, who had joined the Valiants in 1963, was appointed at first as the caretaker manager and then as the player-manager, but he was unable to prevent the team from ending up third from the bottom and being relegated. The last straw in one of the most disastrous campaigns in Vale's history was that the final home match, against Walsall, attracted a crowd of just 3,521.

While the Valiants were in the mire in the 1964-1965 season, Stoke consolidated their First Division status and finished a very creditable eleventh. More new heroes arrived during the campaign, especially Roy Vernon, a Wales international inside-forward, who cost £40,000 from Everton, and the goalscoring left-winger, Harry Burrows, who was signed from Aston Villa for £27,000. By then, the Wizard of the Dribble had become almost the forgotten man, having been overtaken by Stoke's fruits of his labours, but he was still able to savour the knighthood that he had been given in the 1965 New Year's Honours List. He made his final bow as a professional footballer in his one and only first-team appearance of the season, a 3-1 home victory over Fulham on 6 February, five days after his fiftieth birthday, which made him the oldest footballer ever to play in the First Division. He retired from the game at the end of the campaign, having made a grand total of 783 Football League and F.A. Cup appearances in his career, but he later regretted having finished so young!

History shows us that Stoke City were promoted to the First Division in 1963 and went on to spend fourteen years in the top flight, finishing fifth in both 1974 and 1975, on the latter occasion just four points behind the champions, Derby County. They also reached the F.A. Cup semi-finals in 1971 and 1972 and won the League Cup in the latter year to boot. However, had it not been for the visionary idea and immaculate timing of Tony Waddington in signing a 46-year-old outside-right in 1961, it is extremely doubtful that any of this would have come about. Even worse, there is a strong possibility that the Potters would have been relegated to the Third Division in the 1961-1962 season or soon afterwards. Certainly, there was a general feeling in the Potteries, shortly before the Wizard of the Dribble reappeared on the scene, that City's demise would not be long in coming. Stoke's future was looking extremely bleak before Waddington's coup.

The same force that propelled the Potters into a golden age had essentially the opposite effect at Vale as the vast majority of the football interest and therefore impetus in the Potteries was, virtually in an instant, transferred to the Victoria Ground. The Valiants' support gradually seeped away, as more fans went to watch the big names in the premier division, until their average home gate in the

1980-1981 campaign fell to just 2,738. And yet for a season or two before the return of the Magician, they had seemed poised to overtake their Potteries rivals.

Vale spent 32 years below the Second Division after they were relegated in 1957. However, had they signed the Wizard of the Dribble, as they tried to do in September 1959 and should have done later that year or in the two following ones, would they quickly have returned to the second tier and then perhaps finally been promoted to the First Division for the first time in their history, inspired by the Magician? In short, could the Valiants have achieved what Stoke did, or something similar, if only they had beaten their deadly rivals to the signature of the old man on the wing?

Suppose Norman Low had rekindled his interest in Matthews in early September 1961, approximately six weeks before Tony Waddington triumphantly signed the maestro. The Vale manager might well have done that after the side's poor start to the season and particularly after he had dropped his right-winger, Brian Jackson. Indeed, having been on the ball and made a bid for the maestro's services two years earlier, it is hard to understand why Low failed to spot the opportunity this time round when the Wizard of the Dribble could not get a sniff of first-team action at Blackpool.

Before the Magician played his big comeback match at Stoke on 28 October 1961, the team had taken only ten points from their opening fourteen league games and, had they continued to perform at that rate, they would have finished bottom of the table with thirty points and been relegated to the Third Division. However, from Matthews' comeback match until the end of the season, the Potters gained 32 points from 28 games, which propelled them well into the top half.

When Vale dropped Brian Jackson in September 1961, the team had taken four points from their opening six league matches. Had the Wizard of the Dribble then been signed and had precisely the same impact on the Valiants' fortunes as he did have on Stoke's, then the Burslem side would have gained 46 more points and ended up ninth in the table, with fifty points. Thus promotion would have been missed by a clear twelve points. Although the Third Division was generally regarded as being rougher than the Second, the quality of play was not as high and it therefore may well have been that Matthews would have had even more impact at Vale than he did at Stoke. Having said that, it is likely that, even with the Magician on board, the season would have turned out to have been a preparatory one for promotion, rather than have embraced the event itself.

Of course, it is virtually a certainty that, with the famous 46-year-old right-winger in the team, the attendances at Vale Park would have rocketed, just as they did at Stoke. The crowds did not flock in to gaze in awe at the Victoria Ground, but at the old man running down the flank of the pitch. There would not have been many people who would have been put off going to see him perform at Vale Park instead, not least because local people were less partisan then than now. As the Valiants had pulled in higher average league crowds than the Potters in the 1960-1961 campaign and the early part of the following season before Matthews' return to Stoke, it is possible that their gates would have surged even more than City's did, although it is probable that the Potters had more latent fans than Vale did.

Any way round, there would clearly have been a dramatic upsurge in attendances at Vale Park, as a result of which money would have flooded in at the turnstiles and the Valiants would have soon found themselves in a position to pay sizable transfer fees and higher wages for much better players, exactly as Stoke did. Whether footballers of the quality that the Potters were able to attract to their Second Division setup would have been willing to have dropped down to the Third Division (even for the privilege of being able to play alongside the maestro) is arguable, but it is a near certainty that Vale would have been able to have brought in significantly better players than those they already had. Better footballers on show would have attracted higher crowds still and most likely have produced improved results, which would have led to even more interest from the public, just as happened at City.

Therefore, the signing of the Wizard of the Dribble would almost certainly have produced a very similar snowball effect in Burslem to the remarkable one that took place at Stoke. Inspired by Matthews, the Potters won the Second Division championship in 1962-1963, the season after he returned and it may have been that the Valiants would have been promoted at the end of the campaign had the Magician joined them instead. As it was, in the real world, Vale finished third and only four points from taking second place and, with it, a promotion spot. With Matthews playing regularly in the team, new star signings pulling strings on the pitch and huge crowds at Vale Park baying for blood, it is difficult to believe that the Valiants could not have made up the extra four points actually required to gain promotion. Whether they could have improved so much as to have clawed back eight points and an inferior goal average to have pipped Northampton Town for the title is more arguable.

So, in the most likely course of events with the maestro at the club, Vale would have found themselves in the Second Division in 1963, with a very elderly right-winger, several other players of high quality, very strong support and real expectation in the air. It is not improbable that they would have gone forward from there as long as they could have maintained the success breeding success cycle. By then, they very probably would have been the pride of the Potteries and unchallenged by Stoke, who would likely have been languishing in the Third Division, with big financial headaches.

Because of the higher quality opposition in the second tier, the Valiants might have needed a year to adjust to the level and therefore it could well have taken them more than one campaign finally to gain promotion to the First Division, even if they had been able to maintain their impetus. However, they would have had all the ingredients in place for their upward spiral to have continued to progress and so hopes of competing in the First Division would have been far from unrealistic.

In conclusion, because Vale were attracting crowds a little higher than Stoke were prior to Matthews' return and seemingly had a slightly better team than their Potteries rivals, there is no intrinsic reason to suggest that the Valiants could not have achieved success on a similar scale as the Potters managed in actuality. Perhaps they would have had a fourteen-year stay in the top flight, twice finished fifth, twice reached the F.A. Cup semi-finals and won the League Cup as well. However, to get to the Promised Land, Stoke had only one promotion to gain, whereas Vale would have had to have achieved two and therefore their task would have been considerably harder. Also, because events unfolded the way they did in the real world, does not mean that they would do so again, or even similarly, from the same starting point if the dice were recast. Such a lack of inevitability is ensured by the butterfly effect and it could have been that, setting out to travel to Burslem six weeks before he actually did to Stoke, the Wizard of the Dribble would have tripped up getting on a train and sustained a multiple fracture of his right leg in a fluke accident. Thus Vale's future might well have ended up exactly how it has after all! In any case, sadly, for the Vale supporters, the whole conjecture about the great Sir Stanley Matthews is only a dream.

Unfortunately for the Valiants, the story does not end there. Having twice failed to get the signature of their most famous fan and once, to the immense delight of their greatest rivals, having not bothered even to try, the club were determined finally to get their man. In July 1965, soon after the Magician's retirement as a footballer, Vale's player-manager, Jackie Mudie, recommended to the club that they get his famous friend on board. Mudie said: 'Stan is the greatest name in the game. We need the sort of shot in the arm that he can give us.' On the 16th, the board swooped and, three days later, Matthews was appointed as the Valiants' general manager. He said: 'There is only one way Port Vale can get back to the top and that is by attracting and nurturing young footballers. This is the overriding policy I shall be pursuing, but the policy will need patience.'

At Stoke, Tony Waddington probably breathed a sigh of relief that the club this time had lost out to the Valiants for the services of the maestro. Had the Potters appointed Matthews to assist their manager in some capacity, the Wizard of the Dribble clearly would have been in the wings, waiting for a time when "Waddo's" star was failing. However, fortunately for Stoke, Waddington and Matthews, the scenario was avoided.

It was made clear that the Magician and Mudie would be working as a team, although Vale's versatile half-back, Terry Miles, who played under them, later said, 'Stan definitely ran the club and I'd say he ran the team as well, with advice from Jackie.' Harry Poole, the Valiants' second-longest-serving player, agreed and said, 'Although they worked together, Stan was the boss and Jackie was more or less his assistant.'

Almost immediately, the maestro started a series of trials for boys and checked out hundreds of them within a few weeks. In addition, three young Scottish players were signed in anticipation of the 1965-1966 campaign and there was a buzz of excitement and optimism around the club. The team started reasonably well and were tenth in the Fourth Division early in October, but then the limits of Matthews and Mudie as managers began to be seen as Vale won just two of their following seventeen matches, to plummet into the re-election zone. Nevertheless, young players continued to be signed and thrust into the side. Indeed, for an away game at Bradford City on 12 January 1966, all the regular forwards were dropped and replaced by five teenagers, who constituted the youngest five-man forward line ever fielded in the Football League: Alex Donald, Paul Bannister, Roddy Georgeson, Mick Cullerton and Paul Ogden. The Valiants duly lost 2-0, being 'vanquished with cruel ease', according to the *Sentinel*, and four of the debutants were in turn axed for the next game!

The team did not improve, although its average age declined until it reached twenty! By 9 April, Vale were third from the bottom and looking favourites to experience the ignominy of having to apply for re-election, but an unexpected late revival saw them rise three places to finish nineteenth, two points clear of humiliation. However, in the final match of the campaign, on 14 May at Luton Town, the Valiants were trounced 5-0, after being five goals down after 25 minutes, in the absence of the Magician, who had left for a six-week tour of South Africa!

There was something of an improvement in the 1966-1967 season and Vale flirted with a promotion challenge on occasions, but ended up thirteenth, with only four more points than they had managed the previous campaign. Unfortunately, their average league attendance fell from 6,015 to 5,114 and the degree of interest in the first team was well illustrated by the fact that a bigger crowd turned out to watch the youth side play in the quarter-finals of the F.A.'s national cup competition on 6 March 1967 than attended any of Vale's Football League games that season!

On 11 May, Jackie Mudie resigned for 'personal reasons', although Matthews later said it was because 'he'd had enough of it'. The Wizard of the Dribble was therefore left to struggle on alone. Now in complete control of the playing side of the club, the buck clearly stopped with the maestro. One of the first decisions he needed to take was which players to release at the end of the season and amongst them was a fifteen-year-old striker named Ray Kennedy. Matthews described him as being 'very awkward and slow', but Kennedy went on to make 428 Football League appearances for Arsenal and Liverpool and was capped seventeen times by England! Although it is extremely unlikely that Kennedy alone in due course could have transformed Vale's fortunes on the pitch, he might well have brought in a fair fee to help alleviate the club's perennial financial problems.

The 1967-1968 campaign that followed turned out to be a disaster and the Valiants were rock bottom of the Football League after their opening seven matches had yielded no wins and just two points. Although the team won all of their following four home games, scoring four goals each time, their efforts proved to be brief flashes in the pan. The position became so difficult that the Magician resorted to bringing in experienced players to supplement the still somewhat youthful ranks, but, in February 1968, an absolute bombshell broke.

A Football Association/Football League Joint Inquiry, on the 20th, into alleged breaches of the rules on payments to players, found Vale guilty and their officials were 'severely censured' for their 'gross negligence'. The club were fined £2,000 by the F.A. and the same sum by the Football League, but, far more importantly, the latter expelled the Valiants from the competition at the end of the season, although they were allowed to apply for readmission.

The following month, Vale elected a new chairman, Arthur McPherson, who then stated that the club's primary objective was to gain promotion from the Fourth Division and the youth policy was consequently sidelined. Although the services of the Wizard of the Dribble were to be retained as the general manager, to look after the youngsters and the club's administration, it was decided to advertise for a player-manager to handle first-team affairs. The writing was clearly on the wall for Matthews.

The position was so desperate that the Valiants needed to win their final game, at Lincoln City, on 11 May, to be sure of avoiding a re-election as well as a readmission plea to the Football League. As it turned out, they won 1-0 and finished seventh from the bottom.

At the end of the month, the club appointed Shrewsbury Town's player-coach, Gordon Lee, as their new team manager and, on 8 June, they were readmitted to the league by 39 votes to 9. All that was needed to end a very sorry chapter in Vale's history was to decide on the future of the Magician. It was agreed that he would thenceforth spend most of his time looking for new players and that he would only visit the ground two or three times a week. Having effectively been demoted to a scout, Matthews' name was removed from his office door and he drifted out of the picture, still owed £9,000 in salary and expenses, which he had not drawn because of the financial problems of the club.

The Wizard of the Dribble later said: 'Managing Vale was a terrible job. I didn't bother about the first team so much because I was travelling round to get the best kids we could, which gave us a very good youth team, but Vale didn't have the patience to see it through.'

Roy Sproson had a different view: 'The club had their priorities wrong and the first team suffered badly, whilst Stan trusted people, who took advantage of him.'

It became obvious in Matthews' spell as Vale's general manager that he was no master tactician, which was proven by the team's poor performances and lack of achievements under his guidance. Therefore, it can be argued that the Valiants made a serious mistake by appointing him. Indeed, it could be said that the whole problem was created by the board of directors, who employed as their general manager an ex-player with no experience of football management, allowed him to neglect the first team, enthusiastically endorsed his youth policy and then scrapped it when they prematurely ran out of patience with it. As Crewe Alexandra later proved, a system based on youth has to be a long-term proposition to be successful.

However, would Vale have done any better had they not appointed the maestro? Undoubtedly they would have continued with Jackie Mudie as their player-manager, at least for a while, because he had only been confirmed in his post 4½ months before Matthews arrived. Mudie had begun well, with the team gaining thirteen points from his fourteen league games in charge to the end of the dreadful 1964-1965 season. Although, in the event, his efforts did not save the Valiants from relegation, they compared very favourably with those of the old master, Freddie Steele, whose 32 league matches as the manager had yielded just 19 points. Unfortunately, though, Vale fared worse in a lower division the following campaign once the Magician had joined Mudie at the helm. It is therefore more than possible that the latter would have achieved better results without his mentor and this is indicated by Harry Poole's comment that, 'Jackie had more knowledge of football than Stan, who didn't know a lot about management.'

As Mudie was in his post so briefly before Matthews arrived, it is very difficult to speculate how he might have performed on his own, but it is exceedingly unlikely that he would have turned the poor 1965-1966 side into a promotion outfit. Another 17 points and a vastly better goal average would have been required for the Valiants to have finished fourth that season. The following year, Vale ended up fifteen points and goal average adrift of promotion, so again Mudie would have had a big task on his hands to have bridged that gap, although, of course, he might have brought in better new players on his own than he and Matthews did together.

The one and only campaign in which the maestro was in charge on his own (1967-1968) ended up a disaster, with the club being expelled from the Football League and the team finishing with only 39 points in the Fourth Division. Therefore Vale's new manager, Gordon Lee, inherited a very weak side from Matthews and yet he got the Valiants promoted in only his second season in charge. Lee had a knack of keeping things simple and getting the basics right, and not every manager can do that. Indeed, it has been argued that such achievements were beyond the capabilities of the Magician.

So, in summary, with regard to the Wizard of the Dribble, Vale produced a masterclass of how always to be in the wrong place at the wrong time. They failed get the signature of Matthews when he supported them, gave up thirty years later at the first sign of a refusal, allowed their greatest rivals to snatch him from under their noses two years afterwards and, finally, appointed him to a job for which he had no experience. It is therefore difficult to describe the club's performance in relation to the Magician as anything other than inept. Had the Valiants been on the ball on just one of the key occasions, it would have been all the better for them and their future. However, they managed each time to snatch defeat from the jaws of victory, for which their Potteries rivals owe them a great debt of gratitude, whether they know it or not. Indeed, it is quite conceivable that, had the Valiants played their cards right, they, and not Stoke, could have been the top team in the Potteries today. If only Vale could have secured the sublime skills of Stanley as a footballer and not as a manager!

11 John The Baptist

Sir Stanley Matthews and Gordon Lee were like chalk and cheese. Whilst the "Wizard of the Dribble" had conquered the world as a wonderful winger, Lee had plied his trade as a journeyman full-back with Girton Road Gasworks, Hednesford Town, Aston Villa and Shrewsbury Town. Although the "Villans" today are a big club in the Premier League, they were relegated to the Second Division in the 1958-1959 campaign, in which Lee made his first-team debut for them. Indeed, he was employed mainly as a reserve by Villa during his eleven seasons at the club and in total made only 118 Football League appearances for them. The highlight of his playing career was the League Cup winner's medal he received in 1961 for being a member of the triumphant Villa sides which won the two-legged inaugural final.

Whilst the "Magician" was knighted and became Vale's general manager in a fanfare, Lee unassumingly became Shrewsbury's trainer-coach. Also, while Matthews was tarnishing his reputation at Vale, not least through being associated with the illegal player payments scandal, Lee was quietly building up a reputation as a manager of men.

During the maestro's managerial reign at Vale, rarely did the players seem to gel into a team despite the fact that they had some very good individual footballers, not least Harry Poole, John Rowland, Mick Cullerton, Roy Chapman and John Green. Tactics appeared to be at a premium and the outmoded 2-3-5 formation was regularly resorted to.

However, when Lee arrived at Vale Park at the end of May 1968, things rapidly changed. He was described by the chairman, Arthur McPherson, as 'young, full of enthusiasm and typical of the modern track-suited manager'.

Things were in such a sorry state at Vale by then that even the evergreen Roy Sproson was ready to leave, but Lee persuaded him to stay. Sproson later said of the new manager: 'He was a great person to work for. He was as straight as a die, but rather cautious and predictable.'

Lee made his general approach clear when he said, 'We must all work together as a team.' He based the training on fitness and 'the type of situations that can occur during a match' and there seemed to be more determination about the side when they started the new (1968-1969) season. Centre-forward Roy Chapman scored eight goals in his first twelve appearances, but the Valiants lost four of their opening six league matches and sank to the bottom of the table in the middle of September. By then, though, Lee was beginning to steer the ship in new directions, with more emphasis on preventing the opponents from scoring, and a steady revival followed, so that the team finished the campaign thirteenth in the league, with 46 points from the same number of games and an identical number of goals scored and conceded. Thus, at his first attempt, Lee had stabilised the club's playing fortunes.

In the close season, Lee released four experienced forwards, but was only able to replace them with four others signed on free transfers because the club were in financial difficulties as usual. However, the new campaign proved to be a revelation as the team produced a new club record eighteen-league match unbeaten run from the start of the season and remained undefeated until the second half of November, with just six goals being conceded in the opening fifteen games! The manager gave a simple explanation of the success of his starless wonders: 'The secret formula is just fitness and teamwork.' Although Vale lost four consecutive league away matches in the middle of the winter, they recovered strongly to ease their way to promotion in fourth place, with 59 points and only 33 goals conceded. Lee then hit the nail on the head when he said, 'No team could have deserved reward as much for their hard work and strength of character.'

Roy Sproson's view was that, 'There were better teams than us who did not go up, but they lacked the team spirit which we had.' However, team spirit alone can only succeed to an extent and, because the club had managed to record a loss on the campaign (of £3,003), Lee was not given any transfer funds to strengthen the side for the 1970-1971 season. Therefore, not surprisingly, Vale struggled to retain their new-found status and ended up seventeenth, just three points above the relegation zone.

Although for the first time since 1963, the club made a profit on the season (£3,424), the overall deficit of £134,640 meant that, as usual, the manager had little money with which to improve the team for the following campaign. However, the Valiants generally performed better than they had the year before and were comfortable in midtable for most of the season. However, the size of the difficulties that Lee was operating under was revealed only too clearly on 4 March 1972 when just 2,809 spectators turned up to see Vale beat Mansfield Town 1-0 at home. The same day, a crowd of 100,000 watched their arch rivals, Stoke City, beat Chelsea 2-1 at Wembley to win the League Cup, their first major trophy in their history. There was no doubt about who the football beggars in the Potteries were! Nevertheless, the Valiants finished the season fifteenth in the Third Division, with 41 points, five clear of the relegation zone. Unfortunately, the future looked bleak because the average league home attendance had dropped to just 4,366 and the total debt was still £100,130. Even worse, Lee's team of battlers were in no way a counterattraction for the public of the Potteries to Tony Waddington's wonders on show at the Victoria Ground. How they could close the gap on their illustrious rivals was a 64-thousand dollar question that no-one (until John Rudge arrived) was able to answer.

In July 1972, to try to improve their position, Vale splashed out £3,000 and the proceeds of a friendly game for the services of Stafford Rangers' skilful striker, Ray Williams. Although he scored only three times in his first 29 appearances, the Valiants made a serious bid for promotion in the 1972-1973 campaign, not least by generally playing more open football than they had done previously under Lee. In spite of several thrashings which resulted (7-0 at Rotherham United, 4-0 at Bournemouth, 5-0 at Brentford and 5-0 at Southend United), Vale were still in contention for promotion on Easter Monday when they played at home to the already-crowned champions, Bolton Wanderers, in front of a bumper crowd of 14,168. Unfortunately, they let a 2-0 lead slip, to draw 2-2, and ended the season in sixth place, four points and an inferior goal average short of going up.

Although a £14,304 profit had been made on the campaign, the total debt remained stubbornly over £100,000 (including loans owed to the directors) and, in August, striker Sammy Morgan was sold to Aston Villa for £22,222, plus an extra £5,400 through a goalscoring clause, which made a clear statement about the limits of the Valiants' ambitions. With money being tight, no new signings were made for the 1973-1974 season and, by 22 December, after a run of just two victories in seventeen league games, the team were seventh from the bottom and only three points clear of the drop zone. Three weeks later, they remained in the same position, but then, on 13 January 1974, Gordon Lee was appointed as the new manager of Blackburn Rovers. Mark Singer, the Vale chairman, said, 'He has done a wonderful job with little or no money.'

Lee went on to altogether finer things after he had left the Valiants. He led Blackburn Rovers to the Third Division championship in 1975, Newcastle United to the final of the League Cup in 1976 and Everton to the final of the same competition in 1977 and the semi-finals of the F.A. Cup in 1977 and 1980. He also managed Preston North End, became the coach of KR, of Iceland, and then the assistant manager and caretaker manager of Leicester City.

Two questions that can be asked are whether the Valiants could have kept Lee with them and if they could have gone on to greater things with him at the helm. In the cold light of day, neither possibility seems very likely. Lee would clearly have realised that Vale's prospects were extremely limited, because of their small crowds and high debt, and he would therefore have been on a loser to have remained any longer. Realistically, as it turned out, the only way for the Valiants, with their infrastructure, was down. It would have made no sense for Lee to have been in charge when relegation happened, even if he had succeeded in postponing the almost inevitable. Blackburn Rovers were obviously a much better stepping stone for a football manager than were Port Vale and had an average league home crowd of 7,432 in the 1973-1974 season, as compared with the Valiants' 3,959, so Lee moved on.

Roy Sproson took over as the caretaker manager and was appointed permanently to the post in April 1974. Straightaway he announced a radical change in policy by stating, 'Gordon Lee was quite happy with a point a game to play safe, but I believe in trying to entertain the public.' Thus Sproson boldly entered new attacking territory, at least in theory, although the side scored only 23 goals in his 21 matches in charge to the end of the campaign, compared with the 35 they had already netted in 30 games under Lee. Also, 26 goals were conceded with Sproson at the helm, compared with 40 when Lee had been the boss. Therefore, in spite of his proclamation, the matches actually became tighter under the new boss.

Considering Sproson's inexperience as a manager, the team fared reasonably well during the rest of the season and gained twenty points from their remaining 21 games, which was actually a slight improvement on what they had achieved under Lee (22 points in 25 matches). Although, in the event, they finished fifth from the bottom, they were seven points clear of the relegation zone and only the same number of points adrift of eighth place.

The manager promised that there would be a new-look attacking style, with more width, in the 1974-1975 campaign and confidently predicted, 'I think we will do very well.' Although only two of the opening eleven league games were won, a strong revival took the team to second place by the end of December. Early in the new year, 1975, all the players were taken to Benidorm, in Spain, for a four-day break, but the side fell apart on their return and failed to win any of their following six league matches! By 8 March, Vale had had seven players sent off and their atrocious disciplinary record did not help their ailing prospects of going up. However, five victories in March put them back in contention, but just two wins in their final eight games meant they finished sixth, four points short of the third promotion place.

Unfortunately, for the next five years it was all downhill, as Vale's league position worsened each season! The catalyst for the decline in their fortunes was a difficult financial situation. A £16,964 loss had been made on the 1974-1975 campaign, which forced drastic cuts, with seven players being given free transfers and only thirteen being retained! However, £7,000 was spent on bringing the skilful forward, Mick Cullerton, back from Stafford Rangers and signing Stoke's defender-midfielder Terry Lees. The idea seemed to be to secure quality instead of quantity, but a seven-match unbeaten run in the league from the start of the season was followed by six games without a win. Although the team's performances remained inconsistent, they were on the fringes of the promotion race on 9 March 1976 when Brian Horton, the midfield dynamo, was sold to Brighton & Hove Albion for £30,000 because Vale were losing £400 a week. Roy Sproson said, 'It will be difficult to replace a player of his calibre,' and so it proved because the Valiants won only two of their remaining eleven matches and finished twelfth in the table.

It might be argued that Vale could have been promoted if only they had not transferred Horton at that moment. However, because of their financial situation, they were not in a position to turn down a cheque of the size that they were offered, especially as promotion was only an outside possibility. At the time, the team had accumulated 37 points from 35 games, which meant that they would have had to have gained nineteen points (assuming a superior goal average) from their final eleven matches to have pinched third place from Millwall. In that light, the directors seemingly made the right move, although, at the time of the Horton transfer, the "Lions" were actually two positions below Vale in the table, with a point less and a game in hand, and therefore proved that the task was not impossible.

Although the season ended in disappointment, with an average league crowd of only 4,133 it was no wonder that the Valiants were a selling club and, without Horton's transfer, yet another loss (of £5,181) would have resulted. As a sign of the times, just two free-transfer players were added to the squad for the 1976-1977 campaign and Terry Lees was sold to Sparta Rotterdam, of the Netherlands, for £25,000 on the opening day of the season. Therefore, the prospects did not seem too hopeful and the team performed much to expectations, winning just three of their opening 21 league games, despite £12,000 being spent on a new striker, Ken Beamish, from Blackburn Rovers. By the end of the year, Vale had sunk into the relegation zone, but there was then an unexpected revival of form, with the team losing just two of their next eleven league games and fighting their way into the fifth round of the F.A. Cup, from which they were despatched 3-0 by First Division Aston Villa, in front of a crowd of 46,872 on 26 February 1977. Although the Valiants lost half their final fourteen league matches, they struggled over the safety line and finished sixth from the bottom, just three points above the relegation zone.

Unfortunately, the club did not, or were not able to, heed the warning signs of what would probably happen the following year if the side was not strengthened in the close season. A loss of £5,959 on the 1976-1977 campaign and a total debt of £123,863 meant that only three free-transfer players were added to the ranks in the close season and Roy Sproson was told that his job as the manager would be reviewed after fifteen games. On 17 October 1977, when that time had elapsed, Vale were third from the bottom of the division and Sproson was duly sacked. He said: 'My bags have been packed for three years. That's how it is in this job,' and he took the name plate off his office door to 'spare someone else the bother'!

The club appointed ex-Bury boss Bobby Smith as their new manager on 18 November and his assistant, Dennis Butler, confidently pronounced, 'We aim to make Port Vale a force to be reckoned with.' However, the team continued a fourteen-league-match winless run, which lasted until New Year's Eve and left them fourth from the bottom. A phenomenal new income then appeared through the "Vale Lottery", which financed a spending spree on new players, but to no avail as far as the outcome of the season was concerned. Nevertheless, despite winning just two games out of fourteen from 11 February 1978, with four matches remaining it looked as though the Valiants might well save themselves from relegation. However, all four ended in defeat and the team finished fourth from the bottom, three points and goal difference short of safety. The club had returned to where it had been before Gordon Lee had started knocking it back into shape almost ten years earlier.

Hardly had the campaign ended than Bobby Smith departed to become the manager of Swindon Town, but at least the Valiants received £10,500 in compensation for their loss. Dennis Butler declined to join him there in favour of becoming his successor at Vale.

Before the start of the 1978-1979 season, the new manager spent £9,000 on a striker, burly Bernie Wright, from Bradford City and then splashed out a new club record £37,000 on Ken Todd, a busy midfielder from Wolverhampton Wanderers, who had made just four Football League appearances! Although the side made a promising start, losing only one of their opening six league games, Butler decided that the squad needed overhauling and, in just over a month, sold four forwards (Terry Bailey, Mick Moore, John Froggatt and Ken Beamish) for a total of £47,000. They were replaced by a right-back, Gerry Keenan, who cost £15,000 from Bury. In October, Butler bought a midfielder, Felix Healy, and a left-winger, Kevin Tully, for a total of £16,000 and transferred midfielder-defender John Ridley to Leicester City for a then club record fee of £55,000.

Not surprisingly, with all the upheaval, the team's results became erratic and, by the end of October, Vale were just a single point clear of the re-election zone. However, Butler had not finished there and the following month bought another outside-left, Andy Proudlove, for £1,000, from Buxton, and then paid Bury a new club record £40,000 for the services of midfielder Peter Farrell.

In December, the manager again lost patience with the side's performances and bought the Chester central defender, Bob Delgado, for £30,000, although half the fee was recouped by the sale of right-winger Peter Sutcliffe to the same club. In an unprecedented whirlwind of transfer activity in less than four months, almost £250,000 had changed hands, at a deficit to Vale, and therefore it was not the happiest of parties that returned from a 6-2 thrashing at Barnsley on Boxing Day!

Butler was still not entirely happy with the team and the players he had at his disposal, but he managed to control his urge to spend any more money. Nevertheless, the Valiants' performances did not improve and, not surprisingly, the supporters became increasingly frustrated and critical of the side. Incredibly, in the middle of March, the manager responded by calling the fans 'a bunch of yobbos'! Inevitably, a series of angry letters then appeared in the *Sentinel*. In the midst of the turmoil around them, the team stuttered on to the end of the campaign and finished sixteenth, but only five points clear of the re-election zone. Chris Harper, of the *Sentinel*, said the season had 'largely been one long toothache', but things were about to get worse!

The club's efforts had not impressed the supporters and the average league home attendance had slumped to just 3,287, Vale's lowest, out of wartime, since they had been in the North Staffordshire Federation League in 1907-1908! Therefore, it was not surprising that the campaign had proved a financial disaster, with a new club record £52,000 loss, despite the commercial department having raised an amazing £225,000. Butler's player deals, to fund an unsuccessful team, had resulted in a £36,000 transfer deficit and the overall debt had rocketed to £187,000.

Under the financial circumstances and with few saleable assets on the pitch, the manager was only able to sign three free-transfer players for the 1979-1980 season to replace the four who had been shown the door at the end of the previous campaign. Nevertheless, the vice-chairman, Jack Burgess, confidently predicted, 'I believe we should be capable of finishing in the top four.' Hardly had he spoken than the team reeled off six straight defeats from the start of the campaign, including four in the league, which put them firmly at the bottom of the table. The result was that Butler left by mutual consent and Alan Bloor, the youth team boss, became the caretaker manager.

Although an improvement followed under the new boss, Vale were trounced 7-1 at Huddersfield Town on 22 September. Four days later, Bloor's appointment was made permanent! Occasional positive performances pierced the gloom, but the Valiants were trounced 5-1 at York City on 1 December and sank to third from the bottom of the division. The result was that Bloor resigned, saying, 'I do not have what it takes.' Defender Bill Bentley was then put in temporary charge of the team.

The club first offered the vacant manager's post to their ex-star player, and by then experienced manager, Ronnie Allen, but he wisely turned it down. Then Burnley's 35-year-old midfielder, Peter Noble, was approached to become the player-manager, but he also declined the job. Finally, just before Christmas, Vale tried John McGrath, Southampton's 41-year-old reserve team coach, who had applied for the post. Although he held only a minor job and had no managerial experience, he had been strongly recommended to the Valiants' chairman, Arthur McPherson, by a number of First Division managers. So Vale took a chance and, on 22 December, McGrath was persuaded to become the new boss, mainly because he had ambitions to become a manager and it was a big promotion from the job he was doing. Also, the location of Burslem enabled him to return to his Manchester roots. Although McGrath had been a favourite at Newcastle United and Southampton as an uncompromising defender, he was hardly a big enough name to generate real interest amongst the Vale fans, but that was the amount of pulling power that the Valiants had by then.

The new manager proved to be something of a showman and fully realised the value of publicity, so he talked up the club right from the off. On arriving at Vale Park, he said to the media, 'The potential here is tremendous – that is why I took the job.' However, he made his intentions clear to the players, by saying, 'I am looking for total dedication and a hundred per cent effort because without it quality does not mean anything.' He first and foremost intended to fashion a side after his own legacy and it was obvious that there were going to be big changes.

McGrath needed a coach and second in command, and, probably rightly, did not think that appointing anyone from within the sinking ship would be a good idea. His choice fell on John Rudge, an ex-journeyman striker, who was at that time the coach at Torquay United. Although it then remained to be seen, the two Johns constituted a formidable partnership which transformed the Valiants' fortunes.

When McGrath and Rudge arrived at Vale, the club was virtually a laughing stock. The latter later said: 'The place was dead, but we came here full of enthusiasm to try to get a bit of life into it. John was good at beating the drum, so we went to factories to try to generate a bit of interest and we painted the dressing rooms because they were like railway stations.'

McGrath's first game in charge was at home to Scunthorpe United on Boxing Day and was won 1-0. However, the following two matches, which were also at Vale Park, yielded just one point and the new manager had seen enough. He said: 'The trouble with this club is that people are undisciplined. The players are their own worst enemies, but the holiday is over!' Within a fortnight of taking control, McGrath had imposed two fines and very quickly decided which players he wanted to keep. He split them off from those he wanted to jettison and told Rudge to train the latter group separately!

The team took five points from their first six games under McGrath, but the manager was not happy. Consequently, in early February 1980, he signed three new young players and made fifteen existing ones available for sale, saying, 'I want players to show more pride and passion for the club.' McGrath increasingly turned to youth, but, with two matches to play, the Valiants were still fourth from the bottom, a point adrift of safety. Against the odds, both were won and the team moved up a place to avoid a re-election plea by a whisker as a result of having scored more goals than Hereford United, with both clubs having gained 36 points.

The manager's first task had been accomplished, although only just. However, under his direction, Vale had gained 21 points from 23 league games, compared with the 15 that they had accumulated before he had arrived. Therefore, he had had a positive impact on their fortunes despite having inherited a very poor side. For once, it seemed as though the board had got their choice of manager right.

At the end of the season, McGrath not surprisingly had a clear out of unwanted footballers, but his efforts to improve the team were hampered by an even worse than usual financial situation. The club had recorded a loss of £82,069 on the campaign and so the manager was able to bring in just two free-transfer players for the 1980-1981 season ahead. Not surprisingly, it proved to be a struggle, with pitifully poor crowds witnessing a series of substandard performances, and, by the turn of the year, Vale were third from the bottom, two points adrift of safety. Then came complete humiliation on 6 January 1981 when the team were dumped out of the F.A. Cup, by being beaten 3-0 at Enfield, of the Isthmian League, in a third round replay. Chris Harper, of the *Sentinel*, wrote that it was 'the night Vale died in shame'.

However, things simply got worse and the Valiants lost their following three league matches, conceding eleven goals in the process. By 31 January, they were rock bottom of the division, five points inside the re-election zone, and, two days later, the board convened a crisis meeting. Notwithstanding the lack of funds at McGrath's disposal to bring about an improvement, the situation was such that the directors might have parted company with their manager at that point, but, fortunately, they decided to stick with him, perhaps not least because of the lack of money to pay him compensation. Thus the impending McGrath-Rudge revolution came about when it so easily may never have happened. Nevertheless, the chairman, Don Ratcliffe, said, 'We are in a crisis and it calls for speedy action.'

Three days later, the manager was given the money to sign two new players on free transfers: Terry Armstrong, a solid midfielder from Huddersfield Town, and Andy Higgins, a towering central defender from Chesterfield. Neither seemed likely to set the world on fire, but their inclusion (the latter sparingly) had the desired effect of making Vale harder to beat. Then a new goalkeeper, Brian Lloyd, was signed on loan from Wrexham and he proved to be a revelation. Consequently, the team improved and unexpectedly gained 19 points from their final 17 games to finish sixth from the bottom and three points clear of the re-election zone. The manager's assessment was that, 'It has taken time, but the attitude is slowly changing.' The fans were not so sure because the average crowd slumped to 2,738, Vale's lowest ever in the Football League since regular records began!

At the end of the campaign, McGrath further overhauled the squad, handing out six free transfers and selling midfielder Kenny Beech to Walsall for £10,000. In spite of a £12,496 loss, the manager was given money to try to improve the team's fortunes and wisely spent £27,000 in total on the Crewe Alexandra busy midfielder, Geoff Hunter, and Chesterfield's experienced striker, Ernie Moss, as well as signing the ex-Stoke City favourite forward, Jimmy Greenhoff.

With a better side on the pitch, the Valiants won half of their eight opening league games of the 1981-1982 season and moved up to seventh place at the beginning of October. An unbeaten fifteen-match run from 7 November 1981 to 19 February 1982 kept them well in contention for promotion, six points adrift of the target zone, with a win by then being rewarded with three points. Unfortunately, the rest of the campaign was an anticlimax, as only six more victories were gained in Vale's final eighteen games, which meant that they finished seventh, but eighteen points adrift of the promotion places. Nevertheless, the team's fortunes had been turned around, with the achievement of a very respectable league position after the shambolic seasons that had gone before, and pride had been restored at the club. Despite that, McGrath was still unhappy with many of the players at his disposal, so he released eight of them on free transfers.

Although the average league gate had risen by 33 percent, to 3,639, the campaign had proved to be a financial disaster, with a loss of £65,000 being recorded, which had had the effect of increasing the overdraft to a very worrying £235,452. The cost of remaining in the same division with ease had been astronomic and therefore the future looked bleak. Consequently, the manager was left to try to mastermind a promotion challenge with the addition of only four free-transfer players.

As it turned out, financial salvation was just around the corner because, in August 1982, Stoke City paid an astonishing £180,000 fee for Vale's exciting winger, Mark Chamberlain, and their promising goalkeeper, Mark Harrison. Although this initially disrupted McGrath's plans for the team, it enabled him to pay Hartlepool United £15,000 for the services of Bob Newton, a bustling striker, who proved to be a revelation. His addition meant that Chamberlain's brother, Neville, a striker, became surplus to requirements and he was also transferred to the Potters, for £40,000.

After gaining only two points from their opening three matches of the 1982-1983 season, Vale got into their stride and took 25 points from their following ten games to move into third place. By the end of January 1983, the Valiants were second and McGrath was rewarded with a new two-year contract. Indeed, his ability to build a promotion-chasing team from very profitable transfer dealings was not surprisingly considered to be a marvellous feat. The manager was able to celebrate even more loudly on 26 February when the team beat Halifax Town 2-1 at home to hit the top of the table and it seemed that they had timed their run to perfection.

Unfortunately, they then only picked up two points from their next three matches, which prompted McGrath to buy another striker, Jim Steel, from Wrexham for £10,000. Ernie Moss was axed to make way for the new man and then sold to Lincoln City for £1,500, but for once the manager had made a mistake in his deals. Moss had been a mainstay of the table-topping side and had scored a goal every three games during his time at Vale. Steel was to manage just three in thirteen appearances to the end of the campaign and only seven in thirty in total in his brief stay in Burslem. Nevertheless, a haul of 23 points from the final thirteen matches secured third place for the Valiants and with it promotion to the Third Division. In less than 3½ years, McGrath had transformed the team and given the supporters a side to be proud of. It was an impressive achievement. Remarkably and entirely unexpectedly, little after that went right for the manager at Vale.

The average league crowd had increased impressively again, by 32 per cent, to 4,806, which helped to generate a then club record profit of £100,888, although, of course, the main reason was because of the manager's astute transfer dealings. In June, McGrath appeared to have made another fine signing when he paid Wigan Athletic £10,000 for their sharp forward, Eamon O'Keefe, who was a Republic of Ireland international. In anticipation of an exciting campaign ahead, season ticket sales increased by sixty per cent to reach a then club record level.

However, behind the scenes all was not well, as several players refused to sign new contracts and the problem seemed to be a discrepancy in the terms offered. Unfortunately, at the start of the 1983-1984 campaign, four players remained in dispute with the club, but McGrath said, 'If we bend any more the tree will snap.' It was thus an unhappy club that faced the challenge of the Third Division. The difficulties were exacerbated by the manager deciding to switch to a more attacking style, which did not seem to suit the strengths of the players, and he put O'Keefe in midfield, much to the Irishman's dissatisfaction. Not surprisingly, only one victory was obtained in the opening four league matches and that was followed by an all-time club record eighteen games without a win, which lasted until after Boxing Day. Staggeringly, during that period, just two points were gained from fifteen league matches, which dumped the Valiants firmly at the bottom of the table, a stunning thirteen points adrift of safety.

Unfortunately, along the way, the manager committed a transfer blunder by signing Martin Henderson, a striker with good technique, from Chesterfield, in exchange for the effervescent Bob Newton and £8,000. The latter had hit 24 goals in 51 games with Vale, but Henderson managed only seven in 28 appearances before he disappeared from the club without notice after the end of the season! Thus McGrath had dispensed with his two powerful strikers, who had been instrumental in the team's success the previous campaign, and, during the disastrous eighteen-match run, just ten goals were scored.

In November 1983, the chairman, Jim Lloyd, blocked the manager's attempt to sign a new defender, which led to McGrath saying to the *Sentinel*, 'I sometimes wonder whether the club has the necessary ambition.' Lloyd retorted, 'I would feel much happier if he put his full effort into the field of play instead of the irresponsible statements in the media.' Clearly the race had not much longer to run. Remarkably, though, the manager lasted a further game after a debacle at Burnley on 26 November when the Valiants were annihilated 7-0! Finally, on 6 December, McGrath received a letter from the club suspending him on full pay and he left permanently following an amicable financial settlement.

Thus departed the larger-than-life John McGrath, who had done so much to breathe new life into a club on its knees, only to fall by the wayside shortly after his greatest triumph. Although he left behind a team destined for the drop, the infrastructure of the club was a lot stronger than it had been before he had arrived and so not all of his good work had been undone. He went on to manage Chester City, Preston North End and Halifax Town before becoming a much in demand after-dinner speaker. Sadly, he died at his home in Manchester on Christmas Day 1998, aged just sixty.

The rise and fall of the mercurial manager is a story in itself and an intriguing one at that. In addition, a number of questions can be asked about whether aspects of his connection (or otherwise) to Vale could have turned out differently.

To start with, McGrath was neither the first choice as the Valiants' manager in 1979, nor the second. Had Ronnie Allen or Peter Noble accepted the challenge, there would have been no McGrath era at Vale, nor is it remotely likely that John Rudge would ever have been employed by the club.

The directors made a sensible move by initially contacting the very man who had been instrumental in denying them an F.A. Cup final appearance in 1954 because by then Ronnie Allen had a wealth of managerial experience, in England and overseas, and had guided several of his teams to trophies and various other successes. However, with his pedigree, struggling Vale cannot have been an attractive option to him. Nevertheless, had he felt an unbending urge to devote himself to a most charitable cause in Burslem, there would have been no McGrath or Rudge. Whether Allen would in the event have been a positive force at Vale obviously will never be known, but it may have been that, at the tail-end of his career, he would not have been able, or even willing, to have committed the sheer energy that McGrath did, to get the club moving again.

On the face of it, the club's approach to Peter Noble does not seem to have been badly conceived either. Although he had none of Allen's vast experience, the energetic Noble, at 35, seemed a good prospect as a player-manager. However, he wanted to continue playing and did so until 1983. He never became a Football League club manager, but did have the drive and acumen to start up and run a sports shop in Burnley for twenty years, so perhaps he would have been a success in the hot seat at Vale.

Having twice been rejected, the board at Burslem plumped for John McGrath as their new manager. Because he had no previous managerial experience, the club were taking a big risk in appointing him, but, as it turned out, their gamble paid off handsomely. After having employed a series of mediocre and ineffective managers after Gordon Lee had departed, the law of averages alone indicated that Vale were due to appoint a good one! Had they failed to do so this time, it is obvious that a Football League re-election plea would almost certainly have been just around the corner. Indeed, the Valiants were in such a state at the end of 1979 that it is possible they could have become another Bradford Park Avenue and been engaged in a perennial struggle to avoid being voted out of the league. Their already limited support was ebbing away and the club had probably reached a decisive point in its history. Without McGrath to shake things up and get the show back on the road, so ably assisted by John Rudge, Vale may have failed to gain re-election, like Park Avenue in 1970, Barrow in 1972, Workington in 1977 and Southport in 1978. Notably, none of those clubs have ever regained their Football League status!

Once the Valiants had made McGrath the management offer, there does not seem to have been any real reason why he would have turned the post down. Indeed, as a mere reserve-team coach suddenly being offered the job as the main man, it would have been bordering on foolhardy for him not to have seized the opportunity. The main stumbling block might have been if he had had a sentimental attachment to Southampton, but his aim was eventually to become a Football League club manager and so the offer to do so immediately, and within range of his Manchester roots, not surprisingly proved irresistible to him.

So McGrath arrived in Burslem to a baptism of fire, but he took the bull by the horns, survived the ordeal, transformed the club's fortunes and laid the ground for a greater man still, a messiah who came after him. For many a while, it appeared as though McGrath was the saviour himself and, in a way, perhaps he was because he was at the helm when the club's fortunes were at their lowest level, but he did the really hard work and steered Vale to much safer waters before he was axed.

As McGrath was so successful in resurrecting Vale in just three years or so, why was it that things went so badly wrong for him after his greatest success in a much shorter space of time still and could his downfall have been avoided? The first point to make is that it is well known that the sack is always but a step away for a football manager in a notoriously very short-term occupation. In such a competitive situation, where there have to be winners and losers, it is inconceivable that any manager can keep the balls in the air indefinitely. A monumental triumph is quickly forgotten when a corner is turned and the going gets tough, so perhaps there should be no inquest on McGrath because he lasted longer at Vale than most managers at English professional clubs do and he had more success than the majority.

Having said that, his fall from grace, from a pinnacle, was so rapid that it is difficult not to think it should have been avoided. Three main factors seem to have come into play and, had at least one of them have been evaded, McGrath might well have had a chance of continuing as the club's manager – at least for a little longer.

Firstly, before success was achieved (promotion from the Fourth Division) and consolidated (stabilisation in the Third Division), the manager decided to try to undertake further developments, especially with regard to his strike force, one of the most potent parts of the team. Thus, in an attempt to improve the side, he replaced Ernie Moss and then Bob Newton with lesser men, thus undermining much of the Valiants' attacking threat. At the same time, he bought a new striker, Eamon O'Keefe, seemingly without knowing how to fit him into the team, with the result that he played the Irishman out of position in midfield, much to the latter's annoyance. Thus the balance of the side was upset. It is easy to say in hindsight, but McGrath should have avoided these errors.

Secondly, with promotion having been secured, contract disputes broke out between the club and several players. Irrespective of the rights and wrongs of the situation, the problem should have been avoided and most certainly not left to fester as it was. However, McGrath and the directors allowed player power to undermine their efforts to consolidate their new-found Third Division status. It would have been no easy task to have achieved that with a happy ship, but, with disgruntled players in the ranks, not everybody was pulling in the same direction at the same time. Again, a resolution of the situation should have been seen as urgent and the top priority, but it was allowed to drag on.

Finally, when the pressure was on, the manager and the chairman waged a war of words. Who is to say whether McGrath or Jim Lloyd was in the right, but there was one thing for certain – that who would turn out to be the loser was a foregone conclusion. Therefore, it can be argued that the manager should have kept his thoughts to himself in the autumn of 1983 when the team were churning out an endless series of defeats because his comments were like a red rag to a bull. Having said that, he may have felt that he was poised for the axe anyway by then and that he wanted to put his point of view on record.

Whether or not McGrath could have extended his stay at Vale had he played his cards differently, there remains the question of whether the club should have kept him on board, knowing full well what a fine job he had done for at least 3½ years. Ultimately, the chairman was responsible for the Valiants' fortunes and, by the beginning of December 1983, he was faced with a dire situation. The team had accumulated just six points from seventeen league matches, there were no signs of an improvement, time was running out to right the ship and he was at loggerheads with his manager. Something had to give to relieve the pressure. So action urgently needed to be taken and Lloyd took what was realistically the only option in front of him.

Having said that, McGrath's dismissal did not necessarily mean that he had recently become a bad manager, but he had run out of time at Port Vale. Another opportunity quickly came his way when he was appointed as the boss at struggling Fourth Division Chester City in January 1984, but he could not prevent them from finishing at the bottom of the table at the end of the season. He began to rebuild the team, but was sacked in December of the same year, although the "Seals" ended up in sixteenth place that campaign.

His next port of call was Preston North End, who had finished the 1986-1987 season 91st in the Football League. The following year, McGrath guided them to the runners-up spot in the Fourth Division and with it promotion to the next tier. However, he was unable to steer them any higher, with the peak of their achievement being a place in the play-offs in 1989, where they were despatched 4-2 on aggregate in the semi-finals by none other than Port Vale. He departed in February 1990 with the "Lilywhites" involved in a (successful) battle against relegation.

The final club that McGrath managed were Halifax Town, who were also struggling in the basement division when he arrived in October 1991. However, he did not have the resources at his disposal to effect the kind of turnaround that he had at Preston and he departed in December 1992 with the "Shaymen" well on course to finish bottom of the table and be relegated to the Vauxhall Conference League.

Thus there was plenty of life and a fair amount of achievement left in McGrath as a football manager after he had parted company with Vale and his later success as a speaker on the after-dinner circuit amply illustrated that he still had the ability to get audiences to listen to what he had to say. However, in the autumn of 1983, perhaps it was the right time for him to have said goodbye to the Valiants. It was just a shame that he could not have done so on a happier note.

In his relatively short time at the club, John McGrath had created a legacy, which, despite the events preceding his departure, largely remained intact to be grasped by his successor and taken further. The question was whether the directors would find a replacement manager with the ability to accept the inheritance and continue the very good work already done. As it turned out in the fullness of time, McGrath mainly became remembered less for his own considerable successes at Vale than for being the precursor of a golden age in their history, as a kind of John the Baptist figure to the messiah who was to follow him.

12 Rudgie's Rough Diamonds

John Robert Rudge was born in Wolverhampton on 21 October 1944 and was a striker who signed as a professional for Huddersfield Town in November 1961. At that time, the "Terriers" were a fair force in the Second Division and remained so in the five years that he spent with them. As a result, he was restricted to just five Football League appearances, in which he scored no goals, and, by the time that England won the World Cup in 1966, one could have been forgiven for thinking that he would soon disappear into the massed ranks of football also-rans.

In December 1966, Huddersfield transferred Rudge to their Second Division rivals, Carlisle United, and, somewhat surprisingly, he made a rapid impact, scoring seven times in his fourteen league appearances as the "Cumbrians" finished third, six points and goal average adrift of a place in the First Division. The following season, he struck a respectable nine goals in 29 league and cup matches, although Carlisle dropped down to tenth place. In the 1968-1969 season, however, he made only five league and cup appearances for the Cumbrians, without scoring, and was transferred to Third Division Torquay United in January 1969.

At first, Rudge made little impact for the "Gulls", hitting the target just twice in his fourteen league appearances to the end of the 1968-1969 campaign, and it seemed as if his Football League career might be drifting towards an end. However, the following season, he got back on song, with sixteen successful strikes in 35 league and cup matches, which made him Torquay's highest scorer in their mediocre campaign. He kept up the good work in the 1970-1971 season, netting 21 goals in 43 league and cup appearances, which made him easily the top marksman for the Gulls. However, even with his firepower, they could only finish tenth in the table. The next campaign was a lean one for Rudge with Torquay as he managed to score just twice in twelve league and cup appearances before being transferred to their Third Division rivals, Bristol Rovers, in February 1972. However, it proved to be a successful move for him as the Gulls were relegated.

Rudge started his career with the "Pirates" fairly well because he notched three goals in eight league appearances to the end of the 1971-1972 season. However, the next campaign he returned to form and hit twelve goals in 29 league and cup games, to finish as Rovers' second-highest scorer as they mounted a promotion challenge. They ended up in fifth position, four points away from going up and one place above Vale. The Pirates finished the 1973-1974 season as the runners-up and thereby gained promotion to the Second Division, although it was little thanks to Rudge, who made only fifteen league and cup appearances and scored five times.

Even though Rovers struggled to maintain their status in the following campaign, Rudge played just three times in the league, without scoring, and was transferred to struggling Third Division Bournemouth in March 1975. Unfortunately, his seven league appearances until the end of the season for the "Cherries" yielded no goals and they were relegated in 21st position. He was sidelined throughout the whole of the 1975-1976 campaign with a ruptured Achilles tendon and the next season proved to be his last. He struggled in vain to overcome his injury and bowed out as a Football League player with two just goals in eleven league games.

In total, Rudge scored 79 goals in 230 league and cup appearances, which meant that he hit the target once in just under every three matches, a rate which would have been considered borderline for regular inclusion in a side as a striker. Although at times he had threatened to become a goalscorer of repute, for the most part his professional career had not been particularly inspiring, not least because it had been blighted by a succession of injuries. However, history now shows that his best talents were in another field altogether – that of management.

In the summer of 1977, Rudge became the first-team coach at one of his old clubs, Torquay United, where he remained until he got a phone call out of the blue from John McGrath on Christmas Eve 1979. McGrath had been appointed as the new Vale manager only two days beforehand and was looking for a coach with thorough knowledge of Third and Fourth Division players, which was almost entirely outside the experience of the ex-Southampton coach. Rudge was indeed such a man, who had developed an encyclopaedic knowledge of lower division footballers, especially because his club was a pretty unassuming one in the bottom tier of the league and therefore always on the lookout for new players from the pool. However, he was no more than an acquaintance of McGrath, as Rudge later said: 'I'd met him on coaching courses, but he wasn't a bosom buddy.'

Objectively, Rudge was a good catch for McGrath, particularly because, with him on board, the latter would not be going into his job blind to the players in his new world. However, it seems an oddity that Rudge was ever asked to accompany him, especially because the two Johns were not particularly well known to one another. McGrath had played nearly 500 Football League games, so he knew a large number of professional footballers, even if, in the case of many of them, it was only on the pitch. However, since 1961, he had only ever played in the First and Second Divisions and so the lower part of the league was a pretty foreign world to him. Nevertheless, as an ebullient character with a lot of contacts, it is surprising that he did not appoint someone he knew well to be his second in command at Vale. Of course, it may be that none of them fitted the bill, but the speed at which he rang Rudge indicates that McGrath ran out of available contacts very rapidly.

In the event, the reason why the new Vale manager contacted Rudge was less to do with an impression that the latter had made when they had met than the fact that he was recommended by a third party. The identity of the mystery man is unfortunately unknown, but the fact that McGrath took on Rudge on someone else's say-so suggests that either the recommendation was glowing or that the new manager had become desperate for a helping hand as he faced up to the challenge ahead. Although patience was not one McGrath's outstanding virtues, it is difficult to accept that he was in a panic for a coach only two days after being appointed to his new job. Therefore it appears that he had been resoundingly led to believe that Rudge was an assistant not to be missed and, of course, history has proved that assessment to be true.

Therefore, Vale had employed as their new manager a minor coach with no experience of the Fourth Division and he in turn had selected as his assistant a man with whom he was not particularly well acquainted. If the world of human beings was rational and logical, those two events most likely would never have happened. However, people actually live in a universe where they try to make sense of myriad inputs swirling around them and do the best they can under the circumstances. It appears that that is exactly what McGrath did, so that he took a chance that Rudge would become the perfect foil he was looking for. As it turned out, the gamble paid off big time because Rudge proved to be a highly accomplished assistant, who never challenged his master.

Therefore, Rudge's summons to Burslem came about as a result of a tip a now unknown individual gave to McGrath almost immediately after the latter had been appointed as the Valiants' manager. Such are the effects of chance in deciding events that Rudge almost certainly would not have even been in the frame had the monumental piece of advice not been given or a better one been received in time.

So it was very far from certain that Rudge would be called, but, having been offered the Vale post by McGrath, was there any doubt that he would have accepted it? It appears not because a number of factors stacked up to make the job attractive:

Firstly, although the posts at Torquay and Vale were similar and identical in rank, the one in Burslem seemed to promise more opportunity. At that time, the Gulls had a team manager, Mike Green, and a general manager, Frank O'Farrell, and therefore the structure was rather top-heavy. At a small club, like Torquay, this meant that not only was there little chance of Rudge being promoted in the foreseeable future, but also financial problems might lead to a job being shed and the coach's would be the cheapest to dispense with. Also, Green undertook coaching duties as well and in the wings was the reserve-team coach, Mike Hickman, so the club had a crowd of coaches. In addition, Green and O'Farrell had operated fairly successfully as a partnership since March 1977, whilst the latter had vast managerial experience, not least with Manchester United. Therefore, at Torquay, Rudge had competition and was vulnerable.

At Vale, however, there was only one manager and he was a new boy who did not know the ropes. Consequently, the post on offer was fairly secure and gave better prospects for the future.

A second reason why the job in Burslem was relatively attractive to Rudge was owing to the location of Torquay. Although it was a nice place for him and his family to live, he later said that it was 'out on a limb', particularly in relation to the hub of the English professional football world, and 'I was looking for what would be best for my career.' The Midlands was awash with clubs and also offered reasonably easy access to both the North and South, so it was ideally located for an ambitious coach like Rudge.

Thirdly, even a run-down Port Vale seemed to offer a more likely route to success than Torquay did, primarily because of its much larger potential spectator base, and Rudge said, 'I thought there'd be a better opportunity at Vale.' The only downside was that the Gulls were sixteen places higher in the Fourth Division table at the time, but, because things can change so quickly in football, that was insignificant in the scheme of things.

Finally, Wolverhampton, where Rudge had been born, was only 35 miles from Burslem, and he still had contacts there, especially family ones. He said: 'I had ties there. My mother was still in Wolverhampton and I stayed there with her at first.' Because the congestion on the motorways then was nowhere near what it is like now, Rudge was able to commute to work at Vale fairly easily.

Therefore, Rudge travelled to Burslem to meet McGrath and was offered the job on the spot. After thinking about it over Christmas, he decided to take it on and became Vale's coach at the beginning of January 1980. Then, for nearly four years, he worked very hard, happily in the background most of the time, to help his new manager to steady the sinking ship and then propel it upwards to a higher plane. He was quickly rewarded by being upgraded to the assistant manager in December 1980 and later said, 'I played my part in helping John to take Vale forward, but I would never try to take the accolades off him for what he did.'

By December 1983, the wheels had come off the McGrath bandwagon, with the team in dire straits, and he was suspended by the club before an amicable financial settlement was agreed. On the 6th, his deputy, Rudge was appointed as the caretaker manager in what was a commonplace move for a football club. He had until then quietly, but effectively, got on with his job and showed no little skill and ability in his work. He had gained a lot more experience along the way and had clearly developed into a contender for a manager's job. As Vale had lost fourteen of their last sixteen matches with McGrath at the helm, it was virtually impossible that Rudge could do worse and, in any case, the team were virtually doomed to relegation, even at that early point in the season. Therefore, there was little risk to the club by giving Rudge the job temporarily, to see what he could do with it. Even if he made a pig's ear of it, time would be gained to weigh up candidates for a permanent appointment. Therefore, the board made a sensible move and, of course, Rudge was not going to look the gift horse in the mouth. His real chance had finally come and he was determined to make a success of it.

The great advantage of the time that he took over meant that it was almost certain that he would achieve better results that campaign than had his predecessor, but his immediate problem was that the ship was rapidly sinking. With only six points on the board from seventeen league games, victories were urgently needed, but Rudge said: 'We cannot change things overnight. I will introduce my own ideas gradually.' Thus he was quick to show his ability to stay calm within a storm.

However, at first, it seemed as if the downward spiral was continuing unabated because his opening two matches in charge were both lost, by a total of five goals to nil. Thus, by Boxing Day, Vale were seven points behind the club immediately above them and thirteen points adrift of safety. A miracle was therefore needed if they were to survive in the Third Division that season. However, the manager balanced the left side of the team by signing skilful midfielder Kevin Young on loan from Burnley and switched Eamon O'Keefe to the attack. Amazingly, the Valiants then beat the second-placed club, Sheffield United, 2-0 on 27 December and gained ten points from four games in January 1984, to cut the gap from safety to only four points. At the same time, the manager deemed striker Jim Steel to be surplus to requirements and he was sold to Wrexham for £10,000, without being missed by the team. Rudge's magic wand had clearly begun to work.

As the remarkable revival continued, Vale moved off the bottom on 18 February with a 4-3 home win against Newport County. Rudge's appointment to his post was made permanent the next month, with him being given a contract until the end of the following campaign, and he then unsuccessfully tried to re-sign Bob Newton. Undaunted, on 19 March he guided the Valiants to a 2-1 win at relegation rivals Southend United, which took them out of the relegation zone. The *Sentinel* commented, 'John Rudge has achieved mission impossible.' Unfortunately, the team had played more matches than most of their rivals and were unable to maintain their impetus, so that they eventually finished in penultimate position, six points and an inferior goal difference short of safety.

Nevertheless, the new manager had led the side in a most valiant effort so close to preserving their Third Division status from a position that had seemed near impossible. With Rudge in charge, Vale had gained 37 points from 29 games compared with the six that John McGrath had guided them to in seventeen matches. If Rudge's success rate had been repeated throughout the season, the Valiants would have ended up a respectable sixteenth with 59 points, without taking into account the reduced number of points other sides would have got by not beating Vale. There could be no doubt about who had easily been the finer manager in Burslem in the 1983-1984 campaign and it is intriguing to speculate upon how much earlier Rudge's appointment might have proved decisive. Based on his actual average number of points achieved per match that season, and taking into account those gained under McGrath, it would have needed to have happened six games earlier. However, of course, because of the innumerable factors in play, we will never know the number that would have been required or even if Rudge would have succeeded at all with the whole season at his disposal.

Despite being relegated, the Valiants were not in too bad a position because the team's spirits had been revived and a profit of £50,601 had been made on the campaign, although the bank overdraft remained high at £136,053. However, their young striker, Mark Bright, who had scored in five consecutive matches at the end of the season, was sold in June, against the manager's wishes, to Leicester City for £33,333, with top-up payments which eventually doubled the fee. He was the first of a fair number of raw recruits, or 'rough diamonds', as Rudge called them, nurtured by the manager during his time with Vale, whose eventual sale for big money transformed the club.

The manager was allowed the funds for wages to bring in four new free-transfer players for the 1984-1985 campaign, the most important of whom was the wily striker, Ally Brown, who had been released by Walsall. At the same time, Rudge managed to slash the player wages bill by twenty per cent, which was one of the first examples of the financial prudence he showed during the whole of his time with the club.

The manager stabilised the situation during the 1984-1985 season, in which the Valiants finished a respectable twelfth with sixty points. That was all the more laudable as a net transfer credit was achieved, especially through the sale of the unsettled Eamon O'Keefe to Blackpool for £10,000 in March 1985. One of the main successes of the campaign was the emergence of a dangerous striking partnership between Brown and young Robbie Earle, a rough diamond being developed under Rudge's watchful eye. Between them, Brown and Earle hit the target forty times in all competitions.

However, there was another striker on Rudge's radar, the signing of whom in May turned out to be one of the most crucial moments of the manager's long reign at Vale. His name was Andy Jones, he was 22, powerful, strong and quick and had finished the season as the joint-leading scorer in the Northern Premier League. He cost £3,000 from Rhyl and his later big-money transfer provided the catalyst for Rudge to build a side to compete in the second tier of English football. However, Jones very nearly did not join the Valiants at all.

Rudge was on the lookout for rough diamonds, as usual, players with a spark and potential that he could hopefully develop with the right coaching. On the recommendation of Ken Roberts, one of Vale's scouts, Rudge had already watched Jones twice, without seeing anything to convince him that he should take the striker on board. Ever a glutton for work, the manager decided to check him out for a third, and very probably final, time. So Rudge went with his family for a day trip to Rhyl in order to take in their match against Matlock Town while he was there. Unfortunately, when they arrived, he discovered that Jones had one of his knees strapped up and was therefore only a substitute. The game to half-time had been so poor that for once the Vale manager decided to give it up and so suggested to his wife, Del, that they should leave and take their children to the seafront. She said, 'Well, you might as well wait now and watch the second half,' which they did.

As it turned out, Jones duly came on and Rudge later said, 'He did three or four things in that period that impressed me and, although he was only half-fit, I decided to sign him, which I did the next week.' So, had it not been for Del Rudge putting her husband's job before their children's pleasure (which she might well not have done), it is highly unlikely that Vale would have signed Jones and consequently they may never have triumphantly returned to the Second Division.

Even then, the striker was not in the bag because the Valiants' chief scout, Ray Williams, reported that he had heard that Arsenal had arranged for Jones to go there on a fortnight's trial. With no time to lose, Rudge and Roberts rushed to the striker's house. The manager said: 'We knocked on Jonesy's door. He didn't know we were coming and he was a bit hesitant about signing, but I signed him there and then.' Therefore, had Rudge not acted immediately, it may well have been that the striker would have become a big-name player in London or, more likely, returned to Rhyl, having failed his audition.

Despite the urgency to get Jones on board, he was only a substitute for the opening league match of the 1985-1986 season because the recognised first-choice strike force was still Brown and Earle. However, he made his full debut in a 0-0 draw at home to Mansfield Town on 24 August and scored his first goal in a competitive game for the team in a 1-1 draw against Rochdale at Vale Park a week later.

Reinforced by other useful signings, the Valiants mounted a promotion challenge after a slow start and went to the top of the table on 2 November 1985. However, they then went off the boil and had dropped to sixth by the middle of January 1986. Nevertheless, an eighteen-match unbeaten run then proved instrumental in Vale finishing fourth and gaining promotion to the Third Division. The top scorer was none other than Jones, whose play had been polished up somewhat, and he had found the net eighteen times in all competitions.

Hardly had the campaign finished than Preston North End offered Rudge a pay increase to become their manager. The "Lilywhites" had finished in penultimate place in the Fourth Division and were desperate to revive their fortunes. However, they were unable to coax Rudge on board and he said: 'Football is not always about money. I am happy.' Although North End had more potential than Vale, in reality they were offering Rudge a retrograde move to handle a struggling side in an area well distant from his base. Had the Valiants' manager decided to have taken up the challenge, however, it may well have been that the golden age to come in Burslem would never have materialised. As it turned out, Rudge's old mentor, John McGrath, became the new manager of the "Lilywhites".

Despite a loss of £79,474 having been made on the 1985-1986 season, Rudge was allowed to spend a total of £28,000 on three players to boost the team for the Third Division challenge ahead, the most important of whom was the ball-playing, 22-year-old midfielder, Ray Walker, from Aston Villa. His play was not as rough as that of some of the other diamonds that the manager signed during his time at Vale, but Walker developed into a very fine midfield man, not least through being polished by the Burslem coaching system.

In spite of being reinforced, the Valiants struggled to cope with the demands of the new division in the 1986-1987 campaign. Jones had no trouble scoring goals, but no-one else backed him up with any degree of regularity. Rudge was therefore in the market for another striker and found the man he wanted, 21-year-old, swashbuckling Steve Bull, a West Bromwich Albion reserve. However, the Vale manager had a big problem – he could not afford the fee that the Baggies wanted for Bull, so he offered them midfielder Geoff Hunter as part of a package deal, but that did not prove acceptable. The price of the striker might have declined over time to an acceptable level, but, on 20 November 1986, he signed for Fourth Division Wolverhampton Wanderers for £50,000. As is well known, Bull quickly became a legend at Molineux, scoring a total of 102 goals in two consecutive seasons (1987-1988 and 1988-1989) and becoming their all-time top marksman (with 306 successful strikes).

Bull also became an England international and it really whets the imagination to ponder upon what he might have achieved at Vale and what the Valiants might have accomplished with him. However, he might, of course, have fallen over on the car park at Vale Park, immediately after signing for the club, and suffered a career-ending compound fracture of a leg. In that case, presumably Rudge would have been pilloried for wasting a large sum of money on a striker so proficient that he could not even stand on his own two feet! Alternatively, the Valiants would have had two powerhouse strikers of similar styles (Bull and Jones), who might have broken world records or perhaps simply got in one another's way to no good effect.

Anyway, on 22 November, two days after Rudge had lost Bull to Wolves, Vale were defeated 2-1 at Doncaster Rovers and slumped to the bottom of the table. The manager of the Valiants was thus back to where he had started three years before! The position began to look desperate, but Rudge produced a masterstroke in signing the experienced central defender, Bob Hazell, on a free transfer from Reading just before Christmas and fourteen points were gained from the following six matches. Phil Sproson said of Hazell, 'He would not accept defeat and we derived our strength from him.' Although the team's form was erratic thereafter, the undefeated run proved the turning point and Vale finished the season in a respectable twelfth position. In the meantime, Jones, the goal machine, could not stop scoring and, on 28 March, bagged a hat trick in a 6-0 trouncing of Fulham, which remains as the club's all-time record Football League away win. Then the striker surpassed himself on 4 May by netting five times in a 6-1 thrashing of relegated Newport County! His remarkable total of 37 goals in all competitions broke Vale's post-war scoring record out of sight and in less than two years he had risen from obscurity to become a striking sensation, as well as a Wales international.

Unfortunately, the club had recorded a £53,373 loss on the campaign and the total debt rose to a worrying £363,878, which created pressure for player sales. Although Rudge was trying to progress the team, left-back Russell Bromage and midfielder Jon Bowden were transferred to Bristol City and Wrexham respectively for a total of £37,500 before a ball had been kicked in the 1987-1988 season. The only compensation was the purchase of a promising striker, Darren Beckford, another of Rudge's rough diamonds, from Manchester City for £15,000, half of which was paid by the supporters.

Nevertheless, Vale began the 1987-1988 season in excellent league form and were top of the table after six games, having accumulated thirteen points. By then, Jones had already banged in six goals, including all four in a 4-2 defeat of Aldershot in the opening match. However, the Valiants' speedy right-winger, Paul Smith, had in the meantime been transferred to Lincoln City for £40,000 and Jones, the heart of the side, was the next to go. With the team perched at the top, Vale accepted an irresistible £350,000 offer for his services from Charlton Athletic. Although his sale virtually solved the club's financial problems overnight, Rudge said the loss of Jones was like 'cutting off my right arm'.

Unlikely though it seemed at the time, the main man's transfer was the harbinger of a golden age for the club because the funds which then became available to the manager enabled him to build a promotion side and guide the Valiants back to the Second Division for the first time in 32 years. Thus the sale of a single outstanding footballer both took the financial pressure off the club and gave the manager the clout to bring in several new players to improve the team all round. But had Del Rudge not persuaded her husband to stay to see the second half of the match between Rhyl and Matlock Town, Jones would very probably never have signed for Vale and the course of history would have been dramatically changed. It may well have been that Rudge would have had a much shorter stay in Burslem and that the golden age of the 1990s would never have happened.

Nevertheless, in the short term, the loss of the goal machine had a disastrous effect on the team's results, which almost cost the manager his job. £20,000 was spent on the diminutive striker, David Riley, from Nottingham Forest, but, obviously, he struggled to fill Jones' boots. Also, Robbie Earle was sidelined for nearly five months and the goals started to dry up. The team went twelve league games without a win and, on 28 December, sank to sixth from the bottom of the table. The board decided to 'assess' the situation in a month and it appeared that Rudge's reign as the Vale manager was near to ending. However, salvation was at hand.

Mike Pejic was upgraded from the youth coach to the first-team coach to create more of a fighting spirit and the normally cautious Rudge spent a total of £70,000 on Simon Mills, a skilful midfielder from York City, and Gary Ford, an industrious right-winger from Leicester City. At first, there was no improvement and, on 10 January 1987, Vale were five minutes away from failing to beat non-league Macclesfield Town at home in the F.A Cup third round when their eighteen-year-old reserve midfielder, Kevin Finney, finally broke the deadlock. It became generally believed that his goal saved Rudge's bacon, not least because the Vale chairman, Bill Bell, was not the most patient of men. It is easy to speculate that, had the game remained goalless and the Valiants been eliminated from the competition in the replay, Rudge's number would have been up and the dream of a return to the Second Division might well have been nothing but a fantasy.

However, Finney's goal proved to be a turning point in the Valiants' fortunes and a remarkable transformation followed, with the team gaining 29 points from their next twelve league matches! Better still, they found fame and fortune by beating First Division Tottenham Hotspur 2-1 in sensational style at home in the fourth round of the F.A. Cup on 30 January 1988. A terrific crowd of 20,045 paid new club record receipts of £78,357 30p to watch the tie and Vale were boosted by a further £80,000 from selling television filming rights to the game.

Three weeks later, an even bigger crowd, of 22,483, turned up at Vale Park and paid new record receipts of £87,699 30p to see the Valiants fight out a 0-0 draw against Watford, another First Division side, in the fifth round of the cup. Although the replay was lost, 2-0, the club had made a staggering £175,000 profit from just three matches and the stage was further set for the success that was to follow. However, had Kevin Finney slipped in the mud and not scored his late winner against Macclesfield, the club may well have been a lot poorer and John Rudge could easily have been on the dole instead of being a hero in Burslem. So fine is the dividing line between success and failure and such are the vagaries of fate.

Although the team went right off the boil in the final month of the campaign, they finished a creditable eleventh, only ten points and goal difference adrift of fifth place and a play-off position. Far better still was the new club record £410,239 profit that had been made on the season, which finally put Vale on a sound financial footing.

The manager's main new signing for the 1988-1989 campaign was the intelligent and experienced striker, Ron Futcher, who cost £35,000 from Bradford City. He was no rough diamond, but the finished article, and it was money very well spent. Vale were quickly into their stride, taking 23 points from their opening ten league matches, and went to the top of the table after trouncing Cardiff City 6-1 on 17 September and Chesterfield 5-0 two days later. The club then raised £164,800 by selling their unused training ground at Cobridge.

By 14 January 1989, the Valiants were second, five points clear of the third team, with two games in hand, and automatic promotion looked very likely, but they then permanently lost both their commanding central defenders, Bob Hazell and Phil Sproson, within a week of each other, through injury. The manager then threw caution to the wind and paid a staggering £200,000 for the signature of the classy central defender, Dean Glover, from Middlesbrough to help plug the gap. Rudge followed up this move by signing Gary West, a tall centre-half, from Gillingham for £70,000 and also brought back Andy Jones on loan.

Had Jones not been originally sold for a phenomenal fee, Kevin Finney scored against Macclesfield Town, Vale beat Tottenham Hotspur and the club sold their training ground, it may well have been that neither of the new defenders could have been signed. As it turned out, Rudge's moves in the transfer market failed to achieve automatic promotion because the Valiants were edged out of second place on goal difference by Sheffield United. Had they gained just a single point from three home games they lost to also-ran sides in the latter stages of the season, they would have gone up in second place. In the event, it did not matter because Vale triumphed in the four-team play-offs and returned to the Second Division after a 32-year absence on 3 June by beating Bristol Rovers 1-0 in Burslem, to win the final 2-1 on aggregate.

The campaign's leading scorer with 23 goals in all competitions was Darren Beckford, who had developed from a rough diamond into a lethal goal poacher. However, a price had been paid for achieving promotion because an £88,142 loss was recorded on the season, primarily through a £333,084 player transfer deficit. Nevertheless, the Promised Land had finally been reached and Rudge intended that the club would stay there. Consequently, he spent £265,000 in total on Neil Aspin, a solid right-sided defender, from Leeds United and Nicky Cross, a clever striker from Leicester City, to bolster the squad.

Nevertheless, the team initially found the going to be tough in the 1989-1990 campaign and won just one of their opening nine league matches, so that they were fifth from the bottom by the end of September. However, a revival saw Vale gradually move up into midtable and, on 10 January 1990, they pulled off an outstanding 3-2 victory at First Division Derby County in a third round F.A. Cup replay. Although they were trounced 6-0 in the next round seventeen days later by Aston Villa, who were then second in the premier division, around £150,000 had been made from the competition, most of which was marked for ground improvements. In the league, a steady second half of the season resulted in the Valiants finishing a very respectable eleventh and thereby becoming the biggest club in the Potteries, for the first time since 1956, with the relegation of Stoke City to the Third Division. The top scorer once again was the ex-rough diamond, Darren Beckford, with a total of 21 goals bagged in all competitions.

Vale consolidated their place in the Second Division in the 1990-1991 campaign, although it proved to be largely one of anticlimax. Although they won only three of their opening thirteen league games and seemed to be running into relegation trouble, they managed to win regularly enough thereafter to steer clear of the danger zone. In February 1991, Rudge sold Ronnie Jepson, a bustling striker whom the club had groomed, to Preston North End for £80,000 and spent the money on another rough diamond, Robin van der Laan, a hard-working midfielder, from Wageningen, of the Netherlands. The deals proved to be simply the latest astute moves made by the manager as the Dutchman developed into a key player for the club and was later sold at a very large profit. With his assistance, the Valiants finished the 1990-1991 season in fifteenth position, nine points clear of relegation, and Beckford once more topped the club's scoring charts with a total of 23 goals in all competitions. However, a £388,465 loss was made on the campaign, largely because of the cost of ground improvements, which threatened to seriously limit Rudge's team-strengthening plans.

Unfortunately, in June, Vale lost their star striker, Beckford, who moved to Norwich City for a then club record fee of £925,000, and the following month their midfield dynamo, Robbie Earle, left for Wimbledon, although the Valiants banked £775,000 from his sale. The combined income was a staggering reward for the time that had been spent turning both rough diamonds into First Division-class players and all for an initial outlay by the club of just £7,500! In the absence of Beckford and Earle, it is unlikely that Vale would have been promoted in 1989 and, without their goals to look forward to in 1991, a battle against relegation looked on the cards.

Rudge did what he could to cover the gaping hole in the Valiants' attacking threat by signing the intelligent striker, Martin Foyle, from Oxford United for a then club record outlay of £375,000; the formidable centre-forward and centre-half, Peter Swan, from Hull City for £310,000 and the experienced striker, Keith Houchen, from Hibernian for £100,000. So, for less than half the price, the manager replaced two outgoing players with three incomers, but, unfortunately, the net loss of quality proved decisive.

From the outset, Vale found the 1991-1992 season hard going and won only two of their opening eleven league matches, though the cracks were to some extent glossed over by a marvellous 2-2 draw at First Division Liverpool in the third round of the Rumbelows Cup on 29 October. Although the Valiants were brushed aside 4-1 in the replay 22 days later, the 18,725 crowd generated new club record receipts of £126,434 and, by 30 November, the team were twelfth in the league.

However, seventeen league matches without a win, from the beginning of December to the second half of March 1992, saw them plummet to the bottom of the table. By the 21st, they were seven points adrift of safety, having played two games more than fourth from the bottom Plymouth Argyle, and Rudge told a packed open meeting at the club a week later, 'I am not a magician who can keep producing white rabbits out of a hat.' Unfortunately for him that was virtually what he had become at Vale and, because of his regular success in performing near-miracles, it was what many supporters had come to expect of him. Indeed, his achievements had by then become pressures themselves. Nevertheless, Rudge and his team gained eleven points from their following six matches and came close to pulling off a great escape, but eventually fell five points and goal difference short of safety and finished bottom of the table, having scored the joint-lowest number of goals (42). The only sweetener was that the club had made a marvellous £455,465 gross profit, primarily because of a large player transfer surplus, but the total overdraft stood at £410,466.

Following the big disappointment, Rudge dusted himself down and, less than two weeks after the end of the season, signed yet another rough diamond to develop, Ian Taylor, an industrious midfielder from Moor Green for an initial £15,000. As usual, the manager's investment proved to be an excellent one. Determined to see the Valiants regain their lost status at the first attempt, he also signed a number of other new players, most notably Paul Kerr, a stocky midfielder, from Millwall for £140,000.

On 14 August, in an ominous prelude to the 1992-1993 season, Vale's lucrative market was closed down by the council, which promised to limit the funds for Rudge to continue to produce the white rabbits out of his hat. The team made a lacklustre start to their campaign in the Second Division (as the Third Division had been renamed), winning just one of their opening eight games, and were eighth from the bottom on 19 September. However, they then kicked into gear and took 45 points from their following nineteen league matches to sit second in the table on 13 February 1993. Although they generally continued to perform well and gained 36 points from their remaining nineteen games, it still wasn't enough to secure automatic promotion because they were pipped at the post for the runners-up spot by Bolton Wanderers, in spite of having secured an all-time club record 89 points!

The "Trotters" had gained just one point more than the Valiants and the Potters had ended up four ahead, which left a number of different scenarios whereby Vale could have finished ahead of one or both of their rivals.

The most intriguing of these is that, had the Valiants beaten Stoke at home on 31 March, instead of losing 2-0 to them, Vale would have finished as the champions with 92 points and City would have been denied second place and automatic promotion by Bolton on goal difference. Although the Valiants had been well beaten in the vital match, they had been without their best striker, Martin Foyle, and their midfield dynamo, Ian Taylor, who were both injured. Also, Rudge had preferred to start with Keith Houchen rather than the much more mobile Nicky Cross. However, in their F.A. Cup third round replay (one of five titanic struggles between the two rival sides that season) on 24 November, at Vale Park, Foyle and Cross had torn the Stoke defence apart with their movement and been instrumental in helping the Valiants secure a historic 3-1 victory. The situation easily brings a variation of an old proverb to mind: for want of Foyle and Cross (and perhaps Taylor too), the game was lost; for want of the points, automatic promotion was lost and for want of automatic promotion, the season (in the event) was lost.

However, the campaign was nowhere near over because Vale still had the play-offs to contend with and made their way to the final through a 2-1 aggregate win against Stockport County in the semi-finals. Despite having never before set foot inside Wembley Stadium, the Valiants had two visits lined up, just eight days apart! The first match was the final of the Autoglass Trophy, for the lower division clubs, against Stockport on 22 May and a fine display in a 2-1 win secured the cup in front of around 25,000 of their own supporters! The more important play-off game was against West Bromwich Albion, whom Vale had twice beaten in the league, and the result hinged on a dramatic incident. The Valiants had had slightly the better of a tight encounter until the 66th minute when Peter Swan brought down the Baggies' striker, Bob Taylor, who was otherwise clean through on goal. Swan became only the seventh player to be sent off at Wembley, Albion converted the resulting penalty and they then picked off the depleted Vale side to gain a flattering 3-0 victory in front of a crowd of 53,471. If only Foyle and Taylor had been fit on 31 March! If only Rudge had played Cross that night! If only Swan had not fouled Taylor at Wembley! So fine proved the line between success and failure in 1993.

Despite the number of big games played and the longevity of two cup runs, the club managed to make a £62,915 loss on the campaign, which was very worrying, not least for their manager, who was bent on securing promotion at the second attempt. Therefore the only new close season signing of note was Wigan Athletic's left-back, Allen Tankard, who was bought for £87,500. However, Rudge still had in his ranks the ex-rough diamond, Ian Taylor, who had finished the 1992-1993 campaign as the club's leading marksman, with nineteen strikes.

The team began the new season seemingly with a hangover because they won just one of their opening seven league matches and slumped to fourth from the bottom of the table on 14 September. However, they then found their feet and won the following five games to move onto the fringes of the promotion race.

Steady progress continued to be made, so that Vale ended the year in fourth position, but their most impressive form was reserved for an F.A. Cup third round tie against Southampton of the Premiership (as the First Division had been rebranded). The Valiants drew the initial match 1-1 at The Dell on 8 January 1994 through, as the *Sentinel* described it, 'a magnificent display of courage and resolve'. The team finished the job in the replay ten days later, achieving a marvellous 1-0 victory on a very heavy pitch.

Vale were knocked out of the competition in the next round, 2-0 by Wolverhampton Wanderers, but a week later they achieved a splendid 2-1 league victory at the leaders Reading, which was a clear statement of their intentions. They gained 27 points from their next fourteen games, but a 2-1 defeat at their promotion rivals, Stockport County, on 19 April, seemed certain to consign the Valiants to the play-offs for the second successive season. However, the players kept their nerve and finished the campaign with five straight victories to snatch the runners-up spot and automatic promotion at the death, with 5,400 of their fans urging them on to their 3-1 success in their final match at Brighton & Hove Albion on 7 May. The *Sentinel* captured the feeling of the moment when it said, 'The final whistle released a wave of joy on the terraces as a line of police and stewards were unable to stop thousands of jubilant supporters invading the pitch.' Vale were back and John Rudge was immediately offered a new two-year contract by his chairman, Bill Bell, who exclaimed, 'This is a fantastic achievement.'

Although Rudge had said in 1992 that he could not keep producing rabbits out of a hat, most of the time that was exactly what he had continued to do. To create feats of magic almost year in, year out took some doing and one of the most important secrets of his success was his discovery and development of rough diamonds, players with potential, whom he could sign for free or cheaply and sell for big money. In turn, that stabilised the finances of the club and enabled the manager to find more rough diamonds and, occasionally, to pay sums of money previously unheard of in Burslem to get high quality footballers on board. Indeed, there were yet more rough diamonds to come before John Rudge's time was through at Port Vale.

However, there may well have been very few rough diamonds and a distinct lack of magic tricks and rabbits being pulled out of hats at Vale if an unknown person had not recommended the services of John Rudge to John McGrath. If Rudge had not become the Valiants' coach, he almost certainly would never have become their manager. If McGrath had not failed so spectacularly in the 1983-1984 season, Rudge may not have become the manager anyway. Had his wife not put her husband's job before her children's pleasure on a day out to Rhyl in 1985, Andy Jones would probably never have been signed. Had Jones not become a Vale player, he would not have been sold by the club for £350,000 and thereby have helped Rudge to strengthen the team overall. Had Kevin Finney not scored at the death against Macclesfield Town in 1988, Vale would never have earned big money from F.A. Cup matches against Tottenham Hotspur and Watford. Had that money not been made, it is very unlikely that the Valiants would have been able to have afforded to buy Ron Futcher. Had Futcher not joined the ranks, promotion to the Second Division would probably not have been achieved in 1989. Had the former rough diamonds, Darren Beckford and Robbie Earle, not been transferred for huge fees in 1991, Rudge would probably not have been able to have assembled the 1993 Autoglass Trophy-winning team and that which gained promotion in 1994. Had the manager not taken a chance on Ian Taylor, a rough diamond, in 1992, it may have been that those sides would not have succeeded in their endeavours. Finally, if John Rudge had not had the knack of developing rough diamonds, it is virtually certain that this chapter would never have been written!

13 A Stand Too Far

William Thomas (Bill) Bell was born in Burslem on 21 January 1932 and became a supporter of the Valiants in 1948. He was involved in the construction of Vale Park as a maintenance mechanic and later became a garage proprietor. He was co-opted onto the Vale board in May 1984 and became the club's second-largest shareholder in April 1986 when he bought 23,000 shares from the ex-chairman, Don Ratcliffe. Over the following year, Bell became increasingly influential in the boardroom and had very different ideas than the chairman, Jim Lloyd, on the way the club should be run. Effectively, the result was a struggle for control of the club.

On 14 May 1987, Lloyd gave up the fight and resigned as the chairman, saying, 'I have been unhappy for a while with the attitude and support of the Board.' He was replaced by Bell, who made it clear from the outset that he was intending to run a tight ship at Vale. He said: 'The club needs sorting out in some respects. There can be no room for sentiment in football and if there are people here who do not do their jobs, they will have to go.'

Bell inherited a canny team manager, John Rudge, who had been in post for nearly 3½ years and had already guided Vale to promotion from the Fourth Division in 1986. The team had consolidated its position in the third tier of the Football League by finishing twelfth in the campaign before Bell obtained the chair and the Valiants had a red-hot goalscorer, Andy Jones, to boot. Therefore, the playing side of the club was stable and progressing. That Bell had acquired a masterful manager is beyond question and the forging of an 11½-year partnership between the two men, although it did not run smoothly at times, was instrumental in creating a golden age at the club. Broadly speaking, as long as Bell managed the club and Rudge managed the team, all was well, but, on the occasions when the chairman crossed into the realm of football, the show threatened to come off the rails.

Bell was ambitious to make a success of the club, but he inherited the perennial problem that virtually all previous Vale chairmen had faced – there were insufficient paying customers for the business to thrive. Indeed, the average league home crowd in the season preceding his reign had sunk to just 3,312 and the visit of First Division Manchester United to Vale Park in the second round of the Littlewoods Cup on 7 October 1986 had attracted only 10,568 spectators. The campaign itself had produced a £53,373 loss and the overdraft with the club's bank stood at £216,453, the interest on which had cost £26,159. Such was the scale of the problem that Bell (and Rudge) faced. The manager was already proving to be a magician, who could pull rabbits out of a hat, but the question was whether the new chairman could match his performance and help to take Vale on to higher things.

Bell signalled his intention to run the club the way he wanted to by purchasing Jim Lloyd's shares in November 1987, so that he then owned sixty per cent of the total holding. Thenceforth, he was unrestrained by the power of anyone else in the boardroom. It remained to be seen whether his ability was equal to his power.

On 28 December, the team dropped to sixth from the bottom of the table as Vale threatened to get involved in a relegation battle, but Bell removed Rudge's right-hand man, Alan Oakes, and replaced him with Mike Pejic, the youth coach, who was renowned as a hard taskmaster. At the same time, it was made clear that the situation was under review and therefore there could be little doubt that Rudge's job would be on the line if results did not improve. However, improve they did and the manager secured his immediate future when the team sensationally beat First Division Tottenham Hotspur 2-1 at home in the fourth round of the F.A. Cup on 30 January 1988.

Even at this early stage, the chairman was showing a considerable interest in developing the ground and in May the club received a £42,000 grant from the Football Trust to develop a family enclosure, to accommodate 2,000 spectators, in the long-closed area between the Railway Paddock and the Bycars End. Bell said, 'Encouraging families to return to soccer is one of my pet themes and I am thrilled that we can finally get work under way.' The intention was clearly that this would just be the first development because the chairman added, 'We have a five-year plan to improve the ground.'

Less than a fortnight later, the club announced that they were going to have a £20,000 electronic scoreboard installed at the Hamil End of the ground. Vale Park had long been allowed to become run-down, but things were on the move and the technological age was about to come to Burslem! Because nine of the ten available advertising slots on it had been already taken, it was expected that the scoreboard would pay for itself within a year or two.

The chairman, naturally, was looking to help things progress on the pitch as well and said on 10 June, 'We are not in a situation where we need to sell and my policy is to put success before profit.'

Before the start of the 1988-1989 season, the new scoreboard kicked into action and three second-hand plush executive boxes arrived at the ground at a reduced price from Newcastle United, for use by companies who wanted to entertain customers. The five-year plan was well under way and the announcement, on 5 October, that a new club record profit of £410,239 had been made on the previous campaign (mainly through the F.A. Cup receipts and the transfer of Andy Jones), resulted in Bill Bell saying, 'The club is on a firm financial base for the first time in a good many years.'

Then, on 20 October, the chairman told the shareholders at the annual meeting that he had negotiated the sale of the club's training ground at Cobridge for £164,800. As it had been bought for £13,500 only eight years previously and was unused, that represented a particularly good piece of business. Unfortunately, the Bycars End of Vale Park needed money spending on it to make it safe, although Bell said funds from the training ground sale were also earmarked to strengthen the team. The chairman's coup led the club president, Jack Burgess, to remark, 'Bill Bell is a man of enterprise and vision.'

On 1 December, Vale announced that they had submitted plans to the council for the building, at a cost of £80,000, of a special stand to house up to 25 disabled fans at the matches. This was one of Bell's pet projects and was to be the first such purpose-built enclosure in the Football League.

The construction of the Family Enclosure had made good progress and opened on 4 February 1989. It had room for 1,500 supporters, with 600 of them being able to be seated. There was no let-up on the development of Vale Park because, less than two months later, work began on constructing the disabled stand, which by then had expanded into becoming a 48-seater, but it was hoped that three-quarters of the cost would be paid for by local companies.

Despite the impressive improvements of the ground during the season, its highlight came on 3 June when a 1-0 victory in the second leg of the Third Division play-off final meant that Bell became the first Vale chairman in 32 years to be at the helm with the club in the second tier of English football. How much of that was down to him, though, for providing financial support for the manager's efforts would be the subject of much debate over the years. Nevertheless, Bell could look back on a highly successful initial two years in his job.

However, there was more to be done on the ground sooner than he had envisaged in the wake of more stringent safety requirements following the Hillsborough Disaster, which had taken place on 15 April and led to the deaths of 96 Liverpool supporters. The cost of the total envisaged upgrading of Vale Park was estimated at £¼ million, with £119,000 of that amount being met by a grant from the Football Grounds Improvements Trust. Such grants had been available before Bill Bell had ascended into the chair, but the club had not bothered to take advantage of them, with the result that the stadium had fallen into semi-disrepair.

Before the start of the 1989-1990 campaign, exits from the ground had to be widened and terracing and crush barriers improved. The Bycars End was condemned as unsafe, half of the Hamil End was closed pending extensive renewal work and the stadium's capacity was reduced to 12,000. Because of the events completely out of his control in Sheffield in April, the Vale chairman suddenly had a major headache that threatened to destroy all his planning.

Nevertheless, the Disabled Stand opened on the Lorne Street side of the ground on 4 November at a final cost of £100,000 and the Hamil End came fully back into use on 2 December, having cost £175,000 less forty per cent of grant aid to get back up to scratch. Money continued to roll out of the club and Bell was not very happy when the total policing bill for the previous season was announced as £55,202. The chairman said bluntly that the cost was 'absolutely crippling'.

The front of the Bycars End reopened on 3 February 1990, at a cost of £90,000, which increased the stadium's capacity to 23,000. It enabled an impressive crowd of 22,075 to gather to watch a goalless draw against Stoke City in the league that same day.

Although Bell had voluntarily started a programme of ground developments after he had become the Vale chairman, big improvements were now forced on the club, whether the directors liked them or not, because, following the production of the Taylor Report into the Hillsborough Disaster, it was decreed by the government that all First and Second Division stadiums were to become entirely seated by 1994. Therefore, there was a flurry of activity at Vale Park over the summer as 3,750 yellow seats (with a number of white ones which spelled out the initials "PVFC") were fitted in the Railway Paddock and another 1,121 built into the upper part of the Bycars End, which brought the total seating in the ground to approaching 9,000. In addition, a new police control box was built between the Hamil End and the Railway Paddock and the roof of the Bycars End was demolished after being declared unsafe. A plan was then devised to modernise that part of the ground in a £½ million facelift, but an increasing number of mine shafts in and around Vale Park were found and had to be filled and capped, at an estimated cost of £175,000. Despite the promise of financial assistance by the Football League, money was flooding out of the club's bank account and going into the stadium.

Remarkably, the loss on the previous campaign was only £22,000, although the total debt had risen to £289,600. To help keep the club afloat, the admission prices had to be increased, but a new Staffordshire County Council policing bill formula threatened to increase the club's security costs for a season to £¼ million despite Vale Park already being the ninth-most expensive ground to police in the whole of the Football League!

At the annual meeting, on 1 November, Bell announced that the next project was to cover both ends of the ground, but the ex-vice-chairman, Mike Thompstone, said that, 'It is not in the best interests of Port Vale that one man and his family should have overall control.'

By the end of January 1991, the club had received £286,239 in grants from the Football Trust for the work done in improving the stadium over the previous six months. The flurry of activity continued into the spring and Vale disclosed in April that they were planning a major development to create a training ground (including a £½ million all-weather pitch) and sports centre on Bycars Park, just behind the ground. As the land was controlled by the council, part of the idea was to make the facilities available for use by the local community.

The projects continued to roll on and, on 10 May, it was announced that a new 4,000-seater stand would be built on the Bycars End at a cost of over £1 million. As a sign of the times, it was to have a different name, the British Coal Opencast Stand, so called after the sponsors, who agreed to contribute a five-figure sum towards the cost. A chunk of the bill, as usual, was to be met by the Football Trust and the chairman said: 'We are striving for a first-class ground and a Division 1 team. We must have already spent in the region of £1 million of the club's money to bring Vale Park up to the required standard.'

His assessment of the progress made seemed a very fair comment because the activity around the stadium had been like a whirlwind after decades of malaise. However, it was most unfortunate that attendances to match such a monumental effort remained very few and far between despite John Rudge having led the team into the second tier of English football.

An additional problem had also emerged and that was that the council had decided Vale's market, which was generating £100,000 a year, should cease to operate on 31 August. The reason was because the council intended to open their own market in Burslem town centre and did not want any competition against it. The club lodged an appeal against their ruling and Bell said: 'This market is a financial lifeline to the club. If the City Council shut it down it will be responsible for stopping Port Vale's progress.'

In the light of the threat to their market, the club obviously needed more income from other sources, but, unfortunately, on 8 August, an operating loss of £388,465 was announced on the 1990-1991 season and it was disclosed that the debt had risen to a worrying £493,168. It seemed that the only way the Valiants could continue to operate at their existing level of football and keep the stadium improvements on the go was to sell players for big money. In turn, it appeared that the only way that could happen would be through the manager indefinitely signing, coaching and selling on his rough diamonds.

A small move in the right direction was taken by the club increasing their use of stewards at their matches in order to reduce the numbers of policemen on duty and thereby save on their cost. As the price of the club's policing charges had rocketed from £11,300 in the 1987-1988 campaign to £113,567 in three years, the initiative was none too soon!

The British Coal Opencast Stand was opened on 6 November when Vale took on Derby County in a league match. It had, in the event, cost £1.2 million to construct, but half the total had been funded by the Football Trust. The stand contained 4,254 seats and had quite a crowd in to sample it that night, but the total attendance at the game was a disappointing 8,589. Nevertheless, hardly had the stand opened than the chairman stated that the club were hoping to have the Hamil End seated by the start of the following season.

In October, a public inquiry had been held into the future of Vale's market, but, on 20 November, it was announced that the government inspector, George Baird, had decided to turn down the club's appeal. However, the market was allowed to continue until that of the council in Burslem was up and running. The impact on Bell and the rest of the directors was dramatic and immediate. The ground improvements and the club's community programme were suspended because of the forthcoming loss of vital income and the chairman said, 'It is a tragedy for Port Vale.'

Nevertheless, before the end of the month, work began on installing a new system of floodlights at Vale Park, with each one consisting of sixteen lamps instead of the ten used before, in order to meet the Football League's required lux value for the next season. Fortunately, the Football Trust was to pay most of the five-figure cost and, within a fortnight, the whole new lighting system was in place.

However, in March 1992, the Hamil End project hit the buffers as the Football Trust awarded the Valiants only a 25 per cent grant towards the cost of constructing a new £1.86 million 6,000-seater stand. Bell said that the grant was 'not sufficient to go ahead' with the development.

At the same time, the team slumped to the bottom of the Second Division in a winless run that eventually stretched to seventeen league matches. An emergency board meeting was held on 26 March, as a result of which Mike Pejic was sacked and replaced as the first-team coach by Bobby Downes, who had been working as the youth coach. Pejic's dismissal was the consequence of a scuffle that he had been involved in with the reserve goalkeeper, Trevor Wood, but the ex-coach was eventually awarded a four-figure compensation sum by an industrial tribunal.

Nevertheless, the incident was a sign of the pressures at the club at the time and was an indicator of the urgent need for some good results to be achieved quickly. They were and three of the following four games were won, although the improvement came too late to prevent Vale from finishing bottom of the table and suffering relegation to the Third Division on 2 May. Therefore, the club now had a vastly improved stadium at a level of football that hardly called for one of an impressive standard, but at least the chairman resisted the temptation to dismiss the manager and thereby potentially cut off one of the club's major sources of income.

It was then revealed that the policing charges at the matches had increased by up to thirty per cent and Bell said, 'I haven't a clue where we will find the extra money.' In the event, inroads were made into the problem by the recruitment of extra stewards, with the Football Trust helping to pay for their training.

May continued to bring grim news as the council served an enforcement order on the club to force the closure of their market by 20 June. In the event, the council took out a High Court injunction to try to enforce its ruling.

Despite the endless funding and costing setbacks, the appetite of the Vale chairman to continue to develop the ground remained undaunted. Consequently, the club revised their Hamil End plans so that cover and 5,000 seats would be provided for the existing terraces there. The outcome was that the Football Trust awarded a grant of fifty per cent of the cost of the covering and 75 per cent of that of installing the seating. The target completion date was August 1993, but at last the pressure was off because the lower division clubs were no longer obliged to develop all-seater stadiums. Therefore, Bell said, 'We can slow down and spread work over a longer period and it will probably save us £1 million on our original plans [to finish the ground improvements].'

Nevertheless, at the same time, he was pulling off a major coup and it was announced on 10 June that he had negotiated a knock-down (scrap) price for Chester City's ten-year-old grandstand from their former ground at Sealand Road. The total cost of the new scheme was thus reduced to £300,000, but was actually half of that because of grant aid of fifty per cent from the Football Trust. The plan was for the stand to be dismantled, cleaned and painted before being erected at Vale Park. The Vale chairman said, 'We should be able to write off the cost to the club within eighteen months.'

On 14 August, the traders at the Vale market set up their stalls for the final time as the council had won a High Court decision that it should close after that date. A major income stream thus came to an end, at a cost of £65,000 in legal fees. However, the club accounts for the previous season ensured that there would be no immediate big problems because a profit of £455,465 had been made, mainly through a surplus player transfer balance.

The new Hamil End Stand opened on 26 September, aptly to house the Chester City fans in their league clash at Vale that day. Therefore, despite the club's increasing financial difficulties, a new stadium was really taking shape in Burslem from the ashes of neglect.

Despite his dynamism in developing the ground, the chairman had a hands-off approach to the football team and allowed the manager to get on with his job. That was fortunate because Rudge had assembled and fielded an impressive team in the 1992-1993 campaign, who won the Autoglass Trophy on 22 May 1993 at Wembley. Victory was achieved by 2-1 against Stockport County in front of 25,000 or so Vale supporters and, the following day, Bell proudly toured from Talke to Burslem with the manager and players on an open-topped bus, receiving accolades from thousands of fans along the way.

The Lorne Street side of the ground, which was as yet untouched by the chairman's hand of development, was still not up to the new national safety requirements. Therefore, in August, it was announced that the club's next move would be to improve the terraces there.

The club's annual accounts, published in October, showed a loss of only £62,915 on the previous season. That was in spite of the cost of the continuing work on the stadium, a player transfer deficit of £235,000 and the loss of revenue from the market. Nevertheless, Bell said that, 'The directors will be looking to reduce costs wherever possible.'

The price of policing their games continued to be one of the chairman's pet hates and he wrote to Charles Kelly, the chief constable of the Staffordshire force, in January 1994, complaining 'bitterly' about the ongoing cost of their operations at Vale Park. Kelly replied, pointing out that they had only charged the club £18,655 over the last year, and said, 'If in the future Mr Bell can adequately police Port Vale safely and relieve me of the duty nobody would be more pleased than me.' The scene was therefore set for more stewards and fewer police.

7 May proved to be a big day in the club's history because the team got promotion, in second place, back to the First Division (as the Second Division had by then been renamed) by winning their final match of the campaign 3-1 at Brighton & Hove Albion. Once again, great success had been masterminded by Vale's canny manager, but credit was also due to their chairman, who had let him get on with achieving it.

A golden age in the second tier of English football, with Rudge at the helm, followed for Vale, but the architect of the side's success was almost lost before the first ball had been kicked. Belatedly, after promotion had been achieved, the club offered the manager a new two-year contract, but by then Second Division Bradford City were in the hunt for his services. By 17 May, they were confident of landing their man, but hundreds of Vale supporters congregated at the ground to make it clear that they wanted Rudge to stay. At an emergency board meeting, the manager was offered a new three-year deal, which he decided to accept, much to the relief of the fans. The successful manager then made his feelings known: 'If I had been offered a contract at Christmas I would have had no hesitation in signing it. A major reason I am staying is the amazing support we have at this club.'

Although the unnecessary crisis was over, the hesitation and delay of the chairman and the rest of the board in securing Rudge's future was an important episode in the gradual unravelling of their relationship. The incident made crystal clear the overwhelming popularity of the manager amongst the fans and consequently the unpopularity of the position that the chairman had initially taken. It is human nature to baulk at being out of favour and the situation indicated that fan power had pressured, if not actually forced, the hand of authority. Therefore, all did not augur well for the future.

It is understandable that the club wanted to be cautious in handing out contracts, especially with their delicate finances, but it was clearly amiss of the board not to have offered their highly successful manager the security of another, relatively short-term, contract until he had once more proved his worth beyond doubt. At Christmas 1993, Vale had been fourth in the league and had progressed to the third round of the F.A. Cup and the Southern Area quarter-finals of the Autoglass Trophy, so it would have been commonsense to have offered Rudge new terms by then at the latest. However, from seemingly small failures can grow big problems.

In June 1994, the Valiants lost their midfield marksman, Ian Taylor, to Sheffield Wednesday, although they were compensated to the tune of a new club record fee of £1 million. The following month, their central defender, Peter Swan, was sold for slightly above £300,000 to Plymouth Argyle, so the club were suddenly rolling in money, although £275,000 of it was spent on signing two new strikers: Tony Naylor, from Crewe Alexandra, and Lee Glover, from Nottingham Forest.

With a weakened side, Vale found the step-up in level in the 1994-1995 campaign to be difficult and they won only four of their opening fifteen league matches. The situation was not helped by the revelation of a £505,924 loss on the previous season, but, on 24 November, Rudge signed the skilful left-winger, Steve Guppy, from Newcastle United for £225,000 and he proved to be a revelation.

However, the Valiants were dumped out of the F.A. Cup by 1-0 at Third Division Scarborough in the second round on 3 December. The chairman said, 'Results have left us in an unacceptable situation and it has got to alter.' However, Rudge replied: 'I was disappointed with the chairman's comments. I thought that I would have had a bit of support from him at this time.'

Clearly all was not well behind the scenes, but, the same month, Bell's focus switched back to his pet project, the ground. It was announced that the club intended to fill the Hamil End with 4,500 seats, at a cost of £1.4 million, by the start of the following campaign. A five-figure sponsorship deal was then agreed with Caudwell Communications and Motorola, so that the Hamil End was renamed the Caudwell Stand.

It was also revealed that this latest development was part of an overall aim of creating a 25,000 all-seater stadium, which would include the demolition of the existing Lorne Street side of the ground and the construction of a new 6,500-seater stand, with executive boxes, restaurants and the club offices, in its place. The chairman said, 'It will be the biggest project in the club's history.' In the fullness of time, he was unfortunately proved to be right.

That was not even the end of the plans to spend money on Vale Park because the club disclosed in March 1995 that, following problems with the pitch, the top two inches of it would be resurfaced during the summer and a giant cover would be bought to protect it thenceforth from the elements, at a total cost of £750,000.

However, on 1 April, the team lost 2-1 at home to Grimsby Town, which left them in seventeenth place and five points clear of the drop zone, with a match in hand and only seven to play. Although relegation seemed unlikely from that position, apparently the chairman called a board meeting to discuss Rudge's future, but his fellow directors refused to sit around the table. Three weeks later, Vale secured safety by winning 1-0 at Stoke City, to achieve their first league victory at the Victoria Ground for over 67 years. The outcome was a clear-the-air board meeting, which pledged the directors' united support for the manager. The vice-chairman, Dave Bundy, then confirmed that he had been planning a takeover of the club to safeguard Rudge's position! Shortly afterwards, the manager issued a public thank you to the many Vale fans who backed him through the crisis. He said, 'To think that I still have that support is magnificent.'

The manager had cleared another hurdle, but the days of Rudge and Bell working together in harmonious partnership had gone. The seeds of uncertainty had been well and truly sown and the main question appeared to be how long the manager could survive. As long as the results went well, his position was probably unassailable, but it seemed that a period of poor form on the pitch would threaten danger.

Vale had finished the season in seventeenth place, ten points clear of relegation, with an average league home gate of 9,174, their best for 31 years, but the pressure was clearly on to do better still. At the end of July, Rudge acted and paid a new club record fee of £450,000 to York City for their forceful right-winger, Jon McCarthy. Within an hour, the manager had transferred Robin van der Laan to Derby County in exchange for their tall striker, Lee Mills, and £475,000. Rudge clearly meant the Valiants to be an attacking force because he now had two flying wingers and a big centre-forward to get on the end of their crosses.

On 19 August, the new Hamil Road stand opened for the first home game of the 1995-1996 season, with 4,550 seats having been installed at a total cost of £1.5 million. Three sides of the ground were now completed and the last remaining one, the Lorne Street area, was due to be replaced by a new 7,000-seater two-tier stand by 1997, at an estimated cost of £3.5 million. Bell was confident that £1 million of that would be financed from available grants, but he was hoping that the council would also put in a sizable amount. Considering the volatile relationship that the club had had in recent times with the corporation, his hopes might have been considered as wishful thinking. Also, as Vale rarely drew five-figure attendances outside attractive cup ties and Potteries Derbies, it was difficult to understand what the purpose of such a huge undertaking would be, the more so in the light of an operating loss (excluding transfer activities) that had occurred on the previous campaign of £283,898.

Unfortunately, it took the team quite some while to get used to the new two-winger system and they gained only two wins in their opening nineteen league matches, which left them bottom of the table at the beginning of December. However, there was then a remarkable reversal of form, which began with Vale's first home league victory of the campaign on 2 December and saw them take 37 points from their following seventeen games to stand just three points from the play-off zone by the end of March 1996!

The resurrected side also fought their way to the fifth round of the F.A. Cup, along the way beating the holders, Everton, of the Premiership, 2-1 at home in a replay on a wonderful night, in front of a largely ecstatic crowd of 19,197 on 14 February. The club made a profit of £400,000 on the cup run and an ecstatic Bell said: 'There is no pressure to sell players at all. In fact the Board has told John Rudge that we will support him if he comes to us with a player he wants.' Therefore, on the surface, all seemed rosy in the garden once more, but the bottom line was that the team were winning most of their matches.

The valiant victors also battled their way to the final of the Anglo-Italian Cup, in which they were unfortunately hammered 5-2 by Genoa at Wembley on 17 March, in front of a disappointing crowd of just 12,663. Despite the fact that no profit was made from the competition, the chairman was still able to feel great pride at his club's third appearance at the prestigious stadium in less than three years. The partnership between Bell and Rudge remained intact and was still delivering the goods.

Unfortunately, after the end of March, the team went completely off the boil, but still finished a respectable twelfth. However, they ended up only eight points clear of the relegation zone, so the margin for error had not been great.

Although it had taken a long time to happen, it was announced on 26 April that the Valiants and the council had agreed in principle to the joint-construction of a £1.6 million outdoor sports complex at Bycars Park. The idea was the creation of three all-weather, full size, floodlit pitches; three grass pitches; a floodlit five-a-side pitch and changing facilities, all to be shared between the club and the local community. The Vale chairman said, 'We are now going forward, but they have not offered the £4.5 million they have to our friends down the road [for a new stadium].'

The Bell-inspired developments continued apace and, during the close season, the Railway Stand was re-roofed at a cost of £70,000. It was quite remarkable how, with such limited resources at his disposal (other than the profits from Rudge's wheeling transfer deals), the chairman had been able to make such impressive progress on the transformation of the stadium. However, endless success tends to breed overconfidence and Vale's projects were becoming grander and the stakes were getting higher.

For the 1996-1997 season, Rudge was back to having to generate his own money for new players and only an initial £150,000 was raised, from the sale of Lee Glover to Rotherham United. Not surprisingly, the team found the going tough, won only two of their first thirteen league matches and slumped to fifth from the bottom of the table on 16 October. With the manager enjoying hero status in the eyes of most of the supporters, the blame for the (relatively) poor results fell largely on the chairman, who was unable to provide the funds to try to take the side forward. Therefore, he came in for increasingly severe criticism and some abuse from a section of the fans. On 18 October, he snapped and put Vale and their top players up for sale. He gave a seven-day deadline for prospective buyers to come forward and warned that, if they did not, the club could face liquidation! He said: 'I am bitter after ten years of hard work at this club. I could well walk away and wash my hands of the club.' Nevertheless, it was difficult to believe that he would throw in the towel with a substantial amount of money invested in Vale and with most of his pet project completed.

Not surprisingly, he soon had a change of heart and, three days later, said: 'I will continue at the club until I find the right person to take over. If no-one comes in, Bill Bell will stay.' Equally unsurprisingly, nobody appeared with the necessary finance to take over the burden of keeping the club afloat. The reticence of any prospective buyers was no doubt greatly compounded by the announcement, at the end of October, of a loss of £192,912 on the previous season and the existence of a total debt of £1,464,259. So the captain of the ship decided to struggle on, but it was not with the keen heart that he had had when he had first set sail on his journey. The following month, the council approved the Bycars Park scheme and, a few days afterwards, Bell said: 'The club is no longer for sale. I'm staying put. But if there is any more trouble I will walk away.'

In the midst of the excitement, the team made steady progress up the table, to reach seventh on 25 January 1997, but, at the beginning of March, one of Vale's prized flying wingers, Steve Guppy, was sold to Leicester City for an initial £850,000, plus bonus payments based on appearances. Nevertheless, a run of four successive victories moved the Valiants up to fifth, which put them inside the play-off zone by four points with only three matches to play. Although promotion to the Premiership was still some distance away, it had become a realistic possibility. However, the campaign ended in an anticlimax as just one further point was gained, although Vale's eighth-placed finish, with 67 points, was an impressive achievement and the club's best position in the league since 1934. The problem for John Rudge was, of course, that it was unlikely that a club of Vale's stature would be able to equal such a fine accomplishment in the future, let alone surpass it, and therefore the probability was that the only realistic way was down and maybe personally out.

On 28 June, the manager signed a new three-year contract and, in preparation for the new season, paid IFK Norrköping, of Sweden, £150,000 for their skilful midfielder, Jan Jansson. However, Rudge illustrated his mounting problems when he said, 'The game has never been more expensive to run.'

The team made a reasonable start to the 1997-1998 season and were in eighth place at the end of September, despite having sold Jon McCarthy to Birmingham City for a new club record fee of £1.5 million. In anticipation of the transfer, the manager had lined up a replacement, the wholehearted Gareth Ainsworth, and signed him the day after from Lincoln City for an all-time club record fee of £500,000.

By then, the Lorne Street stand project had run into trouble because no outside monies had become available, but, unfortunately, because of the implications of the Taylor Report, it needed to be redeveloped or closed by the start of the following campaign. Fatefully, the chairman's mind was set upon its construction and he said: 'It is my ambition to see the job completed. We have decided to develop our own stadium fit for the Premiership.'

On 27 September, the club unveiled an artist's impression of the fabulous forthcoming stand, with its projected 5,000 seats, fourteen executive boxes, 300-seater restaurant, three conference rooms and plush vice-presidents' suite. Sadly, behind the glossy images, there was little rationale in an intrinsically lower division club, with limited support, developing such a wonderful ground. It was a nice dream, but was rather adrift of reality, even though the Football Trust eventually awarded a £1.2 million grant towards the cost of the new stand's construction.

On the surface, a profit of £621,567 on the previous season made the project appear to be feasible, but the favourable balance sheet was the result of yet another player transfer surplus driven by the manger. The danger was that, if Rudge's financial lifeline dried up, the club would be in big trouble.

Meanwhile, the team dropped down the table to seventh from the bottom by the end of the year, with a dismal run of just three wins in sixteen league matches. Then, completely out of the blue, the Valiants fought Premiership Arsenal to a standstill over two games in the third round of F.A. Cup before bowing out of the competition on penalties at Vale Park on 14 January 1998. The sheer scale of the achievement is amply illustrated by the fact that the "Gunners" went on to accomplish the cup and league double that season!

However, it proved to be a flash in the pan and Vale slumped to the bottom of the division on 1 March following a 0-0 home draw against Stoke City. Although they managed to pull out of the relegation zone, the team still needed to win their final game to guarantee their survival and did so in style, trouncing Huddersfield Town 4-0 away on 3 May. It was just as well they did because they finished a single point clear of the drop in nineteenth place, with only 49 points.

In the light of the struggle on the pitch and an impending further one ahead, the prospect of the giant new stand looked increasingly out of place. However, Bell was undeterred and said, 'It will be the making of Vale Park.' In July, the work began, with the first phase being the demolition of the existing structures, and the close season also saw the start of the building of a new disabled stand through a £¼ million sponsorship by Britannia Building Society.

As the manager prepared for a difficult campaign ahead, striker Lee Mills was sold to Bradford City for £1 million, but only £300,000 was spent on his replacement, Peter Beadle, from Bristol Rovers. As anticipated, the team began badly, gaining just a single point from their opening five league games, which anchored them firmly to the bottom of the table. Rudge commented, 'You have to keep defying the odds and selling at a profit and buying in cheap could be catching up with us.' Rarely were words more truly spoken, but, ominously, the chairman publicly criticised the side's performances and speculation mounted about Rudge's future.

Four consecutive victories in October took Vale up to twelfth and helped to relieve the pressure. However, on 1 November, Gareth Ainsworth, the main attacking threat, was sold by the chairman for an all-time club record fee of £2 million to Wimbledon, while the manager was out of the country. The income did wonders for the club's finances, but boded badly for Vale's survival in the division and Rudge's in his chair.

The annual accounts once more indicated the near-miraculous achievements of the club, with a gross profit of £653,771 having been made on the previous season, entirely because of yet another player transfer surplus. Bell himself said, 'Without this input from player transactions the club would not survive.'

After Ainsworth's departure, the team fell apart and gained only four points from their following thirteen league matches, to leave them second from the bottom in the middle of January 1999. Rudge desperately tried to secure replacements with some of the Ainsworth money and finally managed to land Hibernian's physical right-winger, Tony Rougier, for £175,000 and, on 16 January, the promising Crystal Palace striker, Marcus Bent, for £375,000. They proved to be too little too late as, finally, the manager failed to pull the rabbits out of the hat in time and the chairman (and the rest of the board) at last did the deed that had been threatened on a number of previous occasions, as Rudge was sacked on the 18th after 843 competitive games in charge. Bell said, 'There was no alternative,' but perhaps the manager had become too popular with the supporters for his own good. The main hand that was feeding money into the club was therefore cut off, with the bulk of the fabulous new stand still to be funded. Bell and Rudge had achieved wonders together and it remained to be seen if the chairman could repeat the same success without his greatest asset.

The chairman's next move was to threaten to sell the club if he and his wife suffered more of the abuse that they received after he had taken his decision. Nevertheless, he appointed a new manager before the week was out, the former midfield favourite, Brian Horton, although Vale had to pay Brighton & Hove Albion compensation for his services. Not surprisingly, Horton said, 'My first ambition is to keep the club in the First Division.'

Although the team continued to struggle, ten points from the next nine matches lifted them to fourth from the bottom. However, the new manager was unhappy with the resources he had at his disposal and spent £640,000 just before the transfer deadline on four new players: Dave Brammer, a skilful midfielder from Wrexham; Tony Butler, a tall central defender from Blackpool; Carl Griffiths, a striker from Leyton Orient, and Alex Smith, a tricky left-winger from Chester City.

As their signings were offset only by the sale of Peter Beadle to Notts County for £250,000, Horton had already reversed Rudge's long-term policy of buying cheaply and selling dearly. Such was the price that was paid by Vale to try to retain their First Division status.

The outcome was that twelve points were taken from the final eight games and the Valiants avoided relegation only by virtue of having scored more goals than Bury, who finished third from the bottom. Intriguingly, goal difference, which had been used to decide the relative positions of sides on the same number of points, had been scrapped for this campaign, but, had it not been, Vale would have been relegated. The following season, goal difference was reintroduced, so the Valiants had been amazingly lucky!

The team had gained 22 points from Horton's 18 matches in charge and survived by a whisker. However, would they have done so under Rudge? Obviously, we will never know, but only 25 points had been picked up from his 28 games at the helm and his two final signings, Rougier and Bent, found it difficult to settle in the side and were unable to score. Therefore, it does appear that Horton saved Vale, but Rudge, of course, had the knack of pulling the rabbits out of the hat, especially when it seemed unlikely that he could do so.

Any way round, on 10 June, a Football League appeals panel awarded him £325,000 from Vale in compensation for his dismissal and £22,917 in costs. Bell said, 'The club will suffer,' and so it did, as no further players were bought to add quality to a side which had already barely proved to be adequate for the task.

Nevertheless, hectic construction work ensured that the first half of the new Lorne Street Stand (the section towards the Bycars end of the ground) was seated and open for Vale's first league home match of the 1999-2000 season on 14 August. Although the fixture, against West Bromwich Albion, was relatively appealing, it attracted only 7,891 spectators, all of whom could easily have been accommodated without the help of the new stand. Less than two weeks later, work stopped on the second part of the stand because the club ran out of money to fund it. The chairman said Vale were losing £20,000 a week and had been hit by an unexpected bill of £1 million for filling in mine shafts underneath the stand! A new loan then had to be taken out to enable work to recommence.

After a poor start, the team lay fifteenth in the table at the end of September, but that was as good as it got and in less than a month they had slumped to the bottom. Marcus Bent was then deemed surplus to requirements and sold to Sheffield United for an initial £250,000, which helped to relieve the financial pressure. The announcement, in November, of an all-time club record profit of £760,822 on the previous season also helped to lift the gloom, although the monetary position had deteriorated since then. Therefore, Bell said, 'There will be no more money to spend on players this season,' and, soon afterwards, Carl Griffiths was transferred to Leyton Orient for £80,000.

One of the few successes in the team had been Anthony Gardner, a skilful eighteen-year-old central defender, who had been largely developed under Rudge. However, he was sold to Tottenham Hotspur on 25 January 2000 for £1 million and Vale managed just one more victory from their remaining nineteen league matches from then till the end of the campaign. A further sign of the times was the transfer of Tony Butler to West Bromwich Albion for £140,000 on 23 March and the Valiants were ultimately relegated in 21st place, thirteen points and goal difference adrift of the safety zone. It was the end of a marvellous era.

The priority in the close season was to cut the wage bill as Vale tried to come to terms with their return to the Second Division. Therefore, Tony Rougier was sold to Reading for £340,000 on the eve of the 2000-2001 campaign. The team initially found even competing at a lower level to be difficult and slumped to fourth from the bottom of the table on 8 October, as Horton's job came under increasing pressure. Worse was to come as the Valiants were beaten 2-1 at home in an F.A. Cup first round replay on 28 November by Ryman Premier League Canvey Island and therefore were humiliated, although the manager survived an emergency board meeting the following night.

The financial state of play was revealed all too clearly by the announcement on 18 January 2001 that the club had made a loss of £438,806 on the previous season and there were no longer any developing rough diamonds, who could potentially be sold for large sums to bail Vale out. Also, although Bell said that the priority was to prevent a second successive relegation, the only outlay to try to improve the still-struggling side was a most modest £15,000 paid to Watford for the strong striker, Steve Brooker, on 19 January.

Unfortunately, by the middle of February, the Valiants owed Staffordshire Police around £100,000, having not paid any of their policing fees for two years, with the result that the force were threatening to refuse to cover Vale's home matches! By then, the club were £1.6 million in debt and losing over £20,000 each home game, but the chairman denied that there was a financial crisis.

Fortunately, a twelve-league game undefeated run to the middle of April banished any real prospect of relegation and the team fought their way to the final of the LDV Vans Trophy (as the Autoglass Trophy had been renamed), which they won 2-1 against Brentford, with an impressive performance, at the Millennium Stadium in Cardiff on 22 April. Although the triumph provided another proud moment for the under-pressure chairman and the club's ailing finances were consequently boosted by around £200,000, the victory proved to be Vale's last big achievement on the pitch for a very long time. The remainder of the season petered out in an anticlimax, but the Valiants nevertheless finished in a respectable eleventh position with 62 points.

Unfortunately, in the middle of May, the High Court ordered Bell and his fellow director, Andrew Belfield, to pay the ex-Vale director, Stephen Plant, £110,000 in damages and costs for libellous comments that had been made about him after he had resigned from the board in October 1998. Thus half or more of the LDV profit was unnecessarily thrown away not long after it had been earned!

The pressures were mounting on the chairman and, on 19 June, he said: 'I'm getting a little bit old to be running a football club and I could do with finding someone with a fair amount of money to finish off the Lorne Street Stand and take the club forward.' Thus, by then, the unfinished stand had lost its gloss and become a millstone around his neck, but, of course, there were no fantastic financial fairies waiting in the wings.

Promotion hopes for the 2001-2002 campaign were deflated before a ball had been kicked, with the departure on free transfers of Tony Naylor, the previous season's top scorer, and Alex Smith to Cheltenham Town and Reading respectively, after they had refused new contracts. In addition, Dave Brammer was sold to Crewe Alexandra for £600,000, which, it was announced, would be used to meet the club's pressing debts.

Not surprisingly, the team soon found the going tough and were sixth from the bottom of the division by 22 September, although a gradual revival took them up to fifteenth place by the end of the year. In January 2002, a trickle of work resumed on the Lorne Street Stand and the secretary, Bill Lodey, said, 'We have a little bit of money, so we want to show supporters the scheme has not died.'

However, on 1 March, Vale announced that they had made a loss of £598,333 on the previous season and, by the time of the annual meeting on the 21st, work had again stopped on the new stand as the available money had all been used. Bell estimated that just £200,000 was needed to finish the project, but the money was not forthcoming, least of all from the efforts of the team, who finished fourteenth in a pretty undistinguished campaign.

Vale were pinning much hope on receiving around £400,000 from ITV Digital, for filming rights to their matches, as part of a Football League deal, but, unfortunately, the television company collapsed. It was a body blow to the cash-strapped club and then, just when fine, flowing football was needed to bring the crowds in, the team began the 2002-2003 campaign with four straight league defeats, which put them firmly at the bottom of the table. In a remarkable transformation of form, five straight victories lifted them to ninth and just goal difference short of a play-off position! However, the home crowd for the last of the games in the run, against Notts County, was a mere 3,505. After that, the Valiants won only one of their following ten league matches and had dropped back to sixteenth by 23 November. They also got knocked out of both the Worthington Cup and the F.A. Cup in the first round, so there was then little chance of any substantial monies coming in from their remaining games that season.

In desperation, on 25 November, Bell put his shares up for sale. Although £40,000 worth were quickly sold, the amount raised was nowhere near enough to clear pressing debts of £593,000 owed to the Inland Revenue and on 4 December the club presented a petition to the High Court in Birmingham to go into administration. Without doing so, Vale faced going out of business altogether. Their stunned staff received the devastating news in their plush accommodation inside the club's uncompleted huge new stand – the stand too far!

Although the Valiants had essentially struggled for most of their history after the legalisation of professionalism amongst footballers in 1885, they had survived numerous financial crises over the years and only once been in a situation as desperate, when the original club had been wound up in 1909. What then had been so different this time round in order to bring the club to its knees?

A simple answer is not easy to give because Vale had been heading towards a brick wall for a long time and the process of collapse was slow, tortuous and barely apparent almost until it happened. The most prominent underlying factor seems to have been Bell's determination to undertake and complete his greatest pet project, the stand too far, in fundamentally adverse circumstances. Although it can be argued that this was simply the final piece in the redevelopment of the whole ground, the chairman's upgrading of the stadium had been well in action before the compulsory regulations following the Hillsborough Disaster had come into place. What these did, more than anything, was to increase the urgency of the reconstruction of the ground. Also, when the rules were later relaxed to some extent, it did not stop Bell continuing with more stadium projects. Therefore, the driving force behind the reconstruction of Vale Park was the chairman himself and he clearly took great pride in the numerous successful, and often marvellous, schemes that unfolded after decades of neglect by previous club supremos.

Of course, his desire to improve the facilities at the ground was to be applauded and the Vale supporters generally seem to have been happy with what he achieved until the white elephant of a giant stand hit the buffers. However, the scale of the redevelopments was unnecessary because it was out of proportion to the size of the club's supporter base and that was most apparent in the case of the grandest and most expensive project, the stand too far. That might not have mattered had considerable funds not needed to have been found to finance the various redevelopments. At first, there was not much of a problem because grants towards a sizable proportion of the cost were fairly easily available. Also, the club had a magnificent manager, who was a past master at signing promising players for free or cheaply and selling them on dearly at the same time as progressing the team's playing fortunes.

However, in January 1999, Bell effectively drained away this vital source of income by sacking Rudge. His replacement, Brian Horton, was a different kind of manager, much more concerned with the present than the future, although to a fair extent the difficult circumstances he had inherited helped to dictate his approach. Having said that, after he had taken the helm, money continued to pour into the club from player sales, but the bulk of it was from selling footballers whom Rudge had bought or developed. Although Horton's transfer deals were also done at an overall profit, the amount of the surplus was much reduced and was nowhere near sufficient to be instrumental in funding grandiose stadium projects.

In addition, by the time the Lorne Street Stand development was under way, grants and other sources of income had become harder to obtain and the gap between what the Football Trust could offer and the club could provide from its own resources proved to be ultimately unbridgeable. In the light of the lost revenue from the market and the continuing high cost of policing Vale Park, the construction of a huge new stand was an extremely risky venture indeed. That the Valiants undertook it, especially when a much more modest development would have been more than ample, appears to have been the result of overconfidence, particularly on the part of the chairman, who effectively had complete control of the club. His wonderful and unbroken success in bringing Vale Park to within an ace of finally becoming the "Wembley of the North" cannot have urged him to have been cautious with his final move to finish the jigsaw. The completion of the stand would have been concrete proof of his masterly work, a living legacy that would have stood the test of time for years, or even decades, to come. It would have been the shining icing on his very impressive cake. Perhaps when it had been finished, he would have retired and rode off into the sunset, immensely richer through the sale of the club and its stunning stadium, leaving his legacy emblazoned across the sky in Burslem. However, it was not to be – because of the stand too far.

If the crisis which brought the club to its knees could have been avoided by Bell and the rest of the board adopting a much less grand development for the Lorne Street side of the ground instead of the ill-fated stand too far, what might have been the outcome had they not decided to sack John Rudge? Perhaps the manager's spectacular transfer triumphs would have continued indefinitely and provided the necessary funding for the stand too far to have become the jewel in Bell's crown instead of being his crown of thorns. It may well be that, had Rudge remained, the team would have been relegated in the 1998-1999 season instead of the one after, but the same fate had occurred in 1992 and the Valiants had bounced back only two years later. Also, Rudge was still working on his rough diamonds and it could be, like had happened so many times before, that he would have produced yet another side of quality players to grace Vale Park.

However, times were changing, especially as a result of the 15 December 1995 "Bosman Ruling" in the European Court of Justice, which gave EU players the right to a free transfer at the end of their contracts. The ruling as applied in England meant that, if clubs were not able to persuade their footballers over the age of 23 to sign new contracts when their old ones expired or could not find a buyer for their services, the players could simply depart, no matter how much they had cost or been developed by their clubs. An excellent example of this happening in Vale's case was when Tony Naylor, the team's top scorer in the 2000-2001 season, with twenty goals, left after the end of it and signed for Cheltenham Town on a free transfer. Therefore, the new circumstances would almost certainly have hampered Rudge's ability to sell dearly, but it is likely that the old master would still have had the knack of pulling the rabbits out of the hat, albeit perhaps not quite as frequently as before.

It is tempting to believe that, had the board not sacked John Rudge and/or had Bill Bell not pursued the stand too far, all would have been well and we Vale supporters would have lived happily ever after. However, in the real world, all things end and it is best to enjoy them while they last before we mourn their passing. Like that of Brian Clough and Peter Taylor, the prodigious partnership of Bell and Rudge was not made in paradise, but made it was, survived for a long time it did and many a happy time it gave to numerous Vale fans. Even though the Rudge-Bell era is now long past and becoming a fading memory, perhaps we should look back at it with affection and not regret that the stand too far (which in 2011 had still not been completed) brought about its final passing.

There is one final scenario to consider and that is to suppose that Bell had been a chairman with no vision for the stadium (like many others who had preceded him) instead of one with a grand vision. In that case, the ground would most likely have become increasingly dilapidated through neglect other than where improvements would have been forced on the club by the authorities. Eventually, the Valiants may well have been forced to leave Vale Park because the cost of upgrading the ground would at some point have become prohibitive. In that case, the club's inertia would have mirrored that of their great rivals, Stoke City, who allowed the maintenance of their Victoria Ground to slide to such a point that they were obliged to leave for the Britannia Stadium. So it could have been that Vale would have moved to a new, small, featureless ground at Festival Park, constructed in a joint venture with the council and the property developers, St. Modwen, and paid rent for the privilege of playing there. Perhaps in that light, the indefatigable efforts of Bill Bell to raise the monolithic stand too far do not seem so bad after all!

14 Abandon Ship!

In July 2000, a local barrister, Charles Machin, was appointed to the Port Vale board. At the time, his acquisition seemed a matter-of-fact minor development for the Valiants, but, in the fullness of time, it was to have far-reaching consequences. No doubt the chairman, Bill Bell, thought that having a high-flying lawyer on board might prove to be very handy, but Machin did not intend to be a servant on call to the club and it did not take him long to make his mark.

In November, Machin revealed his plans for the Valiants: 'My 10-year ambition is to see the Vale in the top five clubs in Europe. It is my profound belief the power of God will help get the Vale to the top.'

At that point, the team were seventeenth in the Second Division, so a drastic improvement in their results was clearly needed straightaway and Machin had a plan to get the ball rolling. On 22 November, the *Sentinel* reported that the manager, Brian Horton, had been asked, at Machin's behest, to complete a sixty-section questionnaire on each player in his first-team squad every fortnight for the board. It was not quite the solution that Horton aimed to apply and the initiative threatened his control of team affairs, so he fiercely resisted it. As a result, the club received a letter of complaint from the League Managers' Association, branding Machin as 'belligerent, unco-operative and bizarre'. On 27 November, the battle for the command of team matters was over and the chairman said, 'Brian Horton has my full support.' Thus hardly had Machin begun his transformation of the club than he was unceremoniously stopped dead in his tracks.

The following month, the ex-vice-chairman, Mike Thompstone, urged the fans to form a consortium to take over Vale from Bell because he 'gets upset, throws a wobbly, and the whole club is threatened with closure'. Then, on the 29th, Machin publicly revealed that he represented a Manchester-based buying consortium and threw the idea of a takeover into the arena. Bell, however, said no offer had been tabled and denounced Machin's latest plan, to recruit foreign players for the club: 'It's a load of rubbish. He doesn't know what he is talking about.'

Machin was not a man to take such insults lying down and, the next day, the 30th, he quit the club. By the middle of January 2001, he was actively promoting a Valiant 2001 account, into which he wanted 300 Vale fans to put £1,000 each in order to help to finance a new bid for the club and install him as the chairman. A meeting to this end was held at the Vale Pub on 8 February and it was attended by 400 supporters. The plan was to raise £300,000 to put with £500,000 from the Manchester consortium in order to buy the club. An immediate problem, however, was that Bell regarded Machin's valuation as 'a stupid price'.

Machin explained that fans would have seats on the new board in proportion to their financial input, but that the scheme was dependent on him becoming the chairman. He said: 'I think I am the best person to be the chairman. I can't think of anyone I can trust more than myself.'

On 8 March, the Valiant 2001 account was launched, with supporters being able to deposit a minimum of £500 in The Hanley Economic Building Society, in return for shares in the event of a takeover of the club. By June, £73,000 had been invested and the scheme had received the backing of the ex-Vale directors, Stephen Plant and Ian McPherson. However, although Bell claimed that he was looking to sell the club, he was not interested in meeting Valiant 2001 representatives because, 'I don't think they have money.'

By then, control of Valiant 2001 had been broadened to be run by an expanding steering committee, which, of course, included Machin. By September, Mike Thompstone had come on board and the share funds had risen to £100,000, whilst pledges had been signed for another £120,000. Machin then challenged Bell to open talks, but the chairman remained aloof.

In December, Valiant 2001 offered Bell £1 million for his controlling interest in the club, but the chairman said: '£1 million is nowhere near enough. It's daft.' Therefore, Machin challenged him to name his price and the outcome was a meeting between the club's solicitors and Valiant 2001 representatives on the 18th, but Bell said, in response, 'If they took over I don't think they would last three months.'

Out of the blue, in September 2002, Vale resumed talks with Valiant 2001 and the reason why soon became clear – the club was in serious financial trouble. On 19 November, the consortium made a formal offer to buy Vale, but, as the monetary position rapidly deteriorated, Bell put his 80,000 shares up for general sale at ten pounds each. In a week, just £40,000 worth of his shares had been sold, but Valiant 2001 told him that they would meet his asking price if he gave a written assurance, by 4 December, that he would clear the club of all its debts.

The chairman was not prepared to do that (not least because he was one of the creditors) and instead the club presented a petition to the High Court in Birmingham, the same day, for them to go into administration because they were losing £36,250 a month and were unable to pay pressing debts of £593,000. By presenting the petition, the board had enabled the club to continue to trade and staved off complete collapse.

On 16 December, the High Court ruled that Vale were insolvent, but accepted that they could probably be saved by going into administration. The club was placed into the hands of Poppleton & Appleby, the insolvency practitioners, of 10 Queen Street, Newcastle-under-Lyme, whose task it was to sell Vale as a going concern. Bob Young, the company partner dealing with the task, said the two main problems with the club were too many costs and an insufficient income, the exact same difficulties that had dogged the Valiants for most of their history.

Young appealed to the supporters to turn up to the matches in order to increase Vale's income and then he quickly set about reducing the costs. Seven members of staff were made redundant, the club's wage bill was reduced and he called for urgent talks with the police to reduce their 'absolutely immense' bills. The ground was revalued at £850,000 as a going concern, but only £400,000 if the club liquidated, whilst the total amount owing was £2.85 million.

By Christmas, five different groups had expressed a serious interest in buying Vale, but only Valiant 2001 had tabled an offer, in the region of £800,000. By 22 January 2003, five written offers for the club had been submitted, the highest of which was from Raritan Equities, a subsidiary of Stoke Holding, the company which owned Stoke City! The other bidders were all locally-based: Summerbank Management, of High Street, Tunstall, controlled by Brian Carter; Steve Ball and Iain McIntosh, of Kilnstone Properties; and Mo Chaudry, the millionaire owner of WaterWorld 2000 Ltd, in Festival Park, who ultimately presented the lowest offer and dropped out of the running. The number of bids made it clear that Vale would be saved (at least in the short run), but by whom remained to be seen. Fortunately, the Raritan Equities offer was dismissed following a High Court ruling because it did not comply with the Football League's regulations on the ownership of clubs.

On 19 February, Young named Valiant 2001 as his preferred bidder and, on 13 March, the consortium's increased offer of £1.225 million won the unanimous support of the club's creditors, who included Bill Bell! The chairman's vote proved crucial to the outcome because he was owed almost a third of Vale's unsecured debt and the sale needed to be approved by the holders of 75 per cent of the credit. Bell cast his vote thus on the understanding that Valiant 2001 would give him a consultancy role in the club and the use of an executive box at the team's matches, as well as leasing the club shop from him. Therefore, the veteran chairman took his final decision on the future of Port Vale and it led to scenes that the *Sentinel* described as 'of delight and relief'. Had he voted otherwise, perhaps because of a better personal offer, the club may well have had different owners and possibly very different outcomes.

Although a dispute between Valiant 2001 and the administrators over the exact purchase price delayed the completion of the deal, the contracts were exchanged on 8 April and the consortium formally took ownership of the club on 6 May. The new chairman was the local mortgage broker, Bill Bratt, who had become a leading Valiant 2001 spokesman, and Charles Machin, with a lucrative legal profession to maintain, became the vice-chairman. The other members of the seven-man board were Paul Humphreys, Glenn Oliver, Dave Smith, Mike Thompstone and Geoff Wakefield.

Although Young took an honourable decision in recommending Valiant 2001 to the club's creditors, knowing it to be a consortium of Vale supporters, he was not obliged to act upon sentimental interests. From a business perspective, a club run by a number of its supporters would clearly intend to trade indefinitely and therefore the best utilisation of its assets ought to be realised – if the consortium had the necessary capital to keep the concern going.

However, Valiant 2001 presented the second-lowest bid and, had Young been convinced that a higher bid would have created a more robust company, he may have been persuaded to have backed it instead. Had he done so, the outcomes for Vale would almost certainly have been different in each case.

It is difficult to believe that the Raritan Equities bid was anything other than sinister. It is likely that the Icelandic owners of the company intended to sell Vale Park and the land for a sizable profit, and move the football team to the Britannia Stadium to ground share with Stoke City. By doing so, they would no doubt have had more income to show for the same amount of rent (over £250,000 per annum) that they were paying Stoke-on-Trent Community Stadium Development Company for the use of the ground. The obvious problems with the idea from a Valiants' perspective were that the ground was at Sideway, near the heart of the City supporter catchment area, and that the Potters were already well at home there, having occupied the stadium for nearly six years. Therefore, Vale would effectively have been playing each home game away and it is doubtful whether many of their fans would have been willing to have continued to support the club in a foreign land. Consequently, their attendances would have been likely to have been very low and Raritan Equities would probably have scrapped the unprofitable club altogether after a while, leaving Stoke City unchallenged as the pride of the Potteries. Whether that would have been the Icelanders' original intention or not, the outcome would most probably have been the same.

However, it is easy to imagine that the Valiants' fans would have created a new Port Vale, sooner rather than later, as a junior club in a low-level league, as had already happened with a number of ex-Football League teams, for example Bradford Park Avenue, Newport County and Chester. With the strong support Vale would almost certainly have had (as in 1907), it is almost certain that they would have rapidly climbed up the football pyramid and probably eventually have returned to the Football League, like the traditionally less well-supported clubs, Accrington Stanley, Aldershot Town and Wimbledon.

The highest bid at the death came from Summerbank Management and was of £1.4 million, but the company had not provided proof of their funding and were therefore ruled out. Had they produced their evidence and triumphed over Valiant 2001, their intention was to split the club into two halves: a property company, to own Vale Park, and a football company to run the team. The latter would have leased the stadium and paid rent to the former, controlled by Summerbank. Therefore, the football company would no longer have had its own ground and would ultimately have been reliant on another organisation for its stay at Vale Park. Although Summerbank's intentions may have been good, Vale would have been left in a precarious position, with the risk of becoming homeless.

The final bid of Steve Ball and Iain McIntosh, at £1.3 million, was slightly higher than that of Valiant 2001. Their scheme for Vale did not seem to be particularly fleshed out and thus it was difficult to know what might have become of the club had Young named them as his preferred bidder. However, they were running the Queen's Theatre, in Wedgwood Street, Burslem, so they already had a vested interest in the town, which therefore may have augured well for Vale.

Irrespective of what might have been, Valiant 2001 became the club's new owners and they inherited a team which had finished seventeenth in the Second Division, only five points clear of the drop. Even worse, the side had gained just 27 points from their 26 games after the club had gone into administration and that form repeated through the earlier part of the season would have led to relegation. Even then, they had only reached safety by winning three of their final six matches and, had they drawn them instead, they would have gone down. Therefore, the new owners had the tough challenge of urgently improving the playing standards as well as stabilising the club economically and the twin tasks promised to be difficult to achieve for a consortium rather short on money.

Not surprisingly, the new players who joined the club in the summer of 2003 were signed on free transfers. It was therefore remarkable that Vale kicked off the 2003-2004 campaign with three straight league victories and 23 points from their opening eleven games, which put them top and two points clear on 30 September. However, they then really went off the boil and, just over a month later, had dropped to seventh following four defeats in their next six matches. Perhaps even worse were their performances in the F.A. Cup. Having scraped through the first round against Ryman Premier League Ford United after extra time in a replay, they lost 1-0 at home to Scarborough, of the Nationwide Conference League, in the next round on 7 December.

Unfortunately, by then, the club had run into big financial problems once more.

Bill Bratt revealed that the board had been hit with extra costs of around £400,000 within a month of taking over and, on 9 December, he said that the club could be back in administration by Christmas unless £150,000 was raised or a takeover deal was accepted. By 12 December, four offers were on the table, all of them from different bidders than those at the beginning of the year.

In the meanwhile, Machin was quoted in the December issue of the *Lifelines* newspaper as saying, 'I believe that God's plan is to raise the level of Christian spiritual awareness in and around Port Vale to bring about the salvation of many people.' However, on the 16th, he said, 'If we don't raise £200,000 by the end of the year we are going to be in dire straits.' Machin then urged the board to accept a £530,000 takeover bid from Gianni Paladini, an Italian football agent based in Solihull, even though the initial down payment offered was only a £150,000 interest-free loan. In support of his offer, Paladini said: 'There is nothing to say Port Vale can't go into the Premiership. There will be some big names.'

However, on the 30th, the board decided instead, by a majority of five to two (with Machin and Wakefield in opposition), to accept a rescue deal, eventually to be worth up to around £490,000, from a consortium (of two) led by Peter Jackson, a guarantor of the original Valiant 2001 bid. In the first instance, in return for a seat each on the board, Jackson and his partner, Stan Meigh, a television dealer, bought £150,000 worth of shares to stabilise the club's finances. Bratt said, 'It was a good job they did because the club was hours away from having its Football League licence revoked,' but Paladini's response was that, 'I feel like crying because I was thinking big time for Port Vale.'

Paladini's bid for the club thus came to nothing and Glenn Oliver said, with regard to the Italian's plans, 'Grown-ups do not believe in Santa.' However, could Paladini's actions, had he taken over at Vale, have spoken as loudly as his words? Oliver's comment seemed a pretty sober statement at the time and yet Queen's Park Rangers won the Football League Championship in 2011 and thereby gained promotion to the Premier League when Paladini was their chairman. Having said that, money had flooded into the club from sources not associated with the Italian, who was accused of corrupt financial dealings. So Paladini achieved a lot more than many people thought he would, but he was also denounced for being underhand, as some feared he was. Therefore, there can be little doubt that there would have been interesting times ahead for the Valiants had Paladini become their chairman.

So Vale were saved from possible extinction for the second time in a year, but the price that was paid was an irrevocable split on the board between "The Jackson Five", as Machin sneeringly referred to the majority members, and the Valiant 2001 founder and Wakefield. The outcome was that the two minority members were voted off the board at an EGM on 17 March 2004 and they were replaced by Jackson and Meigh. Machin did not take kindly to having been forced off the ship and said: 'I will not go away. I will haunt the corridors of power like Marley's ghost.' However, in due course, go away he did.

Although the founder of Valiant 2001 had departed, he had played an important part in Vale's history because, without him and his organisation, one of the other bidders in 2003 would have taken over the club, perhaps with a less positive outcome. It is interesting to speculate on whether Machin could have remained a force in Burslem had he played his cards differently, but, because he was primarily a blazing individual rather than a team player, it is doubtful if he could have acted other than how he did.

In the meantime, Vale had kept in contention for promotion and, on 7 February, were seventh, one point off the play-off zone. Four days later, however, the manager left his job by mutual consent with the board. Horton was unhappy with the support he was getting from the directors and with the state of negotiations for a new contract. The club did not move heaven and earth to keep him and Martin Foyle, the youth team director, was appointed in his stead on the same day.

Foyle was able to keep Vale's challenge going, but eventually they fell short of a play-off spot by goal difference, in finishing seventh with 73 points. The decisive game had come on 30 March when the Valiants had drawn 3-3 at home to Swindon Town after throwing away a 3-0 lead. Had the team not conceded the equalising goal, seven minutes from the end of the match, they would have replaced the "Robins" in fifth place and condemned them to another year in the Second Division. In turn, had Vale succeeded in doing that, they would have met Brighton & Hove Albion in the semi-finals of the play-offs. As both of the Valiants' league games against the "Seagulls" had been closely contested and ended in 1-1 draws, the Burslem side clearly would have been in with a reasonable chance of beating them, so that it could have been Vale and not Albion who eventually triumphed in the play-off final and were promoted that season.

In addition, once Foyle had taken the helm, the team had gained 28 points from 17 games compared with the 45 obtained from 29 matches when Horton had been in charge. Therefore, if Foyle had been the Valiants' manager throughout the season, and had been able to inspire the team to exactly the same level of performance as he had from 14 February, they would have picked up three more points, which would have been decisive and moved them up to fifth position and into the play-offs.

However, in the real world, Vale remained in the Second Division, although at least they had some cause for celebration because their energetic striker, Steve McPhee, had finished as the division's equal top scorer, with 25 league and two cup goals. Unfortunately, though, because the club's finances remained tight, the players' wages budget for the following campaign was cut back. Therefore, McPhee rejected a new contract and moved on, to the Portuguese club, Beira-Mar, on a free transfer, which was a big blow to the Valiants.

Although no money was spent on new players for the 2004-2005 campaign, Bratt said, 'I reckon we will have a good season.' He was right in the sense that Vale had been elevated to League One, as the Second Division had been rebranded, but otherwise he was to be sorely disappointed. Nevertheless, the team got off to a good start, gaining ten points from their opening five league games, but the bubble then burst. Matters were not helped by the sale, at the end of September, of their leading scorer, Steve Brooker, to Bristol City for an initial £150,000 and a further £50,000 in appearances payments. Thereafter, the campaign was a struggle.

At the beginning of December, it was announced that the club had made a loss of £504,144 in their first fourteen months of trading under their new owners, although the board were at pains to assure the supporters that the financial situation was stable. The accounts were presented at the annual meeting on 13

December, at which the shareholders voted by 119 to 3 to limit individual holdings in the club to a maximum of 24.9 per cent. Bratt explained that the purpose of the new rule was 'to ensure no single shareholder can acquire undue influence or control over the company'.

Nevertheless, by February 2005, the directors were having to make personal loans to the club in order to pay the players' wages. Moreover, the delicate position was not helped by hooligans breaking into the ground on 28 March and causing damage at an estimated cost of £20,000!

The team limped to the finishing line in the league and ended up eighteenth, only five points and goal difference clear of relegation. So the situation had become precarious on the playing front, as well as the financial one.

Although £50,000 was cut from the 2005-2006 season's youth budget, that of the first team was increased in an attempt to achieve promotion, although, as usual, no fees were paid for new players. However, Preston North End were ordered by a Football League tribunal to pay Vale £35,000 plus possible add-on payments (which, in the event, amounted to around £17,500) for the services of their promising striker, Dave Hibbert. Bratt, ever optimistic, said of the campaign ahead, 'I think we can get into the play-off situation at the very worst,' but, unfortunately, he was again to be disappointed.

In the event, the team began well and took fourteen points from their first seven league matches, to stand in third place on 3 September. However, they then went off the boil and disappointing home crowds led Bratt to say, 'We need to get fans back into the club, otherwise it will be gone.' Nevertheless, Vale announced in November that they had only suffered a loss of £51,074 on the previous season, although the total debt stood at a worrying £964,000. However, the club's finances became more secure the following month through the negotiation of a £2.25 million low-interest loan from the council in return for the provision of community facilities at Vale Park.

In January 2006, the Valiants' physical striker, Billy Paynter, and their commanding centre-half, Sam Collins, were sold to Hull City for an initial combined fee of £215,000, with an extra £50,000 resulting from the former's appearances, which put the club on a much sounder financial footing. However, by selling their most marketable players, the deals made a clear statement about how far away Vale were from making a concerted assault on the Football League Championship (as the First Division had been rebranded). In addition, just £20,000 of the sum was spent on a replacement striker, the skilful Leon Constantine, from Torquay United. As Paynter had scored just two goals in his 17 matches and Constantine netted twelve in his 35 appearances to the end of the season, it seemed that the Valiants had undertaken a marvellous piece of transfer business with the two players.

Although the team's efforts in the league were mediocre, they battled their way to the fourth round of the F.A. Cup and earned the club around £250,000 in prize money and profits on the gates, which was very helpful in the circumstances. In February, the club's finances were further boosted when the pop star fan, Robbie Williams, bought £249,000 worth of shares. The outcome was that Vale announced plans to complete the Lorne Street Stand at a cost of £½ million.

The side finished the campaign in thirteenth position, with 60 points, and were thus still nowhere near reclaiming their coveted place in the division above. As a result, Foyle had his player budget increased slightly and Bratt said, 'Next season, we expect to be in the play-offs.' Nevertheless, as usual, no fees were paid for new players in support of the aim, although Bratt became the club's first ever full-time, paid chief executive.

Immediately before the start of the 2006-2007 campaign, Vale sold their flying right-winger, Chris Birchall, for an initial £250,000 and a further £50,000 in appearances payments, to Coventry City and therefore weakened the side before a ball had been kicked. However, the team got off to their normal good start, this time winning their opening four league games and standing at the top of the table on 19 August, but, lacking money to strengthen the side, the Valiants soon dropped into midtable. Nevertheless, they fought their way to the fourth round of the Carling Cup for the first time in the 47-year history of the competition, but were then beaten 3-1 after extra time by Premiership Tottenham Hotspur in front of a crowd of 34,560 on 8 November. However, just over three weeks later, they inexplicably suffered a 4-0 trouncing at League Two Hereford United in the second round of the F.A. Cup!

Fortunately, there was better news on the financial front as the club announced that they had made an operating profit of £352,648 on the previous season, which was primarily the result of player sales. At the annual meeting, on 11 December, Mike Lloyd, the local music entrepreneur, and Graham Mudie, the son of Vale's former player-manager, Jackie, were elected onto the board. By then, the cost of completing the Lorne Street Stand had grown to £2.3 million and, although the council and North Staffordshire Regeneration Zone had agreed to fund £1.22 million of the sum, Vale still needed to find over £1 million towards it! Nevertheless, Bratt expected the work to be virtually finished by March 2008.

Despite the continuing need for money, £70,000 was spent on a new scoreboard and then, on 17 January 2007, the Valiants paid £30,000 for Luke Rodgers, a small, aggressive striker, from Crewe Alexandra. His cost was well more than offset by Vale by the sale of their left-winger, Jeff Smith, to Carlisle United eight days later for £60,000. However, the team ended up a disappointing twelfth in the league. The one really bright light had been the performance of Leon Constantine in scoring 26 goals in all competitions, but he was out of contract and unfortunately decided to leave because he had been booed by some of the fans. Thus Vale lost his striking abilities without any financial compensation.

Although a series of new players were signed for the 2007-2008 season, none of them cost a transfer fee and yet Bratt's dreams of the team going up burned as brightly as they ever did before a ball had been kicked. He said: 'We should be in the running for promotion. I've put a tenner on us to go up.' Sadly, he could not have been more wrong.

The team struggled from the first whistle and, by the end of August, Vale had sold their all-action striker, Akpo Sodje, to Sheffield Wednesday for £250,000, which only made matters worse on the pitch. Only one of the opening seven league games was won and the Valiants sank to second from the bottom of the table on 22 September. Although Foyle had insisted he would not resign, he departed by mutual consent on the 26th after emergency talks with the chairman. The assistant manager, Dean Glover, was then appointed as the caretaker manager, whilst Bratt announced that the club were looking to replace Foyle with someone with similar qualities! The side gained six points from Glover's six league matches in charge, which was a better total than Foyle had achieved from his seven games, but that ratio applied to the remainder of the campaign would not have saved Vale from relegation.

On 2 November, the Farsley Celtic manager, Lee Sinnott, was appointed as the Valiants' new boss by the votes of five directors to four. A split board on the matter did not augur well, especially as the team were third from the bottom at the time, but Bratt optimistically said, 'Getting into the play-offs is still not impossible.' Sinnott emphasised the importance of commitment and hard work, and doubled the time of the players' training, but the 'winning mentality' that he wanted to create did not arrive. On the contrary, the side gained just a solitary point from his first five matches in charge and slumped to the bottom of the table on 24 November, but even worse was to follow.

On 1 December, the team struggled to an embarrassing 1-1 home draw in the second round of the F.A. Cup with Chasetown, who were eighth in the British Gas League, Midlands Division 1, five levels and 108 places below Vale. The *Sentinel* described the performance as 'abysmal'. Nevertheless, Luke Rodgers said: 'We will go to Chasetown and beat them. I will make sure of it.' However, ten days later, the striker missed two penalties as the Valiants lost the replay 1-0, to suffer from statistically the biggest F.A. Cup giant-killing act of all time, and were therefore totally humiliated. The *Sentinel* called it 'the club's worst result in living memory' and a fair number of fans chanted, 'You're not fit to wear the shirt!' Remarkably, Sinnott tried to put a positive slant on the debacle and said the experience 'will stand us in good stead'! Of course, it takes some doing for the same player to fail to score with two penalties in a single game and therefore, on that count alone, Vale should have won the tie, although not many crystal balls would have predicted them to have won the cup that season had they done so!

Fortunately, the good news was announced that the club had made a pre-tax profit of £172,815 on the previous campaign, although the total debt had risen to £4.07 million. Also, the fact that around £1½ million had been committed to pay the hugely underperforming players' wages for the season did not help and, just when the directors needed it the least, Charles Machin and Geoff Wakefield called for them to transfer their shares to a new fan-based trust, Valiant 2008!

However, Sinnott had plenty of plans to improve the playing situation, one of which was the signing of Chasetown's tall striker, Kyle Perry, and their composed central defender, Chris Slater, in January 2008. Of course, had the manager acted earlier and exchanged the whole Vale team for that of Chasetown before the fateful F.A. Cup tie, the Valiants would still have been in the competition!

On 4 February, with the team firmly anchored at the bottom of the table, Sinnott said: 'There has been an improvement. We got up to 150 passes forward in the last four games.' However, as time went on and the side performed no better, the chairman came in for increasing criticism and abuse and received intimidating letters, one of which contained a death threat! Belatedly, Vale won three consecutive matches in late March and early April, but it was far too late for the victories to have any impact on the outcome of the campaign, except that they helped the team to finish in penultimate place, twelve points and goal difference adrift of safety. Even then, had Luton Town not had ten points deducted for going into administration, the Valiants would have ended up well and truly bottom in their disastrous season. Perhaps most worrying of all,

Sinnott's 33 league games in charge had yielded only 27 points, which made his record even worse than that of Glover, who had preceded him.

To try to generate interest in the sinking ship, the board came up with the excellent idea of slashing season ticket prices to less than eight pounds a match for the following campaign if 5,000 fans pledged to buy them by 30 May. In the event, 5,875 pledges had been received by the deadline and so the active supporter base had been increased dramatically by a single initiative. The question then became whether the scale of the team's performances in the 2008-2009 season could match that of the fans. The manager certainly thought so, even though no fees were paid for new players, and he said confidently, 'We're looking to get into the play-offs at least.'

However, by 20 September, Vale had been knocked out of two cup competitions and had won only two of their opening seven league games, but Sinnott said, 'I believe I am a bloody good manager.' Two days later, he was sacked by a board vote of six to three, with six of the directors' opinions being ascertained by telephone! Having been in charge for less than eleven months, it could be argued that Sinnott had been given plenty of time to wreak havoc, but not long enough to succeed. Also, as the campaign was just six weeks old and the Valiants were sixteenth in the league, the situation had nowhere near reached a crisis, but, presumably, the directors who voted for him to go thought things would get worse still if he didn't.

Although Bratt then said, 'We haven't got the money to appoint from the outside,' another two defeats followed before the board decided to give the poisoned chalice to Dean Glover, the caretaker manager who had not been considered good enough to have been appointed permanently the previous autumn! Although Glover said, 'I am very honoured,' he must have realised from the outset that he was a makeshift choice, which cannot have bred confidence in him. Any number of scenarios therefore might well have produced better results and cost significantly less money than the managerial decisions the board took in just over a year regarding Foyle, Glover, Sinnott and Glover again.

The financial position of the club was also very difficult, with a loss of £383,738 being announced on the previous season and the total debt standing at £3.69 million. Bratt was therefore moved to say, 'I feel the board and I have taken the club as far as we can.'

Under Glover, the team's results only improved marginally on those during the early part of the season with Sinnott at the helm and, in February 2009, the pressure began to build. At Vale's match at Macclesfield Town on the 25th, a big banner was unfurled, which read, 'Glover Out, V2001 Out, PVFC Up For Sale'. Then, after a 3-1 home defeat by bottom of the league Luton Town three days later, around 200 fans staged a protest, with the organiser, Shaun Mellor, saying, 'We want Valiant 2001 to actively put the club up for sale.' Although it was not realised at the time, this ripple of discontent eventually became a tsunami, which swept the idea of a supporter-controlled club into oblivion.

Amidst increasing calls for Glover's head, the side slumped to sixth from the bottom on 8 April, although they rallied to finish a place higher, but with only 48 points. However, had Bournemouth and Luton Town not had points deducted for irregularities, Vale would have ended up two positions lower still. Arguably, it was their worst ever season in the Football League over 46 matches and, obviously, something had to give. The board made sure that it was Glover who paid the price and his contract was not renewed even though the results had improved slightly after he had taken over. However, the difference was marginal and had no significant effect on the outcome of the campaign, so the board might as well not have dismissed Sinnott and thereby prevented the club from needlessly having to pay him compensation.

The supporters' patience was wearing thin and it became a matter of considerable importance for the directors finally to get a managerial appointment right, even if it was only by the law of averages. They seemed to have done so when they produced a coup and presented the experienced and frequently successful Micky Adams as their new team boss on 5 June. One of his first moves was to contact his predecessor and 'pick his brains', but Adams still decided that the style of play would change to 'in-your-face football', which required high levels of fitness.

The same month, Bratt was awarded an MBE for his services to sport, but Dave Smith decided to step down from the board to concentrate on his business commitments. He was therefore the first of the Valiant 2001 directors to abandon the potentially sinking ship voluntarily.

Adams brought in five new free-transfer players for the 2009-2010 season, the most notable of whom was the veteran striker and new assistant manager, Geoff Horsfield, who managed just one full game before a series of injuries forced him into retirement! Although the team fought their way to the third round of the Carling Cup, with impressive victories over both Sheffield clubs, who were in the Championship, a 3-1 defeat at Notts County on 26 September meant they had only gained ten points from their opening nine league matches. Adams had seen enough and put the whole first-team squad on the transfer list, but the side then responded positively and produced an unbeaten run of eight league and cup games!

However, the gloss was taken off the turnaround by the news that the club had suffered a £281,541 loss on the previous campaign, although the total debt had been reduced to £3.62 million. The shareholders were certainly unhappy about the situation because, at the annual meeting on 14 December, there was a hand vote against Mike Lloyd and Graham Mudie being reappointed as directors, although they survived easily enough on a share vote, which followed. The development was an ominous sign of general dissatisfaction, but Bratt seriously misread the signal and said, 'I think it was a bit of a protest vote.'

The manager had succeeded in making the team tough to beat, which had been his first priority, but, by Christmas, they were still only sixteenth in the table, albeit ten points clear of the relegation zone. It was then that Adams decided they were relatively safe and changed his tactics to a more attacking approach, to see if they could make inroads into the play-off positions. Nevertheless, by 27 March 2010, Vale were still only thirteenth, but they took fourteen points from their following six matches to surge up to their minimum target of seventh, with just two games to go. There was a real feeling that promotion had become a distinct possibility, but the season ended in an anticlimax as only one more point was added. The Valiants had finally fallen four points short of a play-off spot, but the transformation of the team's fortunes over the campaign had proved an impressive advert for the manager's skills.

Nevertheless, it is interesting to speculate as to whether the team could have got into the play-offs had Adams changed to more attacking tactics earlier in the season. While mainly playing not to be beaten, 26 points had been gained from 21 games, but 42 had been accumulated from 25 matches after the manager's switch to a more offensive approach. If the latter success had been repeated throughout the campaign, Vale would have finished fourth with 77 points. However, because the players' confidence was low at the start of the season, Adams, most probably rightly, dared not initially risk employing open play because of the potential of suffering a string of defeats. However, had he switched the tactics to the offensive perhaps nine or ten matches earlier, it is possible that the four-point gap from a play-off place might have been bridged, if the players' confidence had allowed it.

However, Adams was not satisfied with the resources he had at his disposal and wanted to strengthen all the areas of the team for the 2010-2011 season. Therefore, he brought in four new players, although none of them, as usual, cost a transfer fee. By then, such was the state of the club's trading.

Nevertheless, the directors could have been forgiven for believing that the Adams feel-good factor had removed the bulk of the pressure of discontented supporters from their shoulders. However, it was then that a major problem developed from an unexpected source. By June, Vale were in preliminary talks with a New York businessman, Mike Newton, who was bidding to invest £400,000 into the club. Unfortunately, at that point, the chairman publicly predicted that an even bigger financial loss than previously would result from the campaign just gone, which was something that the fans did not want to hear, especially as, at long last, promotion seemed to be around the corner. Under the circumstances, Newton thus appeared to many supporters to be the saviour of the club, but the rub, as far as the board were concerned, was that the businessman expected to become the new chairman in return for his money.

Newton was looking for action, but was concerned that he had found inertia, so he flew to England in late July to meet the directors and gave them seven days to accept his proposals. The board, quite reasonably, wanted to take the necessary time to weigh up his offer, but Newton continued to force the pace. He outlined his plans to Vale fans at The Leopard, in Burslem, on 1 August and challenged Bratt to share the stage with him at a public meeting at the Jubilee Hall, in Stoke, eleven days later. Newton then courted Valiants' supporters at the opening match of the season before increasing his offer to the club to £½ million. On the 19th, the board rejected his proposal, reportedly by a vote of five to three (Lloyd, Humphreys and Thompstone), because it would be 'to the detriment of the club', but the split vote indicated to many fans that the main objective of the majority directors was to try to hold onto their power. Newton then said, 'I'm not going to go away,' but he soon abandoned his enterprise nevertheless.

The board had survived behind their castle walls, but they had achieved a Pyrrhic victory because Newton had dazzled the crowds beyond with his exciting verve and dash. Although he had flashed into and out of Vale's history in almost an instant, like a meteor, much irreparable damage had been done to the board by his visit and Newton proved to be a harbinger of much more dramatic things to come.

In the meantime, the football season was under way and "Micky's marvels" also started off at a meteoric speed, taking a marvellous 22 points from their first nine league matches, to stand four points clear at the top on 28 September. The only real lowlight had been a 6-0 trouncing at Premier League Fulham in the second round of the Carling Cup on 25 August, but that seemed to have been just a blip. The team's sensational results led Bratt to say, 'I'm fairly certain Micky will get us promoted this year,' but once again his hopes were to be dashed.

The team then went off the boil and took only three points from their following four games before scraping a 1-1 draw at Dartford, of the Blue Square League South, in the first round of the F.A. Cup on 6 November. However, Vale rediscovered their form, won the replay 4-0 and returned to the top of the League Two table with an emphatic 5-0 victory at Stockport County on 23 November.

However, the club announced a £372,649 loss on the previous campaign, although the total debt had been reduced slightly to £3.49 million. The loss made grim reading for the supporters who already believed that the club was underachieving by being in League Two. However, another apparent saviour appeared, as Mo Chaudry publicly launched his second attempt to take over the club, just a week before the annual meeting. He aimed to buy around £1.3 million worth of shares, become the chairman and appoint his own board. He said, 'To take the club forward, I need a controlling interest.' The day afterwards, he formally submitted his proposals to the board, who, uncharacteristically, moved quickly and unanimously rejected his scheme just three days later. The Pakistani businessman said in response: 'I don't intend going away. If required, I am willing to buy the club 100 per cent, but it can only happen if the fans put enough pressure on the directors.' Thus Chaudry instigated a most aggressive bid and plenty of Vale supporters were receptive to it.

The AGM took place on 14 December in a heated atmosphere, with 100 disgruntled fans holding an anti-board protest outside. The chairman told the meeting that the board had agreed to meet Chaudry, but that did not stop many shareholders from barracking him, and Peter Jackson, Stan Meigh and Mike Thompstone failing to be re-elected as directors on a hand vote. Thompstone then resigned and abandoned the embattled ship, although Jackson and Meigh were emphatically re-elected on a share vote. Nevertheless, the board, stunned by fan power, invited Chaudry to resubmit his bid in more detail, which he did. Therefore, on this occasion, the directors had acted decisively, but then did a U-turn under pressure, so their inconsistent actions cannot have inspired confidence amongst the supporters.

Still reeling from the havoc caused by Chaudry's audacious bid, the board were hit with another bombshell when, with the Valiants second in the table, Adams joined Sheffield United in a 'dream job' as their new manager on 30 December. There were very strong pull factors in his decision because he was a supporter of the "Blades", who were two tiers higher, and the pay offered was altogether more lucrative than at Vale. However, the directors had committed an unnecessary blunder by having him present at the ill-fated AGM, so Adams saw first hand the turmoil the club was in. He said: 'The level of hostility aimed towards the board was frightening. It was a shock.' Therefore, the alternative to his new employment was an insecure job with a club in crisis and to remain at Vale Park, in the circumstances, cannot have been an attractive option to him. It is obvious that the board should have shielded him from such goings-on, although he would very likely have departed anyway.

Horsfield and Mark Grew, the head of youth, were put in caretaker charge of the team, but, unfortunately, the two new bosses guided the team to a 5-0 thrashing at promotion-chasing Rotherham United, in their first match in charge on New Year's Day 2011! Their reign lasted just four more days.

On 6 January, the board appointed the experienced manager, Jim Gannon, as their new team boss. Bratt said, 'His record and credentials speak for themselves,' but, ominously, Gannon's history included being sacked by Motherwell in 2009 because the club had decided that his relationships with the staff and directors had become untenable.

The new manager said, 'To finish outside the top seven would be a failure,' and therefore, from the outset, supplied the rope that could be used to hang him! He was very quickly under pressure because his first five games in charge produced four defeats and a home draw against struggling Barnet. Then, before his tenure had lasted a month, a deputation of players presented grievances to the board about how he was running the show. Thus, hardly had Gannon warmed his chair, than he had lost the confidence of his playing staff, which was obviously disastrous.

Meanwhile, the directors asked Chaudry to sign a confidentiality agreement ahead of their discussions about his bid, but the businessman flatly refused and pronounced that their request was 'a smokescreen'. He set up an online petition supporting his bid, which attracted over 1,000 signatures in less than a week, and he created a sympathy vote for himself, with a never-ending succession of outraged comments in the media. In addition, he took a leaf out of Mike Newton's book and presented his bid to 300 fans at a public meeting, at Baddeley Green Working Men's Club on 19 January. Thereafter, he continued to control the pattern of play, with an endless series of unexpected and unorthodox manoeuvres, which appeared to startle the directors, although ultimately they were safe within their castle walls, or so they thought.

The failures of Gannon and the team increased the pressure on the directors and a "Black and Gold Until It's Sold" campaign was set up by disgruntled supporters, to conduct peaceful protests against the board, much to the joy of the Chaudry camp. A second fans' group, "Starve 'Em Out", was designed to add to the pressure by persuading supporters to cease attending the home matches. The WaterWorld owner's next move was to demand an EGM to decide the club's ownership, but Bratt said, 'Mr Chaudry's true intention is to get the club on the cheap and gain control of the property for his portfolio.'

Events became completely surreal on 19 February, when Gannon abandoned the team bus to Aldershot, following a dispute with Horsfield, before the latter was ordered to alight by the chairman a little further down the M6! Four weeks later, Vale were beaten 3-0 at Accrington Stanley and dropped to eighth, amidst very unpleasant scenes involving the travelling supporters, which was all more than the beleaguered board could take. Gannon was sacked two days afterwards. Although his reign was shambolic, the directors were ultimately responsible for it because, once again, they had appointed the wrong manager and he was sacrificed before he inadvertently sacrificed them! Grew, who had been overlooked in favour of Gannon, was then appointed as the caretaker boss, with the unenviable task of trying to salvage the Valiants' promotion bid.

Although Gannon had guided Stockport County to promotion from League Two in 2008, the relationship problems he had had at Motherwell should have alerted the Vale board to potential difficulties ahead by appointing him and therefore his chaotic reign could easily have been avoided. Also, once he was in post, he unnecessarily created problems by attempting wholesale changes to a promotion-chasing team. Had he instead just made fine adjustments to a system that was primarily working and gained the confidence of the players, an altogether more positive outcome may well have been achieved.

In the middle of March, a poll of shareholders, conducted by the fans' group, the North London Valiants, claimed 77 per cent of the shareholders had no confidence in the board. As the tension mounted, Paul Humphreys resigned as a director and, on 4 April, Bratt abandoned his chief executive role to the experienced Perry Deakin, but his problems were far from over.

Seventeen days later, having got the necessary shareholder support, the North London Valiants submitted a request to the board for an EGM, which they were obliged to call. Then, at the end of April, Graham Mudie resigned from the board, having lost the support of his sponsor, Broxap, a street furniture manufacturer.

There was no end to the bad news for the remaining members of the board because the season petered out on the pitch, with the team finishing eleventh, with 65 points, three points and goal difference adrift of a play-off spot. The anticlimax, of course, added yet more pressure for change.

However, the nearly season clearly should have been the really season because the team needed only 45 points from their final 28 league matches to have gained automatic promotion and just 33 points to have clinched a play-off place! However, the results achieved by the successive managers declined in turn. Under Adams, 36 points were gained from twenty games, which performance, if it had been repeated throughout the campaign, would have produced a total of 83 points and secured the runners-up spot. Therefore, it seems that there would have been a strong possibility of Vale having achieved promotion had Adams stayed, although, ominously, his final two matches at the helm had been lost, so it may have been that the team were already going off the boil by then. In turn, the sixteen points achieved from Gannon's fourteen matches in charge, if applied to the rest of the season, would have yielded 53 points and secured sixteenth position, but the ten points from ten games that Grew guided the side to would have produced just 46 points and seen Vale relegated to the Blue Square Bet Premier League in penultimate position!

In the real world, a present from paradise fell into the lap of the directors on 10 May because relegated Sheffield United sacked Micky Adams and the popular ex-Vale boss was promptly re-engaged! Nevertheless, it was too late to save them from facing the music at the forthcoming EGM.

In the run-up to the meeting, Chaudry announced that he had agreed to buy Broxap's 10,000 shares, in return for the latter voting for change at the EGM, which was a serious blow to the Vale directors. Then an apparently decisive event occurred on the 27th when Robbie Williams handed his proxy vote to the Supporters' Club, who were in favour of removing the board. It looked almost certain that the game was up and that the directors would be removed en masse at the meeting.

However, Broxap had wanted the full return on their £50,000 share investment, but Chaudry had only offered £40,000 and an advertising package, whilst the deal was dependent on the former's vote. Also, neither shares nor money had changed hands because the club had suspended the trading of holdings (on 27 April) prior to the EGM. The door was thus left wide open for the directors to strike a deal for the full £50,000 the night before the meeting in return for the Broxap vote for the board. The last-minute move by the directors proved to be decisive because at the EGM, on 1 June, Bratt, Lloyd and Oliver survived the resolution to remove them by the narrowest of margins (1.08%, 0.65% and 0.22% respectively), although Meigh and Jackson were ousted by very slender majorities (0.52% and 0.49%).

An interim board had been planned by the Chaudry camp, to pave the way for the businessman to take over the club, and the vote for its three directors proved equally tight at the meeting. Mark Sims was elected by a majority of 1.06%, but Michael Clough and Mike Thompstone were rejected by 0.06% and 1.77% respectively.

In the aftermath of the meeting, Chaudry said, 'I won't walk away,' but, in the event, abandon hopes of seizing the ship he did. Not surprisingly, Sims did not then take up his seat. He would certainly have been a lone figure in the midst of his opponents. Bratt resigned as the chairman at the end of July because, 'The club needs to go in a new direction,' and he was replaced by Lloyd. Two months later, it was announced that the new chairman and Deakin had negotiated a long-awaited investment deal in the club, of £8 million, with an American synthetic pitch company, Blue Sky International, which therefore seemed to promise a somewhat rosier future. A condition of the deal was the resignation of Bratt from the board, to which he agreed because, 'I'm a supporter of the club and I wanted the money to be invested.' That left just Glenn Oliver of the original Valiant 2001 directors and he said that he would step down at the AGM. The rearrangements of the board continued in October with the election of Deakin, who had bought £100,000 worth of shares, and Peter Miller, a sports executive, who had invested £¼ million to become the largest shareholder. Just a week after climbing on board, Miller replaced Lloyd as the club's chairman. Therefore, the events of the EGM and its aftermath had certainly worked out very differently from what had been predicted. The swirling intangibles of fate had truly spoken!

Several questions still remained to be answered and the first and most obvious was whether the pre-EGM board could have survived and flourished had the directors played their cards differently. Eight years is a long time to serve on a football club board and, after the heady days of 2003, complacency gradually set in, both amongst the directors and the ordinary fans. In the beginning, the board members, as leaders of a supporter-based consortium, were apparently the first amongst equals, even though real democracy was an illusion. Because a grass-roots democratic framework was never established, the directors gradually lost touch with the fans in general until most of the latter simply regarded the former as just a board like any other. From then on, the directors survived on their number of shares and their ability to produce a successful team on the pitch, which they clearly did not. Had the club really been supporter run, the framework would very probably have survived indefinitely and, had the directors discovered a reliable manager who could deliver the goods, they might have been hailed as heroes or, more likely, been allowed to get on with their boardroom politics undisturbed.

Secondly, there is the question of whether the board in effect brought the impact of Chaudry upon themselves and whether they could have handled his aggressive bid better. A fundamental mistake had been made over years, especially by Bratt, in revealing to the media numerous potential investments in the club, which came to nothing. Thus, the expectations of the supporters had each time been built up before being dashed, which, of course, created disillusionment and the widespread view that nothing would ever change. Consequently, the disenchanted fans were ripe to be seduced by the charms of a messiah. It is therefore clear that announcing investments when they had actually materialised would have been an infinitely more sensible approach for the board to have taken and given a much greater chance of a positive outcome.

Having sat tight and seen off Mike Newton, it was a reasonable assumption that the same strategy would work again with Chaudry and generally it was the one that the directors adopted except when the WaterWorld boss forced them to make a move. Bratt said, 'He wanted column inches, so we decided to leave him to it and stopped replying.' However, Chaudry was altogether more persistent than Newton had been and was a past master at working the media and the supporters, so his campaign endlessly gained impetus. Had the board adopted a proactive and combative approach, instead of trying to survive another siege, they may well have captured the minds of more of the fans and the votes of more of the shareholders, but it seemed that their tenure was safe until the Robbie Williams proxy, a key to the castle, was put in the hands of the besiegers. Then, when the position had become desperate, the directors finally proved that they could be men of action, although it proved to be too late for some, and ultimately all, of them.

Finally, there are the questions of why Chaudry's bid failed, especially in the light of the huge support that it had attracted, and whether he could have succeeded had he played his cards differently. His all-action approach had kept the board mainly on the back foot and attracted numerous mesmerised supporters to his side as he fought a virtually flawless offensive that had taken him to within an ace of victory. Only the final move remained, but it was the crucial one that would decide the outcome of the whole campaign. In order for the WaterWorld boss to clinch victory, it was vital that he had the 10,000 Broxap shares in the bag. The comments and actions of Robert Lee, the Broxap chief executive, indicate that, had Chaudry unconditionally offered the full £50,000 for their shares, their vote would have been cast in favour of change and the Pakistani businessman would then have taken overall control of the club. Lee said that Broxap had felt 'cheated' by Chaudry's 'inadequate' £40,000 offer and so the company swapped horses when a better one arrived at the death. Therefore, for want of a nail (or £10,000), the kingdom was lost and won.

No-one will ever know what would have happened had Chaudry taken over Vale, as he came so close to doing. Perhaps, as Bratt had suggested, the WaterWorld owner would have put the club into administration and utilised its assets for his own benefit or maybe he would have used his business acumen and flair to have guided the Valiants to a new golden age. However, had he succeeded in preventing so many future Valiants from abandoning the ship, or bus, he would at least have made an improvement on what had gone before.